Materials & Methods for BUSINESS RESEARCH

Library Edition

By Linda J. Piele, John C. Tyson, and Michael B. Sheffey

A Division Of Neal·Schuman Publishers, Inc.

Published by The Libraryworks
A Division of Neal-Schuman Publishers, Inc.
64 University Place, New York, N.Y. 10003

Printed and bound in the United States of America

Library of Congress Cataloging in Publication Data

Piele, Linda J
  Materials & methods for business research.

  (Bibliographic instruction series)
    1. Economic research—Handbooks, manuals, etc.
2. Economic research—Bibliography. 1. Tyson,
John C., joint author. 2. Sheffy, Michael B., joint
author. 3. Title. 4. Series.
H62.P4645   650'.072   80-20332
ISBN 0-918212-15-4

Contents

Editorial Board

Preface

Materials & Methods for Business Research is the fourth publication of the "Materials & Methods" bibliographic instruction series developed by Carla Stoffle, Assistant Chancellor for Educational Services at the University of Wisconsin--Parkside, and Henry F. Dobyns, Visiting Professor of Anthropology, University of Florida at Gainesville. Basic to the series is the discipline-oriented workbook, developed and tested in the classroom by librarians and teaching faculty. Intended to guide students through the maze of information sources encountered during their studies, the workbooks are based on the principle that the more students know about the materials and methods required for effective information gathering in their subject discipline, the more productive they will become.

This library edition of *Materials & Methods for Business Research* is comprised of the workbook and an instructor's manual. The workbook introduces students to—and requires them to use—a wide variety of reference tools. Chapter by chapter, guides, subject dictionaries, encyclopedias, biographical sources, indexes, abstracts, bibliographies, periodicals, and government publications are explored. The instructor's manual offers suggestions to librarians and teachers; explains the features of the workbook; provides grading, assignment, and scheduling instructions; and includes individualized fill-ins and answers for problems and questions found in the workbook.

Both the instructor's manual and the workbook are available separately, designed for course adoption. This one-volume, hard cover edition has been published to serve as a reference tool in and of itself, as well as a text for staff training in bibliographic instruction.

Materials & Methods
for
Business Research
Instructor's Manual

Table of Contents

Preface

Materials & Methods for Business Research is designed to familiarize business students with the basic types of information sources available in the field, to introduce important examples of each type, and to prepare students to use those information sources efficiently and effectively. The workbook consists of brief textual discussions of individual types of sources, and assignments requiring students to use important examples of each type. Instruction and immediate practical application are thus blended to maximize student learning.

The workbook is modeled on the lab manuals used in many science courses. This format was selected after examination of, and experimentation with, several alternative methods for teaching library research skills. There are several advantages in teaching these skills in this manner: (1) the content is broken down into small units that can be mastered easily; (2) the exercises immediately reinforce the textual and class presentation of information; (3) the students actively participate in the learning process; (4) students receive immediate feedback about their progress; (5) student confusion or failure to master the skills can be easily and immediately detected; (6) additional instruction can be provided for those who need it, while those who do not can proceed at their own pace; and (7) the number of students that can be taught simultaneously can vary significantly, and almost any course setting, from a separate course to a module within a course, can be used.

As well as introducing principal types of information sources, and principal examples of each type, the workbook is designed to provide students an opportunity to use the sources in a systematic way. It discusses research strategies and the mechanics of the research process, and requires, in the last assignment, that students undertake a research project utilizing the previously learned sources and skills.

The development of the workbook was funded in part by a joint grant from the Council on Library Resources and the National Endowment for the Humanities and is the product of three years of experimentation by librarians and business faculty at the University of Wisconsin-Parkside. Its development followed that of workbooks in several other disciplines at UW-Parkside, and in concept and format it is based on the model established by them. The categories of information sources chosen to be covered in individual chapters are based on those discussed in Lorna Daniells' *Business Information Sources* (Berkeley: University of California Pr., 1976), Edwin Coman's *Sources of Business Information* (Berkeley: University of California Pr., 1964), Webster Johnson's *How to Use the Business Library, with Sources of Business Information* (Cincinnati: Southwestern, 1972), Carl White's *Sources of Information in the Social Sciences* (Chicago: American Library Association, 1973), Thelma Friedes' *Literature and Bibliography of the Social Sciences* (New York: Wiley, 1973), and Jean Gates' *Guide to the Use of Books and Libraries* (New York: McGraw-Hill, 1973).

This Instructor's Manual is divided into eight sections. Section One describes the organization and scope of the workbook and identifies its objectives. A description of how best to use the workbook is provided in Section Two, as well as suggestions for its use in settings other than a one credit course. Specific suggestions regarding instructional procedures, the role of the library staff, and sources used are given in Section Three. An itemized checklist comprises Section Four, identifying nine tasks for the instructor to accomplish. Section Five provides sample instructions to guide the faculty member in preparing instructions to the students for the course.

A Checklist of Titles Used, in Section Six, enables the instructor to determine whether the library owns the exact editions of titles used for the assignments. And Sections Seven and Eight are included to save the instructor the time-consuming chore of creating and testing individual question sets for use with the workbook.

1
Arrangement and Scope
of the Workbook

The specific objectives of the workbook are to teach students:

1) to identify and use specialized business reference sources such as guides, subject dictionaries and encyclopedias, handbooks, yearbooks, loose-leaf services, indexes, abstracts, and bibliographies;
2) to locate sources of statistical data;
3) to locate articles and book reviews in business periodicals and newspapers;
4) to locate and use government publications;
5) to identify sources of information found outside of a library;
6) to utilize specific research techniques and search strategies for efficient and effective information gathering;
7) to cite periodicals, books, and documents according to standard bibliographic form.

The workbook is organized into fourteen chapters. Each of the first thirteen describes the purpose and utility of one category or type of publication. Examples of each type are annotated. The sources used as examples were selected after a review of business bibliographies and guides, and on the basis of three criteria: they are all in the English language; they are generally available in medium-sized college libraries; they are important examples of the types of sources most useful to business majors. The difficulty of including sources relevant to the specialized needs of different types of business majors (e.g., marketing and accounting) has been addressed by choosing examples for each individual chapter from one or two functional areas of business, and by including additional examples from other areas in the Appendix for that chapter.

The assignments accompanying each chapter insure that students immediately use the sources and techniques discussed. The questions pose specific study or research problems. Since needless frustration can only hinder learning, there are no "trick," or even very difficult, questions. Each question is phrased in a manner that reiterates points made in the text about the general utility of a type of source and/or the special utility of an individual source. Tools which are especially appropriate for finding information about companies and industries are emphasized by including questions on them in a special section of many assignments. Students are each assigned one company, and the industry of which it is a part, to follow through this series of questions. This will help to clarify what each source can contribute to building a comprehensive profile of a particular company and/or industry.

To introduce students to sources that list reference works, the first chapter focuses on guides to the literature. Chapters Two through Eight introduce substantive reference works: handbooks, subject dictionaries and encyclopedias, yearbooks and almanacs, directories, loose-leaf services. Chapters Nine and Ten introduce the principal types of finding aids: indexes, abstracts, and bibliographies.

The focus of the workbook then shifts away from reference materials. In Chapters Eleven and Twelve, scholarly and trade journals, professional business periodicals, and newspapers are discussed; government publications and the finding aids essential to their use in research are the subject of Chapter Thirteen. Chapter Fourteen, the last chapter, consists of a discussion of strategies, mechanics, and methods for efficient library research. Students are asked to define a research topic and prepare a bibliography, using as many of the types of sources introduced in the previous chapters as may be appropriate. This summary assignment requires students to review the preceding chapters. It reiterates for them the interrelated utility of the sources discussed in the separate chapters, and demonstrates to them that in a relatively short time they have learned much about the library's resources and how to use them.

On the average, the workbook absorbs roughly 30 hours of out-of-class student time. Individual assignment sheet questions should require no more than 20 to 30 minutes, although at first they often require more time since students are generally unfamiliar with reference sources.

2
Use of the Workbook

At the University of Wisconsin-Parkside, the workbook is used by a librarian to teach a one credit course offered through the Management Science Division. The class meets in the library, thereby creating a lab environment where students must locate and use specified publications to complete their assignments. With the exception of periodicals, which must be kept on reserve for the duration to insure their availability, all of the noncirculating publications used in the assignments are left in their normal place in the library. A comfortable familiarity with the reference area is one of the benefits students derive from using the workbook.

At the introductory meeting, the librarian describes the workbook, its purposes and organization, and the procedures that will be followed. Students who have had no previous library instruction are given a tour of the library and are offered supplementary instruction on the card catalogue. Attendance at subsequent class sessions is optional, although most students do attend. At these sessions the librarian provides additional information about the uses and organization of the types of sources discussed in the assigned chapters, and answers questions. Students are expected to have read the appropriate chapters and completed the assignments before each class period.

To discourage self-defeating forms of student cooperation, the assignments are individualized. Although every student reads the same question, each is asked for a different item of information. Each question contains a "fill-in" space or spaces designated by the black underlines. Twenty different sets of fill-ins—containing the specific information requests—are provided in Section Seven. Copies of these fill-in sheets are distributed to the students along with instruction sheets (see Section Five). When more than 20 students are enrolled in the course, some sets of fill-ins are given to more than one student. Each student is asked to transfer the "fill-in" information from the sheet to the workbook.

Assignments may be turned in during the class period or may be placed in a specially marked container next to the reference desk in the library. Assignments are corrected daily by the librarian (using the answer sheets in Section Eight), and are placed on designated shelves in the reference area so that students may pick them up and continue their work without delay. Credit is not given for a chapter until all questions are answered correctly. When students must make a correction, they are instructed to ask the reference librarian on duty for help. The reference librarian thus becomes a tutor, providing the student with whatever instruction is necessary to correct a mistake. And, the student becomes familiar not only with the library's resources, but also with its personnel and their willingness to assist students.

The workbook and course are graded on a credit/no credit basis. No credit is given until all the questions in all of the assignments are correctly answered and the bibliography assigned in Chapter Fourteen has been completed to the satisfaction of the librarian teaching the course. The specific criteria used in grading the bibliography at the University of Wisconsin-Parkside are included with the instructions handed out to the students when they begin the workbook (see Section Five).

The workbook can effectively be used in settings other than a one credit course. A number of business students unable to attend during scheduled class time have completed the course on an independent basis. A few have chosen to complete the workbook without enrolling for credit at all. Other workbooks at the University of Wisconsin-Parkside are generally used as an integral part of three credit research methods courses taught by a faculty member, with a librarian teaching the two to four weeks of the course that focus on library research. Other possible settings include: other business courses with a research focus; continuing education programs; and graduate library science programs. In credit business courses, faculty may wish to employ team techniques similar to those used at the University of Wisconsin-Parkside.

For noncredit uses of the workbook in school or public libraries, the instructor or librarian may want to provide the students with the answer sheets so that they can correct their own assignments. In these cases, the instruction sheets, assignment fill-in sheets, and answer sheets can be distributed to the students all in one packet.

3
Specific Suggestions

INSTRUCTIONAL PROCEDURES

The value of library research skills is not always readily apparent to students. The instructor may want to introduce the workbook with a discussion of student research needs and problems, and a discussion of the purposes of the workbook.

The time students should be given to complete the workbook depends on the course format. A semester is too long a period. Given too much time, students tend to fall behind, and then do several chapters in a rushed, short period of time. On the other hand, if given too little time students do not carefully read and digest the information. The results are usually careless mistakes in the assignments. The workbook should not be assigned during the last four weeks of any quarter or semester.

Because all students use the same titles to complete the assignments, there is a possibility that some students will have to wait while others use particular sources. This is especially likely if the students work on the assignments during the class period. If students do the assignments during the class period, frustration over having to wait for the sources can be minimized by having them work on the questions in differing orders (some starting with the first question, others with the second, others with the third), or, whenever possible, by having multiple copies of an assigned source.

At the start, students may have a tendency to try to complete the assignments without carefully reading both the text and the questions. The instructor should emphasize that the assignments can be done correctly and efficiently only after a careful reading of the material. The instructor should warn students about problems they may encounter if they do not examine the reference sources carefully. In some cases, the too casual student will find a partially correct answer but not the best answer for a question.

The organization of some sources, such as indexes and abstracts, is fairly complex. It is advisable to supplement the workbook and class discussion of those sources with transparencies and/or handouts demonstrating their use.

The fill-in sheets in Section Seven should be photocopied for distribution to the students. If more than 20 students are enrolled in the course, some fill-in sheets will have to be given to more than one student. To forestall, if not prevent, students with the same sets identifying each other, the instructor may wish to modify the book numbers on the fill-in sheets so that they may be easily identified for grading purposes only.

Assignments should be corrected and returned to the students as quickly as possible. Immediate feedback is a requirement for optimal effectiveness of the workbook as an instructional source. A system which allows students to hand in assignments as they complete them and pick up corrected exercises from a shelf in the library rather than during the class period has the advantage of providing immediate feedback, and further implements the library as laboratory concept.

Although the workbook can be graded on any basis, a pass/fail system is suggested since it provides a more relaxed atmosphere for the students and poses fewer problems of administration than other grading systems.

The assignments need not be corrected by a faculty member or professional librarian; however, those assignments which contain errors should be seen by the instructor or the librarian. In some cases, although the student may have used the source correctly, a careless mistake writing down the answer could have been made. The instructor must decide how rigidly students will be held to supplying answers exactly as they appear on the answer sheets in Section Eight. There can be a fair amount of flexibility as to what will be accepted. The determinative test should be whether the student has demonstrated an understanding of how to use the source. Many questions ask the students to identify the page on which they found the information requested. This is generally asked to aid the instructor or reference librarian in determining why a student erred in locating the substantive information called for in the question. If the student provides the information correctly but not the page number, the instructor may decide that no useful educational purpose is served by having the student recheck the page number.

ROLE OF THE LIBRARY STAFF

The general reference staff can be very helpful to students if staff members are informed about plans for using the workbook, the schedule for the assignments, the nature of the questions, the exact location of the sources, and any special instructions given the students.

For students unfamiliar with the library, the

staff may provide some initial general instruction about such things as the physical location of materials, the arrangement of the card catalogue and periodicals, and any special symbols or location devices used in the library.

Publications should be left on the shelves if they are part of a noncirculating collection, such as the reference collection, in order to provide the students with a realistic research environment. The work of the library staff will be kept to a minimum if the materials do not have to be handled by the reserve staff every time students use them. However, for publications in the general stacks and other publications whose use involves long delays before they are returned to the shelves (periodicals for example), the reserve collection may be the only viable location.

To minimize student frustration, it is essential that publications, other than those in the reserve collection, be on the shelves in their proper location. Circulation and reference staffs should be provided with a list of the titles and classification numbers of these publications, and asked to watch for them to insure their return as quickly as possible after use. It may be of help to tag or mark publications with a colored tape to indicate to staff that these are materials that should be reshelved immediately. If they are accidently misshelved, they are likely to be noticed more quickly if they are marked.

SOURCES

The library's holdings should be checked using the alphabetical list of annotated sources in Section Six. For books and indexes, the edition and/or volumes used in questions are identified. Journals are cited by the year, volume, and/or issue number. If a publication annotated in this workbook is not owned by the library and a decision is made not to purchase it, an appropriate publication, annotation, and question can be substituted.

If large numbers of students (more than 20 to 25 at a time) will be using the workbook, the instructor may want to have the library provide additional copies of some publications. Large groups can be accommodated without multiple copies, but this may require additional preparation and planning.

New editions of reference works may cause some problems for instructors using the fill-ins and answers supplied in Sections Seven and Eight. In some cases, only the page number of the answer will change. In other cases, yearbooks for example, the information requested may be unavailable or changed in the new editions. Therefore, if a new edition of a source is used, the questions will have to be checked and correct answers substituted on the answer sheets in Section Eight. Old editions may be kept on the reference shelves for several years to reduce the frequency of changes in questions and answers required by change in editions. If this procedure is used, students should be warned to use the appropriate editions.

When a publication for which there is an assignment cannot be located, the instructor may opt for any one of several alternative procedures. Students can be asked to use the publication in another library; a substitute question can be prepared; in cases where questions are taken from several volumes of a source and only one volume is missing, students can be provided with different fill-ins; or the question can always be dropped. Multiple copies of one-volume works would, of course, eliminate the problem. Students could also be told that there will be no excuse accepted for not completing an assignment in an effort to obviate the possibility that publications will disappear while the course is in progress.

4
Instructor's Checklist

1. Check the sources annotated in the workbook against the holdings of your library. Be sure your library owns the issues or editions used in the questions. Section Six contains an alphabetical list of the sources, with the appropriate issues or editions specified.

2. For distribution to the students, prepare a list of the publications for which there are questions and place the call numbers for the publications on the list. You may want to arrange the publications in alphabetical order by title or list them by chapter. A sample list is contained in Section Five.

3. Prepare instruction packets for the students.

Section Five contains a sample of instructions. Be sure to include:

    a. a question fill-in sheet, with instructions to write the sheet number and the fill-ins on the assignment pages in the workbook;

    b. a schedule for the assignments;

    c. information about the grading system; and

    d. special instructions regarding such things as the turning in and returning of assignments, and publications which have been placed in the reserve collection or in other special locations in the library.

4. Make necessary arrangements regarding the publications which must be placed on reserve, moved, or in some way marked.

5. Notify the reference, circulation, and cataloging staffs in writing about the instruction program and any special procedures they should follow while the workbook is in use. Provide them with copies of the instructions given to the students.

6. Provide a copy of the workbook to the reference staff so that staff members may examine it before they are approached for help by students working on their assignments.

7. Prepare a student evaluation form for feedback about the usefulness of this instructional program and suggestions on ways in which procedures and materials can be made more effective.

8. Prepare a list of criteria that will be used in evaluating the student bibliographies and research "logs." These criteria should be communicated to the students in the instruction sheets (see the sample in Section Five).

9. Prepare a grade sheet to record completed assignments for each student. For each assignment, record the date of completion. Be sure that the number for the set of question fill-ins and answers assigned to each student is recorded next to the student's name. This will allow you to be sure that students do not turn in answers to fill-ins not their own on a particular assignment and will enable you to replace correctly and easily their fill-in sheet should they lose it.

5
Samples of Materials for Distribution to Students During the First Class Period

The sample set of instructions on the following pages include a schedule for completing the workbook based on a one credit module meeting once a week for six weeks, as well as details on assignments and how they can be graded. A sample list of sources with call numbers has also been provided. It is arranged to facilitate student use of the workbook.

6
Checklist of Titles Used in Assignments

This list is provided to facilitate checking the holdings of your library against the titles used in the assignments. Please pay particular attention to the date of the edition for each title. The answers provided in Section Eight are taken from the editions specified in this checklist.

Accountant's Handbook of Formulas and Tables. 2nd ed. Lipkin, Lawrence, Irwin K. Feinstein, and Lucile Derrick. Englewood Cliffs, N.J.: Prentice-Hall, 1973.

American Statistics Index. Washington, D.C.: Congressional Information Service, 1973–.
　—1977
　—1978

Ayer Directory of Publications. Philadelphia: Ayer Pr., 1880–.
　(Formerly titled *N. W. Ayer and Son's Directory of Newspapers and Periodicals.*)
　—1979 edition.

Public Affairs Information Service. *Bulletin.* New York: 1915–.
　—vol. 63, 1977
　—vol. 64, 1978

Business Information Sources. Daniells, Lorna M. Berkeley, Calif.: University of California Pr., 1976.

Business Periodicals Index. New York: Wilson, 1958–.
　—vol. 17

Business Services and Information: The Guide to the Federal Government. Philadelphia: Management Information Exchange, 1978.

CIS/Index to Publications of the United States Congress. Washington, D.C.: James B. Adler, 1970–.
　—1977

Commercial Atlas and Marketing Guide. Chicago: Rand McNally, 1884–.
　—1979

Commodity Year Book. New York: Commodity Research Bureau, 1939–.
　—1979.

Core Collection: An Author and Subject Guide. Boston: Baker Library, Harvard Business School. 1970–71–.
　—1977–78

Current Contents: Social and Behavioral Sciences. Philadelphia: Institute for Scientific Information, 1961–.

Directory of Business and Financial Services. 7th ed. Grant, Mary M. and Norma Cote. New York: Special Libraries Association, 1976.

Continued on p. 15

S A M P L E

INSTRUCTIONS

<u>Assignments</u>

The assignments in this workbook are individualized. No two students in the class are asked to look up the same item of information. Attached are the fill-in portions of the questions. This set is unique to you. Please write your name and the number of the set on the cover, title page, and on each assignment page of your workbook. Then, for each assignment, write the fill-ins on the underlined spaces in the questions. Staple the fill-in sheet to the back cover of your workbook; you may want to refer to it later to insure that all information was copied correctly.

<u>Schedule</u>

The following is a schedule of due dates for all assignments. You may work ahead, but please avoid falling behind. Assignments may be turned in during the class period, or you may place them anytime in the bin marked "Deposit Workbooks Here," next to the Reference Desk. The corrected copies will be placed on the "Pick Up Workbooks Here" shelves, also next to the Reference Desk. They will be arranged alphabetically by your last name.

September 15	Introduction
September 22	Chapters 1-3 due
September 29	Chapters 4-6 due
October 4	Chapters 7-9 due
October 11	Chapters 10-11 due
October 18	Chapter 14 + Bibliography

S A M P L E

Grading

The workbook will be administered on a complete/incomplete basis. Each assignment will be checked and errors will be identified. Credit will not be given for an assignment until all questions have been answered correctly.

The final assignment, the preparation of a bibliography and a journal recording the steps taken and sources used in the research, must be completed to the satisfaction of your instructor.

The bibliography will be checked against the following criteria:

1. The appropriateness of the titles cited as sources of information for a research paper in an advanced business course. Factors which will be considered include the copyright dates, the publishers' reputations, the reputation of the journals.

2. The appropriateness of the titles cited as sources for the specific topic being researched.

3. The number of titles cited. Although the suitable number of titles will vary from subject to subject, a bibliography of less than 15 titles raises, in most cases, the question of completeness.

4. The correctness of the bibliographic citation forms.

The journal should reflect the use of a reasonable variety of reference sources in the research. There must be a sound reason given in the journal for consulting each reference source.

S A M P L E

Special Information

Please read carefully the "Note to the Student" section in your workbook. If you follow the suggested procedures, your work will be much less burdensome. Also, keep the following in mind:

1. Only those sources which are annotated in the workbook have questions in the assignment section of each chapter.

2. All publications except periodicals will be found according to the classification numbers provided on the attached list.

3. Periodicals will be kept at the Reserve Desk.

S A M P L E

LIST OF SOURCES WITH LIBRARY OF CONGRESS CALL NUMBERS

Chapter 1 - Guides to the Literature

Guide to Reference Books
REF. Z 1035.1 S43 1976

Business Information Sources
REF. Z 7164 C81 D16

Encyclopedia of Business Information Sources
REF./OFF Z 7164 C81 E5 1976

Management Principles and Practice: A Guide to Information Sources
REF. Z 7164 07 B25

Chapter 2 - Handbooks

Handbook of Modern Personnel Administration
REF. HF 5549 F29

Purchasing Handbook
REF. HF 5437 A6 1973

Handbook of Industrial and Organizational Psychology
REF. HF 5548.8 H25

Accountant's Handbook of Formulas and Tables
REF. HF 5661 L53 1973

Chapter 3 - Subject Dictionaries and Encyclopedias

International Dictionary of Management
REF. HD 19 J58 1975

International Encyclopedia of the Social Sciences
REF. H 40 A2 I5

Roberts' Dictionary of Industrial Relations
REF. HD 4839 R612 1971

Encyclopedia of Management
REF. HD 19 H4 1973

Chapter 4 - Directories

Guide to American Directories
REF. Z 5771 G8

Sample

Standard & Poor's Register of Corporations, Directors & Executives
REF. HF 5035 S8

Thomas' Register of American Manufacturers
REF. T 12 T612

Encyclopedia of Associations
REF./OFF. HS 17 E5

Who's Who in Finance and Industry
REF. CT 6470 A1 W6

Chapter 5 - Services

Directory of Business and Financial Services
REF. HF 5003 H3

Moody's Complete Corporate Index
REF. HG 4961 M6

Moody's Transportation Manual
REF. HG 4971 M74

Moody's Public Utility Manual
REF. HG 4961 M7245

Moody's Bank and Finance Manual
REF. HG 4961 M65

Moody's Industrial Manual
REF. HG 4961 M67

Moody's OTC Industrial Manual
REF. HG 4961 M7237

Moody's Municipal and Government Manual
REF. HG 4931 M58

Standard Corporation Records
REF. HG 4501 S7663

Moody's Handbook of Common Stocks
REF. HG 4905 M815

Standard Federal Tax Reporter
REF. KF 6335 A6 C6

Chapter 6 - Yearbooks and Almanacs

Statesman's Yearbook; Statistical and Historical Annual of the
  States of the World
REF. JA 51 S7

Commodity Year Book
REF. HF 1041 C56

Dow Jones-Irwin Business Almanac
REF. HF 5003 D68a

Chapter 7 - Comprehensive Statistical Sources

Statistical Abstract of the United States
REF. HA 202 A38

Handbook of Basic Economic Statistics
REF./OFF. HC 101 H23

Standard & Poor's Statistical Service
REF. HG 4921 S78

American Statistics Index
IND. Z 7161 A5

A Guide to Trade and Securities Statistics
REF./OFF Z 7164 C8 B3

Survey of Current Business
PER.

Chapter 8 - Marketing and Industrial Statistics

Measuring Markets: A Guide to the Use of Federal & State
  Statistical Data
REF. HC 106.6 A6 1974

Editor and Publisher Market Guide
REF. HF 5905 E38

Survey of Buying Power Data Service
REF. HF 5437 S32

Commercial Atlas and Marketing Guide
ATL. G 1201 G1 R3

Industry Surveys
REF. HC 106.6 S74

U. S. Industrial Outlook
REF. HC 106.5 A17

Sample

Chapter 9 - Periodical Indexes and Abstracts

Public Affairs Information Service. Bulletin
IND. AI 3 P3

Business Periodicals Index
IND. HF 5001 B8

Funk and Scott Index of Corporations and Industries, United States
IND. HG 4961 F8

Social Sciences Citation Index
IND. Z 7161 S65

Work Related Abstracts
IND. HF 5549 A2 W6

Current Contents: Social and Behavioral Sciences
IND. Z 7163 C97

Chapter 10 - Bibliographies

Core Collection: An Author and Subject Guide
REF. Z 7164 C81 H32

Subject Guide to Books in Print
REF./OFF. Z 1215 P973

Subject Catalog: A Cumulative List of Works Represented by Library
   of Congress Printed Cards
CAT. Z 881 A1 C325

Chapter 11 - Periodicals

Fortune
PER.

Harvard Business Review
PER.

Industry Week
PER.

Magazines for Libraries
REF./OFF. Z 6941 K2 1978

Guide to Special Issues and Indexes of Periodicals
REF. Z 6951 S755 1976

Chapter 12 - Newspapers

Wall Street Journal Index
IND. HG 1 W26

New York Times Index
IND. AI 21 N452

Ayer Directory of Publications
REF. Z 6951 A97

Chapter 13 - Government Publications

Business Services and Information: The Guide to the Federal Government
REF. JK 468 I5 M3

Monthly Catalog of United States Government Publications
IND. Z 1223 A18

CIS/Index to Publications of the United States Congress
IND. KF 49 C62

Dow Jones-Irwin Business Almanac. Levine, Sumner N. Homewood, Ill.: Dow Jones-Irwin, 1976–.
— 1979
Editor and Publisher Market Guide. New York: Editor and Publisher, 1884–.
— 1979
Encyclopedia of Associations. Detroit: Gale Research, 1956–.
— 14th edition
Encyclopedia of Business Information Sources. Wasserman, Paul. Detroit: Gale Research, 1976.
Encyclopedia of Management. 2nd ed. Heyel, Carl. New York: Von Nostrand Reinhold, 1973.
Fortune. New York: Time, 1930–.
— vol. 91
Funk and Scott Index of Corporations and Industries, United States. Cleveland: Predicasts, 1960–.
— 1978
Guide to American Directories. 10th ed. Klein, Bernard. Rye, N.Y.: B. Klein Publications, 1978.
Guide to Reference Books. 9th ed. Sheehy, Eugene P. Chicago: American Library Association, 1976.
Guide to Special Issues and Indexes of Periodicals. 2nd ed. Devers, Charlotte M. New York: Special Library Association, 1976.
A Guide to Trade and Securities Statistics. Balachandran, M. Ann Arbor: Pierian Pr., 1977.
Handbook of Basic Economic Statistics. Economic Statistics Bureau of Washington, D.C. 1947–.
Handbook of Industrial and Organizational Psychology. Dunnette, Marvin D. Chicago: Rand McNally, 1976.
Handbook of Modern Personnel Administration. Famularo, Joseph S. New York: McGraw-Hill, 1972.
Harvard Business Review. Boston: Harvard University Pr., 1922–.
— vol. 52
Industry Surveys. Standard & Poor's Corporation. New York, 1973–. 2 vols.
Industry Week. Cleveland: Penton Publishing Co., 1882–.
— vol. 184
— vol. 185
International Dictionary of Management: A Practical Guide. Johannsen, Hano and G. Terry Page. Boston: Houghton Mifflin, 1975.
International Encyclopedia of the Social Sciences. New York: Macmillan, 1968. 17 vols.
Magazines for Libraries. 3rd ed. Katz, William. New York: Bowker, 1978.
Management Principles and Practices: A Guide to Information Sources. Bakewell, K. G. B. Detroit: Gale Research, 1977.

Measuring Markets: A Guide to the Use of Federal & State Statistical Data. U.S. Department of Commerce. Washington, D.C.: U.S. Government Printing Office, 1974.
Monthly Catalog of United States Government Publications. U.S. Superintendent of Documents. Washington, D.C.: Government Printing Office, 1885–.
— 1978.
Moody's Handbook of Common Stocks. Moody's Investors service. New York: 1900–.
— 1979
Moody's Manuals. Moody's Investors Service. New York: 1900–.
Moody's Transportation Manual
Moody's Public Utilities Manual
Moody's Bank and Finance Manual
Moody's Industrial Manual
Moody's OTC Industrial Manual
Moody's Municipal and Government Manual
— 1979
New York Times Index. New York: New York Times, 1913–.
— 1970
— 1971
— 1972
Purchasing Handbook. 3rd ed. Aljian, George W. New York: McGraw-Hill, 1973.
Roberts' Dictionary of Industrial Relations. Rev. ed. Roberts, Harold S. Washington, D.C.: Bureau of National Affairs, 1971.
Social Sciences Citation Index. Philadelphia: Institute for Scientific Information, 1972–.
— 1978
Standard & Poor's Register of Corporations, Directors & Executives. Standard & Poor's Corporation. New York: 1928–.
— 1979
Standard & Poor's Statistical Service. Standard & Poor's Corporation. New York: 1970–. (Formerly *Standard & Poor's Trade and Securities Statistics.*)
Standard Corporation Records. Standard & Poor's Corporation. New York: 1925–.
— vol. 40
Standard Federal Tax Reporter. Commerce Clearing House. Chicago: 1913–. 15 vols.
— 1980
Statesman's Yearbook; Statistical and Historical Annual of the States of the World. New York: St. Martin's Pr., 1864–.
— 1979–80
Statistical Abstract of the United States. Washington, D.C.: Government Printing Office, 1879–.
— 1978

Subject Catalog; A Cumulative List of Works Represented by Library of Congress Printed Cards. U. S. Library of Congress. Washington, D.C.: 1950–.
—1970–74

Subject Guide to Books in Print. New York: Bowker, 1957–.

Survey of Buying Power Data Service. New York: Sales and Marketing Management, 1977–.
—1979

Survey of Current Business. U.S. Department of Commerce. Washington, D.C.: U. S. Government Printing Office, 1921–.
—March, 1979

Thomas Register of American Manufacturers. New York: Thomas Publishing Co., 1905–. 12 vols.
—1978

U.S. Industrial Outlook. U.S. Department of Commerce. Washington, D.C.: U.S. Government Printing Office, 1973–.
—1979

Wall Street Journal Index. New York: Dow Jones, 1958–.
—1977

Who's Who in Finance and Industry. Chicago: Marquis Who's Who, 1936–.
—20th edition

Work Related Abstracts. Detroit: Information Coordinators, 1972–.
—1976

7
Assignment Fill-In Sheets

Copies of the assignment sheets should be distributed to the students with instructions to: (1) write the fill-in sheet number (which appears on the upper right hand corner) on each assignment page of their workbooks; (2) write the appropriate information in the underlined spaces provided for each question; and (3) staple the fill-in sheets to the back cover of the workbook for future reference. The "Q" indicates question numbers in the assignments.

Book No. 1

CHAPTER ONE
Q.2.   Contemporary Philosophy
        a. encyclopedia
Q.3.   public relations and communications
        a. handbook
Q.4.   the history of management
Q.5.   alkali

CHAPTER TWO
Q.2.   controllable variation
Q.3.   accident proneness
Q.4.   administrative regulations
Q.5.   organizations and their environment

CHAPTER THREE
Q.3.   achievement motivation
Q.4.   Adair v. United States
Q.5.   basic management concepts
        the management movement
Q.6.   actuals

CHAPTER FOUR
Q.2.   Deltamax
COMPANY: Boeing Corporation
INDUSTRY: Aerospace
Q.7.   aviation and missile industries
Q.8.   a. aerospace

CHAPTER FIVE
Q.2.   a casualty loss
        an ice storm
Q.3.   William W. Adams
Q.4.   BTA
Q.5.   a. Aerospace
Q.7.   Aircraft-manufacturing
Q.8.   net sales
Q.9.   b. aircraft engines and engine parts

CHAPTER SIX
Q.2.   Spain
Q.3.   Feb. 10, 1978
Q.4.   aluminum
        a. of cast aluminum in N.Y. in 1974

CHAPTER SEVEN
Q.1.   production and business activity
        Economic Indicators
Q.2.   a. transportation equipment
Q.3.   aircraft and parts manufacturing industry
        a. production and related workers
Q.4.   indexes of industrial production
        "Production Indexes and Labor Statistics"
        defense and space equipment
        a. 1975

Q.5.   Industry
        transportation equipment
        a. for the total net sales of aerospace vehicles
Q.6.   aerospace companies stock price indexes
Q.7.   1978
        Energy Resources and Demand
        manufacturers fuel substitution capability .

CHAPTER EIGHT
Q.1.   California
Q.2.   Tucson, Arizona
Q.3.   Ashland
Q.4.   Gadsen, Alabama
Q.5.   b. Lockheed
        profit margins
Q.6.   aerospace (SIC 3721)
        a. value added

CHAPTER NINE
Q.4.   advertising mediums
        v. 64, 1978
Q.5.   appliance stores
Q.6.   S.D. Hunt
        Journal of Marketing Research, v. 11, 1974, p. 86
Q.7.   management by objectives

CHAPTER TEN
Q.2.   advertising research
Q.3.   advertising
Q.4.   Aerospace Industries

CHAPTER ELEVEN
Q.2.   Volume 52, Jan./Feb., 1974
        a. John T. Hackett
Q.3.   Volume 91, January 1975
        a. "A Hall of Fame for Business Leadership"
Q.4.   Volume 184, No. 1, Jan. 6, 1975
        b. Dixie Bearing, Inc.
Q.5.   *Academy of Management Journal*
Q.6.   a. aviation/aerospace
        b. March

CHAPTER TWELVE
Q.1.   Nome, Alaska
Q.2.   Niger Republic
        1972
Q.3.   c. aviation industry
Q.4.   a. aviation
        b. San Bernardino, California

CHAPTER THIRTEEN
Q.2.   affirmative action & equal opportunity employment
Q.3.   retail trade
Q.4.   *Economic and Financial Impact of OPEC Oil Prices*
Q.5.   Aerospace industries–Alabama–Huntsville

Book No. 2

CHAPTER ONE

Q.2. an introductory course in religion
      a. encyclopedia
Q.3. management information systems
      a. handbook
Q.4. the management audit
Q.5. asbestos

CHAPTER TWO

Q.2. acid test ratio
Q.3. age and senility
Q.4. advertising and bid lists
Q.5. job satisfaction theories

CHAPTER THREE

Q.3. operations research
Q.4. Adams v. Tanner
Q.5. basic management concepts
      scientific management
Q.6. adaptive control

CHAPTER FOUR

Q.2. Delphi Glass Blocks
COMPANY: American Motors Corporation
INDUSTRY: Automobile
Q.7. automotive industry
Q.8. automobile

CHAPTER FIVE

Q.2. a casualty loss
      beach damage
Q.3. Agway, Inc.
Q.4. CA-2
Q.5. a. Automobile
Q.7. Automobiles
Q.8. net sales
Q.9. b. automobiles and other motor vehicles, wholesale

CHAPTER SIX

Q.2. Sri Lanka
Q.3. Feb. 20, 1978
Q.4. iron and steel
      a. of heavy melting steel scrap (Chicago) in 1974

CHAPTER SEVEN

Q.1. labor turnover
      Monthly Labor Review
Q.2. a. motor vehicles and equipment
Q.3. automobile manufacturing industry
      a. production and related workers
Q.4. installment credit figures
      "Automotive, Machine Tools, Rubber and Tires"
      cars sold on credit (%)
      a. 1974

Q.5. Industry
      transportation equipment
      a. for the total factory sales (from U.S. plants) of passenger cars
Q.6. automobile advertising outlays
Q.7. 1978
      Energy Resources and Demand
      electric purchases, by SMSA & SIC 2-digit industry

CHAPTER EIGHT

Q.1. Colorado
Q.2. Texarkana, Arkansas
Q.3. Barron
Q.4. Jasper, Alabama
Q.5. b. General Motors
      profit margins
Q.6. automobiles (SIC 3711)
      a. value added

CHAPTER NINE

Q.4. distribution
      v. 64, 1978
Q.5. automobile laws and regulations
Q.6. D. McGregor
      Harvard Business Review, v. 34, 1957, p. 89
Q.7. management consultants

CHAPTER TEN

Q.2. automation
Q.3. display of merchandise
Q.4. Automobile Industry and Trade

CHAPTER ELEVEN

Q.2. Volume 52, Jan./Feb., 1974
      a. Peter F. Drucker
Q.3. Volume 91, January 1975
      a. "President Ford's Hard Choices on Energy"
Q.4. Volume 184, No. 2, Jan. 13, 1975
      b. Kelly Co., Inc.
Q.5. *Academy of Management Review*
Q.6. a. automotive industry
      b. March

CHAPTER TWELVE

Q.1. Flagstaff, Arizona
Q.2. Nigeria
      1972
Q.3. c. auto industry
Q.4. a. automotive trade
      b. Fairfield, Connecticut

CHAPTER THIRTEEN

Q.2. affirmative action compliance
Q.3. the Small Business Administration
Q.4. *Role and Control of International Communications and Information*
Q.5. Automobile industry and trade — United States

Book No. 3

CHAPTER ONE

Q.2. a linguistics course
    a. survey
Q.3. credit management
    a. handbook
Q.4. sensitivity training
Q.5. automotive

CHAPTER TWO

Q.2. accounts payable turnover
Q.3. antifeatherbedding
Q.4. African markets
Q.5. leadership and decision making

CHAPTER THREE

Q.3. trade and markets
Q.4. Adkins v. Children's Hospital
Q.5. basic management concepts
    incentive systems
Q.6. activity

CHAPTER FOUR

Q.2. Ball-Chicago
COMPANY: Dow Chemical Company
INDUSTRY: Chemical
Q.7. chemical industry
Q.8. chemical

CHAPTER FIVE

Q.2. a casualty loss
    blackout losses
Q.3. Aiken Drive-In Theatre Corp.
Q.4. CB
Q.5. a. Chemical
Q.7. Chemicals
Q.8. net sales
Q.9. b. chemicals and allied products, wholesale

CHAPTER SIX

Q.2. Sweden
Q.3. Feb. 21, 1978
Q.4. fertilizers
    a. of nitrogen (elemental, bulk liquid) in 1974

CHAPTER SEVEN

Q.1. commodity prices
    Survey of Current Business
Q.2. a. chemicals, allied products
Q.3. chemicals manufacturing industry
    a. production and related workers
Q.4. figures on the production of plastic materials
    "Textiles, Chemicals, Paper"
    polyethylene resins
    a. 1974
Q.5. chemicals and allied products
    a. for production of commercial aluminum sulphate

Q.6. chemical industry analysis
Q.7. 1978
    Government and Defense
    defense industries and DOD-owned facilities shipments under Federal
    Gov't contract

CHAPTER EIGHT

Q.1. Iowa
Q.2. Fresno, California
Q.3. Bayfield
Q.4. Anchorage, Alaska
Q.5. b. DuPont
    sales record
Q.6. chemicals and allied products (SIC 28)
    a. value added per production worker hour

CHAPTER NINE

Q.4. export marketing
    v. 64, 1978
Q.5. banking laws and regulations
Q.6. M. Bird
    Journal of Advertising Research, v. 6, 1966, p. 4
Q.7. Age Discrimination in Employment Act of 1967

CHAPTER TEN

Q.2. "big business"
Q.3. packaging
Q.4. Chemicals — Manufacture and Industry

CHAPTER ELEVEN

Q.2. Volume 52, Jan./Feb., 1974
    a. William G. Goggins
Q.3. Volume 91, January 1975
    a. "Why that Soviet Buying Spree Won't Last"
Q.4. Volume 184, No. 3, Jan. 20, 1975
    b. Devilbiss Co.
Q.5. *Administrative Management; The Systems Magazine for Administrative
    Executives*
Q.6. a. chemicals/chemical process industry
    b. November

CHAPTER TWELVE

Q.1. Burbank, California
Q.2. Ghana
    1972
Q.3. c. chemical industry
Q.4. a. chemicals and chemical engineering
    b. San Francisco, California

CHAPTER THIRTEEN

Q.2. air pollution control
Q.3. trade regulation
Q.4. *SBA Program Authorization Levels*
Q.5. Chemical industries — Safety measures

MATERIALS & METHODS FOR
BUSINESS RESEARCH

Fill-ins by Book

Book No. 4

CHAPTER ONE
Q.2. Introduction to Literature
       a. handbook
Q.3. marketing
       a. handbook
Q.4. research and development management
Q.5. aviation

CHAPTER TWO
Q.2. breakeven point
Q.3. compensable injury
Q.4. apparel (buying procedures for)
Q.5. communication in organizations

CHAPTER THREE
Q.3. cooperatives
Q.4. Apex Hosiery Co. v. Leader
Q.5. industrial engineering
       process engineering
Q.6. all commodity volume

CHAPTER FOUR
Q.2. Diamonite
COMPANY: Anheuser-Busch
INDUSTRY: Brewing
Q.7. liquor industry
Q.8. brewing

CHAPTER FIVE
Q.2. a casualty loss
       carpet beetle damage
Q.3. Irwin S. Anderson
Q.4. CCA-7
Q.5. a. Brewing
Q.7. Breweries
Q.8. net sales
Q.9. b. Beer and ale, wholesale

CHAPTER SIX
Q.2. Tunisia
Q.3. Mar. 8, 1978
Q.4. barley
       a. of no. 3 malting barley at Minn. in 1974-75

CHAPTER SEVEN
Q.1. prices
       Economic Indicators
Q.2. a. food and kindred products
Q.3. food manufacturing industry
       a. production and related workers
Q.4. figures on the consumption of malt liquors
       "Agricultural Products"
       beer statistics (annual)
       a. 1976

Q.5. Industry
       food and kindred products
       a. for production of beer
Q.6. breweries stock price indexes
Q.7. 1978
       Industry and Commerce
       exports value and related employment in manufacturing establishments

CHAPTER EIGHT
Q.1. Kentucky
Q.2. Sacramento, California
Q.3. Kenosha
Q.4. Fairbanks, Alaska
Q.5. b. Coors
       sales record
Q.6. beverages, alcoholic (SIC 2082)
       a. value added

CHAPTER NINE
Q.4. market research
       v. 64, 1978
Q.5. bonds
Q.6. L. Schramm
       Journal of Collective Negotiations, v. 6, 1977, p. 245
Q.7. Afro-Americans in management

CHAPTER TEN
Q.2. business forecasting
Q.3. cost accounting
Q.4. Brewing Industry

CHAPTER ELEVEN
Q.2. Volume 52, Jan./Feb., 1974
       a. Alan Teck
Q.3. Volume 91, February 1975
       a. "First Aid for Recession's Victims"
Q.4. Volume 184, No. 4, Jan. 27, 1975
       b. B & K Instruments, Inc.
Q.5. *Administrative Science Quarterly*
Q.6. a. beverages
       b. July

CHAPTER TWELVE
Q.1. Greeley, Colorado
Q.2. Tanzania
       1972
Q.3. c. beer industry
Q.4. a. beverages, brewing, and bottling
       b. Stamford, Connecticut

CHAPTER THIRTEEN
Q.2. investigating work accidents
Q.3. trademarks
Q.4. *Securities Investor Protection Act Amendments of 1977*
Q.5. Brewing industry — Law and Legislation — United States

Book No.   5

CHAPTER ONE
Q.2. Introduction to Astronomy
      a. handbook
Q.3. marketing research
      a. handbook
Q.4. business policy
Q.5. bean

CHAPTER TWO
Q.2. co-insurance
Q.3. the death of an employee
Q.4. automotive parts
Q.5. cross-cultural issues and motivation

CHAPTER THREE
Q.3. antitrust legislation
Q.4. Bailey v. Drexel Furniture Company
Q.5. management and the behavioral sciences
      Hawthorne experiments
Q.6. analytic job evaluation

CHAPTER FOUR
Q.2. Dynadet
COMPANY: Georgia Pacific
INDUSTRY: Forest products (Lumber & woodworking)
Q.7. lumber and woodworking
Q.8. lumber

CHAPTER FIVE
Q.2. a casualty loss
      erosion
Q.3. Babst Services, Inc.
Q.4. C.F.R.
Q.5. a. Lumber Industry
Q.7. Lumber and Wood Products
Q.8. net sales
Q.9. b. Forest nurseries

CHAPTER SIX
Q.2. Luxemburg
Q.3. Mar. 14, 1978
Q.4. lumber and plywood
      a. hardwood lumber oak, red, #1 common in 1974

CHAPTER SEVEN
Q.1. unemployment insurance
      Monthly Labor Review
Q.2. a. lumber and wood products
Q.3. lumber and wood products industry
      a. production and related workers
Q.4. figures on imports of sawmill products
      "Buildings & Building Materials"
      lumber (summary)
      a. 1976

Q.5. Industry
      lumber and products
      a. for production of douglas fir
Q.6. forest products industry analysis
Q.7. 1978
      Industry and Commerce
      manufacturers shipments, inventories and orders

CHAPTER EIGHT
Q.1. Maryland
Q.2. Stockton, California
Q.3. Kewaunee
Q.4. Juneau, Alaska
Q.5. b. Boise Cascade
      sales record
Q.6. lumber (SIC 24)
      a. value added

CHAPTER NINE
Q.4. radio advertising
      v. 64, 1978
Q.5. the book industry
Q.6. W.F. Sharpe
      Management Science, v. 9, 1963, p. 277
Q.7. discrimination in employment

CHAPTER TEN
Q.2. consumer demand
Q.3. disclosure in accounting
Q.4. Wood-using Industries

CHAPTER ELEVEN
Q.2. Volume 52, Jan./Feb., 1974
      a. Louis T. Wells, Jr.
Q.3. Volume 91, February 1975
      a. "Bankruptcy, Italian Style"
Q.4. Volume 184, No. 5, Feb. 3, 1975
      b. NCR Corporation
Q.5. *Advanced Management Journal*
Q.6. a. lumber/forest industries
      b. May

CHAPTER TWELVE
Q.1. Pocatello, Idaho
Q.2. Tunisia
      1972
Q.3. c. lumber industry
Q.4. a. lumber, building, materials, woodworking
      b. San Francisco, California

CHAPTER THIRTEEN
Q.2. analyzing jobs
Q.3. small business
Q.4. *Sales Representatives Protection Act*
Q.5. Lumber trade — Prices — United States

Book No.   6

CHAPTER ONE
Q.2.   General Chemistry
         a. encyclopedia
Q.3.   sales management
         a. handbook
Q.4.   conflict in organizations
Q.5.   bicycle

CHAPTER TWO
Q.2.   coefficient of correlation
Q.3.   dismissals
Q.4.   buying policies
Q.5.   decision making strategies

CHAPTER THREE
Q.3.   competition
Q.4.   Baltimore and Ohio Railroad Co. v. Interstate Commerce Commission
Q.5.   management and the behavioral sciences
         group dynamics
Q.6.   annuity

CHAPTER FOUR
Q.2.   Dyna Lok
COMPANY: Diamond International Corporatoin
INDUSTRY: Paper containers
Q.7.   packaging and shipping supplies
Q.8.   paper

CHAPTER FIVE
Q.2.   a casualty loss
         jet sonic boom
Q.3.   John P. Emshwiller
Q.4.   Ct. Cls.
Q.5.   a. Packaging Industry
Q.7.   Paper-Containers, Boxes, Cartons
Q.8.   net sales
Q.9.   b. Paperboard boxes, folding

CHAPTER SIX
Q.2.   Madagascar
Q.3.   Apr. 4, 1978
Q.4.   paper
         a. of boxboard in 1974

CHAPTER SEVEN
Q.1.   construction and real estate
         Survey of Current Business
Q.2.   a. paper and allied products
Q.3.   paper and products manufacturing
         a. production and related workers
Q.4.   figures giving paper production as a percent of capacity
         "Textile, Chemical, Paper"
         paper ration
         a. 1974

Q.5.   Industry
         pulp, paper and paper products
         a. for shipments of folding paper boxes
Q.6.   paper packaging industry analysis
Q.7.   1978
         Industry and Commerce
         manufacturing capacity utilization

CHAPTER EIGHT
Q.1.   Michigan
Q.2.   Colorado Springs, Colorado
Q.3.   LaCrosse
Q.4.   Ketchikan, Alaska
Q.5.   b. Maryland Cup
         sales record
Q.6.   paper and board (SIC 2621)
         a. value added for corrugated and solid fiber boxes

CHAPTER NINE
Q.4.   salesmen and salesmanship
         v. 64, 1978
Q.5.   CBS, Inc.
Q.6.   R.G. Ibbotson
         Journal of Business, v. 49, 1976, p. 11
Q.7.   fair employment practices

CHAPTER TEN
Q.2.   cost control
Q.3.   business cycles
Q.4.   Paper Making and Trade

CHAPTER ELEVEN
Q.2.   Volume 52, Jan./Feb., 1974
         a. Leonard M. Lodish
Q.3.   Volume 91, February 1975
         a. "Mr. Micawber's Disciples"
Q.4.   Volume 184, No. 6, Feb. 10, 1975
         b. Louisiana Power & Light
Q.5.   *Association Management*
Q.6.   a. packaging
         b. October

CHAPTER TWELVE
Q.1.   Tallahasee, Florida
Q.2.   Sierra Leone
         1972
Q.3.   c. packaging industry
Q.4.   a. packaging, boxes, barrels, cartons
         b. San Jose, California

CHAPTER THIRTEEN
Q.2.   apprenticeship and training
Q.3.   advertising
Q.4.   *Small Business and the Quality of American Life*
Q.5.   Paper-making machinery — Handbooks, manuals, etc.

Book No.   7

CHAPTER ONE
Q.2. an introductory geology course
    a. handbook
Q.3. advertising
    a. handbook
Q.4. decision making
Q.5. bolts and nuts

CHAPTER TWO
Q.2. collection period for accounts receivable
Q.3. drugs
Q.4. the buyer-seller relationship
Q.5. consumer psychology and motivation

CHAPTER THREE
Q.3. innovation
Q.4. Bunting v. Oregon
Q.5. financial management
    depreciation
Q.6. approximation of laws (EEC)

CHAPTER FOUR
Q.2. Haydite
COMPANY: Iowa Beef Processors
INDUSTRY: Meat packing
Q.7. food industry
Q.8. meat

CHAPTER FIVE
Q.2. a casualty loss
    job dismissal
Q.3. Electrical Fittings Corp.
Q.4. D.C.
Q.5. a. Food Industry
Q.7. Meat Packing
Q.8. net sales
Q.9. b. Meat packing plants

CHAPTER SIX
Q.2. Burundi
Q.3. Apr. 6, 1978
Q.4. meats
    a. of steer beef carcass, choice, at Midwest markets in 1974

CHAPTER SEVEN
Q.1. federal finance
    Economic Indicators
Q.2. a. food and kindred products
Q.3. food manufacturing industry
    a. production and related workers
Q.4. figures on per capita consumption of poultry
    "Agricultural Products"
    meat
    a. 1974

Q.5. Industry
    food and kindred products
    a. for total production of beef and veal
Q.6. meat packing, cattle on farm, slaughter and average price
Q.7. 1978
    Science and Technology
    R & D spending by industry, actual data compared to estimates . . .

CHAPTER EIGHT
Q.1. Missouri
Q.2. Wilmington, Delaware
Q.3. Lincoln
Q.4. Sitka, Alaska
Q.5. b. Oscar Mayer
    profit margins
Q.6. meat and poultry products (SIC 2011)
    a. value added for meat packing plants

CHAPTER NINE
Q.4. sales promotion
    v. 64, 1978
Q.5. candy factories
Q.6. S.W. Kohlhagen
    Journal of International Business Studies, 1975, p. 33
Q.7. distribution management

CHAPTER TEN
Q.2. decision-making
Q.3. customer relations
Q.4. Meat Industry and Trade

CHAPTER ELEVEN
Q.2. Volume 52, March/April, 1974
    a. Robert W. Fri
Q.3. Volume 91, March 1975
    a. "Why They Call it Fat City"
Q.4. Volume 185, No. 1, Apr. 7, 1975
    b. RCA Service Co.
Q.5. *Compensation Review*
Q.6. a. food/food industries
    b. April

CHAPTER TWELVE
Q.1. Springfield, Illinois
Q.2. Dahomey
    1972
Q.3. c. meat industry
Q.4. a. meats and provisions
    b. Mill Valley, California

CHAPTER THIRTEEN
Q.2. investigating bonus plans
Q.3. accounting and auditing
Q.4. *Small Business Development Center Act*
Q.5. Meat industry and trade — United States

CHAPTER ONE
Q.2. a mineralogy course
      a. handbook
Q.3. personnel management
      a. handbook
Q.4. efficiency audit
Q.5. book

CHAPTER TWO
Q.2. cycle
Q.3. emotional problems
Q.4. buying procedures for commodity classes
Q.5. conflict in organizational development

CHAPTER THREE
Q.3. mergers
Q.4. Carey v. Westinghouse Electric Corp.
Q.5. corporate planning
      break-even analysis
Q.6. arbitrage

CHAPTER FOUR
Q.2. Keytape
COMPANY: Warner Lambert
INDUSTRY: Pharmaceuticals (Drug)
Q.7. drug industry
Q.8. pharmaceutical

CHAPTER FIVE
Q.2. a casualty loss
      smog damage
Q.3. Lawrence G. Empey
Q.4. E.O.
Q.5. a. Drug Industry
Q.7. Drugs — Medicines, Cosmetics
Q.8. net sales
Q.9. b. pharmaceutical preparations

CHAPTER SIX
Q.2. Chile
Q.3. Apr. 24, 1978
Q.4. bismuth
      a. per pound of bismuth, in 1974

CHAPTER SEVEN
Q.1. prices
      Monthly Labor Review
Q.2. a. chemicals, allied products
Q.3. chemicals manufacturing industry
      a. production and related workers
Q.4. figures on sales of medicinal chemicals
      "Textile, Chemical, Paper"
      synthetic organics
      a. 1974

Q.5. General
      domestic trade
      a. for estimated total sales (unadjusted) for drug and proprietary stores
Q.6. drug manufacturers, rates of changes in sales and profits
Q.7. 1978
      Science and Technology
      R & D spending by industry, including energy applications and pollution
      control

CHAPTER EIGHT
Q.1. New Mexico
Q.2. Jacksonville, Florida
Q.3. Manitowoc
Q.4. Bisbee, Arizona
Q.5. b. Upjohn
      sales record
Q.6. drugs (SIC 2831)
      a. value added for biologicals

CHAPTER NINE
Q.4. women's market
      v. 64, 1978
Q.5. the canned food industry
Q.6. L. Bogart
      Journal of Advertising Research, v. 10, 1970, p. 4
Q.7. manager unionization

CHAPTER TEN
Q.2. economic forecasting
Q.3. customer service
Q.4. Drug Trade

CHAPTER ELEVEN
Q.2. Volume 52, March/April, 1974
      a. Dean S. Ammer
Q.3. Volume 91, March 1975
      a. "Outsider in the Throne Room at Kaiser"
Q.4. Volume 185, No. 2, Apr. 14, 1975
      b. Mapp Products
Q.5. *Director*
Q.6. a. drugs/cosmetics industries
      b. April

CHAPTER TWELVE
Q.1. Gary, Indiana
Q.2. Mali
      1972
Q.3. c. drugs
Q.4. a. drugs and pharmaceuticals
      b. Marina del Rey, California

CHAPTER THIRTEEN
Q.2. career planning
Q.3. agricultural industries
Q.4. *Small Business Issues and Priorities, 1977*
Q.5. Drug trade — United States

Book No.   9

CHAPTER ONE
Q.2.   an introductory music course
         a. handbook
Q.3.   production and operations management
         a. handbook
Q.4.   ethics
Q.5.   box

CHAPTER TWO
Q.2.   earnings per share of common stock
Q.3.   exit interviews
Q.4.   centralized purchasing
Q.5.   assessment center, managerial

CHAPTER THREE
Q.3.   patents
Q.4.   Coppage v. Kansas
Q.5.   project management
         the Gantt Chart
Q.6.   asset stripping

CHAPTER FOUR
Q.2.   Key-bak
COMPANY: Rexnord
INDUSTRY: Construction & materials handling equipment
Q.7.   building supplies and construction
Q.8.   equipment

CHAPTER FIVE
Q.2.   a medical expense
         acupuncture
Q.3.   Acme Manifolding Co., Inc.
Q.4.   DC
Q.5.   a. Construction Equipment
Q.7.   Construction (Heavy) and Supplies
Q.8.   net sales
Q.9.   Construction machinery and equipment

CHAPTER SIX
Q.2.   China, Republic of
Q.3.   May 8, 1978
Q.4.   iron and steel
         a. of heavy melting steel scrap (Chicago) in 1974

CHAPTER SEVEN
Q.1.   domestic trade
         Survey of Current Business
Q.2.   a. machinery, except electric
Q.3.   machinery manufacturing industry (except electrical)
         a. production and related workers
Q.4.   figures on total number of residential construction permits issued in the west
         "Building and Building Materials"
         new construction permits
         a. 1974
Q.5.   Industry
         metals and manufactures
         a. for orders for industrial materials handling equipment (seasonally
              adjusted)

Q.6.   construction machinery industry analysis
Q.7.   1978
         Science and Technology
         scientists and engineers employed in private industry and in R & D and
              energy-related activities

CHAPTER EIGHT
Q.1.   North Carolina
Q.2.   Pensacola, Florida
Q.3.   Marathon
Q.4.   Casa Grande, Arizona
Q.5.   b. Caterpillar
         profit margins
Q.6.   construction machinery (SIC 3531)
         a. value added

CHAPTER NINE
Q.4.   advertising
         v. 63, 1977
Q.5.   the cigarette industry
Q.6.   W. Oberg
         Harvard Business Review, v. 50, 1972, p. 61
Q.7.   manager training

CHAPTER TEN
Q.2.   electronic data processing
Q.3.   industrial management
Q.4.   Construction Equipment

CHAPTER ELEVEN
Q.2.   Volume 52, March/April, 1974
         a. George Cabot Lodge
Q.3.   Volume 91, March 1975
         a. "Lawrence Klein and His Forecasting Machine"
Q.4.   Volume 185, No. 3, Apr. 21, 1975
         b. NVF Co.
Q.5.   *Journal of General Management*
Q.6.   a. building/construction
         b. February

CHAPTER TWELVE
Q.1.   Cedar Rapids, Iowa
Q.2.   Zaire
         1972
Q.3.   c. construction industry
Q.4.   a. construction, contracting, building, excavating
         b. Minneapolis, Minnesota

CHAPTER THIRTEEN
Q.2.   consumer affairs & business
Q.3.   business ethics
Q.4.   *Fuel Efficiency Incentive Tax Proposal: Its Impact Upon the Future
         of the U.S. Passenger Automobile Industry*
Q.5.   Construction equipment

Book No. __10__

CHAPTER ONE
Q.2. a survey course in French literature
      a. dictionary
Q.3. industrial research
      a. handbook
Q.4. environment and management
Q.5. brewing

CHAPTER TWO
Q.2. exact simple interest
Q.3. handicapped applicants
Q.4. centralized purchasing vs. decentralized
Q.5. participant observation

CHAPTER THREE
Q.3. productivity
Q.4. Dominion Hotel v. Arizona
Q.5. business logistics
      purchasing
Q.6. autonomous work groups

CHAPTER FOUR
Q.2. Linksem
COMPANY: Aluminum Company of America
INDUSTRY: Aluminum
Q.7. metals industry
Q.8. aluminum

CHAPTER FIVE
Q.2. a medical expense
      an air conditioner
Q.3. Charlton & Co.
Q.4. E.P.C.
Q.5. a. Aluminum
Q.7. Aluminum
Q.8. net sales and operating revenues
Q.9. b. Aluminum ore

CHAPTER SIX
Q.2. Columbia
Q.3. May 15, 1978
Q.4. bauxite
      a. of bauxite, F.O.B. mine in 1974

CHAPTER SEVEN
Q.1. money, credit and security markets
      Economic Indicators
Q.2. a. primary metal industries
Q.3. nonferrous metals manufacturing — foundries industry
      a. production and related workers
Q.4. figures on aluminum consumption in the U.S.
      "Metals"
      aluminum consumption (annual)
      a. 1975

Q.5. Industry
      metals and manufactures
      a. for aluminum production
Q.6. aluminum companies stock price indexes
Q.7. 1977
      Government
      chemicals composition proposed reporting requirement, impact on
      chemicals industry basic R & D

CHAPTER EIGHT
Q.1. Oklahoma
Q.2. Savannah, Georgia
Q.3. Marinette
Q.4. Prescott, Arizona
Q.5. b. Reynolds Metals
      sales record
Q.6. aluminum (SIC 3334)
      a. value added

CHAPTER NINE
Q.4. distribution
      v. 63, 1977
Q.5. communications satellites
Q.6. R.L. Steiner
      Journal of Marketing, v. 40, 1976, p. 2
Q.7. manager appraisal

CHAPTER TEN
Q.2. executive ability
Q.3. communication in management
Q.4. Aluminum

CHAPTER ELEVEN
Q.2. Volume 52, March/April, 1974
      a. Stewart A. Smith
Q.3. Volume 91, March 1975
      a. "What We Should Have Learned About Controls"
Q.4. Volume 185, No. 4, Apr. 28, 1975
      b. Warner & Swasey Co.
Q.5. *Journal of Management Studies*
Q.6. a. mines/mining industry
      b. January

CHAPTER TWELVE
Q.1. Kansas City, Kansas
Q.2. Zambia
      1972
Q.3. c. aluminum industry
Q.4. a. metal working and metal trade
      b. San Francisco, California

CHAPTER THIRTEEN
Q.2. consumer affairs & regulations
Q.3. consumer credit
Q.4. *Federal Subsidy for Certain Air Transportation*
Q.5. Aluminum industry and trade — Environmental aspects — United States

IM 27

Book No.   11

CHAPTER ONE
Q.2. an introductory course in biology
      a. handbook
Q.3. materials management
      a. handbook
Q.4. financial managers
Q.5. building

CHAPTER TWO
Q.2. inventory turnover
Q.3. health problems
Q.4. competitive bids
Q.5. questionnaires and field research methods

CHAPTER THREE
Q.3. regulation of industry
Q.4. Dorchy v. Kansas
Q.5. industrial engineering
      process analysis
Q.6. back-selling

CHAPTER FOUR
Q.2. Linestrain
COMPANY: International Business Machines Corporation
INDUSTRY: Computer manufacturing
Q.7. computers and data processing
Q.8. computer

CHAPTER FIVE
Q.2. a medical expense
      alcohol addiction
Q.3. Jessie Chase
Q.4. F.R.
Q.5. a. Computer Manufacturing
Q.7. Computers
Q.8. net sales
Q.9. b. Computing equipment, electronic

CHAPTER SIX
Q.2. Costa Rica
Q.3. May 21, 1978
Q.4. plastics
      a. index of phenolic molding compound in 1975

CHAPTER SEVEN
Q.1. productivity
      Monthly Labor Review
Q.2. a. electric, electronic equipment
Q.3. machinery manufacturing industry (except electrical)
      a. production and related workers
Q.4. indexes of industrial production
      "Production of Indexes and Labor Statistics"
      commercial equipment
      a. 1974

Q.5. General
      business indicators
      a. under industrial production for business equipment (seasonally
          adjusted)
Q.6. computer and related equipment, annual factory shipments
Q.7. 1977
      Industry and Commerce
      defense industries and DOD-owned facilities shipments under Federal
      Gov't. contract

CHAPTER EIGHT
Q.1. Rhode Island
Q.2. Boise, Idaho
Q.3. Marquette
Q.4. Tempe, Arizona
Q.5. b. Honeywell
      sales record
Q.6. computers and related equipment (SIC 3573)
      a. value added

CHAPTER NINE
Q.4. merchandising legislation
      v. 63, 1977
Q.5. the copper industry
Q.6. P. Kotler
      Journal of Marketing Research, v. 1, 1964, p. 43
Q.7. managerial shortages

CHAPTER TEN
Q.2. the food industry and trade
Q.3. communication in personnel management
Q.4. Computer Industry

CHAPTER ELEVEN
Q.2. Volume 52, March/April, 1974
      a. George W. Schiele
Q.3. Volume 91, April 1975
      a. "Reshaping the American Dream"
Q.4. Volume 185, No. 5, May 5, 1975
      b. Kepner Tregoe, Inc.
Q.5. *MBA*
Q.6. a. automation
      b. September

CHAPTER TWELVE
Q.1. Bangor, Maine
Q.2. Ghana
      1971
Q.3. c. computers
Q.4. a. automation and computers
      b. Boston, Massachusetts

CHAPTER THIRTEEN
Q.2. investigating consumerism
Q.3. corporations
Q.4. *Implementation of the Consumer Product Safety Act*
Q.5. Computer industry

Book No. __12__

CHAPTER ONE
Q.2. Introduction to Spanish Literature
      a. dictionary
Q.3. auditing
      a. handbook
Q.4. forecasting
Q.5. candy

CHAPTER TWO
Q.2. labor wage rate variation
Q.3. homosexuality
Q.4. incentive agreements
Q.5. recruiting and personnel selection

CHAPTER THREE
Q.3. wage and hour legislation
Q.4. Donham v. West-Nelson Co.
Q.5. labor relations
      collective bargaining
Q.6. bandwidth

CHAPTER FOUR
Q.2. Ling-seal
COMPANY: Atlantic Richfield
INDUSTRY: Oil (Petroleum)
Q.7. oil and gas industry
Q.8. petroleum

CHAPTER FIVE
Q.2. a medical expense
      a chiropractor
Q.3. Coeur d'Alene Country Club v. Viley
Q.4. F.R.D.
Q.5. a. Petroleum
Q.7. Petroleum
Q.8. total operating revenues
Q.9. b. Oil and gas well drilling

CHAPTER SIX
Q.2. Cuba
Q.3. Aug. 3, 1978
Q.4. petroleum
      a. index of crude petroleum at wells in 1974

CHAPTER SEVEN
Q.1. foreign trade of the U.S.
      Survey of Current Business
Q.2. a. petroleum, coal products
Q.3. petroleum and coal products
      a. production and related workers
Q.4. figures giving the total number of wells drilled in the U.S.
      "Energy, Electric Power & Fuels"
      wells drilled
      a. 1974

Q.5. Industry
      petroleum, coal and products
      a. for the refinery operating ration for crude petroleum
Q.6. oil pipeline statistics on interstate operations
Q.7. 1977
      Industry and Commerce
      energy use reduction in the ten high-energy consuming industry groups

CHAPTER EIGHT
Q.1. Tennessee
Q.2. Peoria, Illinois
Q.3. Milwaukee
Q.4. El Dorado, Arkansas
Q.5. b. Sun
      profit margins
Q.6. pipelines (SIC 461)
      a. freight movement via pipelines

CHAPTER NINE
Q.4. radio advertising
      v. 63, 1977
Q.5. data base systems
Q.6. L.P. Bucklin
      Journal of Marketing, v. 37, 1973, p. 39
Q.7. management information systems

CHAPTER TEN
Q.2. industrial sociology
Q.3. marketing management
Q.4. Petroleum Industry and Trade

CHAPTER ELEVEN
Q.2. Volume 52, March/April, 1974
      a. Paul S. Nadler
Q.3. Volume 91, April 1975
      a. "The Revolution of Rising Entitlements"
Q.4. Volume 185, No. 6, May 12, 1975
      a. Oakite Products, Inc.
Q.5. *Management Decisions*
Q.6. a. petroleum/gas/oil
      b. November

CHAPTER TWELVE
Q.1. Cambridge, Maryland
Q.2. Tanzania
      1971
Q.3. c. petroleum industry
Q.4. a. petroleum, oil and gas
      b. Springfield, Illinois

CHAPTER THIRTEEN
Q.2. hiring racial minorities
Q.3. executives
Q.4. *Impact of Weather-Related Energy Shortages on Small Business*
Q.5. Petroleum industry and trade — Costs

Book No. 13

CHAPTER ONE
Q.2.   General Physics
       a. handbook
Q.3.   management
       a. handbook
Q.4.   grid theory
Q.5.   cement

CHAPTER TWO
Q.2.   price variation
Q.3.   layoffs
Q.4.   internal pricing
Q.5.   criteria variables classification

CHAPTER THREE
Q.3.   bureaucracy
Q.4.   Duplex Printing Press Co. v. Deering
Q.5.   labor relations
       labor arbitration
Q.6.   bed and breakfast deal

CHAPTER FOUR
Q.2.   Mikaloid
COMPANY: Crown Zellerbach
INDUSTRY: Paper
Q.7.   paper industry
Q.8.   paper

CHAPTER FIVE
Q.2.   a medical expense
       clothing
Q.3.   William C. Coe
Q.4.   C.C.M.
Q.5.   a. Paper
Q.7.   Paper — Pulp
Q.8.   net sales
Q.9.   b. Paper products, sanitary

CHAPTER SIX
Q.2.   Czechoslovakia
Q.3.   Aug. 4, 1978
Q.4.   paper
       a. of wood pulp, unbleached sulphate in 1973

CHAPTER SEVEN
Q.1.   total output, income and spending
       Economic Indicators
Q.2.   a. paper and allied products
Q.3.   paper and products manufacturing
       a. production and related workers
Q.4.   figures giving new orders of paperboard
       ''Textile, Chemical, Paper''
       paperboard
       a. 1974

Q.5.   Industry
       pulp, paper, and paper products
       a. for the total production of all grades of woodpulp
Q.6.   paper companies stock price indexes
Q.7.   1977
       Industry and Commerce
       manufacturers shipments, inventories, and orders

CHAPTER EIGHT
Q.1.   Washington
Q.2.   Springfield, Illinois
Q.3.   Monroe
Q.4.   Bluefield, West Virginia
Q.5.   a. Scott Paper
       sales record
Q.6.   paper and board (SIC 2621, 2631, 2661)
       a. value added

CHAPTER NINE
Q.4.   retail trade
       v. 63, 1977
Q.5.   the dye industry
Q.6.   R.W. Little
       Journal of Marketing, v. 34, 1970, p. 32
Q.7.   management methods

CHAPTER TEN
Q.2.   international finance
Q.3.   marketing channels
Q.4.   Paper Making and Trade

CHAPTER ELEVEN
Q.2.   Volume 52, March/April, 1974
       a. James W. Culliton
Q.3.   Volume 91, April 1975
       a. ''Putting the Cuffs on Capitalism''
Q.4.   Volume 184, No. 7, Feb. 17, 1975
       b. Western Union Telegraph Co.
Q.5.   *Management Review*
Q.6.   a. paper/pulp
       b. December

CHAPTER TWELVE
Q.1.   Salem, Massachusetts
Q.2.   Tunisia
       1971
Q.3.   c. paper industry
Q.4.   a. paper
       b. Oradell, New Jersey

CHAPTER THIRTEEN
Q.2.   copyright practice overseas
Q.3.   government and business
Q.4.   *Impact of Base Closings on Small Business*
Q.5.   Paper making and trade — Vocational guidance

CHAPTER ONE
Q.2. an introductory engineering course
      a. handbook
Q.3. office management
      a. handbook
Q.4. Hawthorne investigations
Q.5. chocolate

CHAPTER TWO
Q.2. quantity variation
Q.3. time off the job (establishing a policy)
Q.4. lease agreements (types of)
Q.5. theory building

CHAPTER THREE
Q.3. capitalism
Q.4. Elgin, Joliet & Eastern Ry. v. Burley
Q.5. corporate planning
      creativity training
Q.6. below-the-line promotion

CHAPTER FOUR
Q.2. Mighty Grip
COMPANY: Federated Department Stores, Inc.
INDUSTRY: Retailing (Department stores)
Q.7. chain, department and discount stores
Q.8. retail

CHAPTER FIVE
Q.2. a medical expense
      contraceptives
Q.3. Florica Constantinescu
Q.4. I.R.B.
Q.5. a. Retail Trade
Q.7. Retail Stores — Department
Q.8. net sales
Q.9. b. Stores, variety

CHAPTER SIX
Q.2. Ecuador
Q.3. Aug. 8, 1978
Q.4. wool
      a. of Australian wool (64's, type 62, duty paid at U.S. mills) in 1975

CHAPTER SEVEN
Q.1. finance
      Survey of Current Business
Q.2. a. general merchandise stores
Q.3. general merchandise stores
      a. nonsupervisory employees
Q.4. figures giving end of month inventories
      "Income & Trade"
      department stores
      a. January, 1977
Q.5. General
      domestic trade
      a. total estimated sales (unadjusted) for department stores

Q.6. department stores, retail sales monthly
Q.7. 1977
      Industry and Commerce
      manufacturing capacity utilization

CHAPTER EIGHT
Q.1. California
Q.2. Sioux City, Iowa
Q.3. Oconto
Q.4. Beckley, West Virginia
Q.5. b. Marshall Field
      profit margins
Q.6. department stores (SIC 5311)
      a. year-to-year percent change in average hourly earnings

CHAPTER NINE
Q.4. sales promotion
      v. 63, 1977
Q.5. employee discipline
Q.6. M. Etgar
      Journal of Risk Insurance, v. 44, 1977, p. 211
Q.7. management style

CHAPTER TEN
Q.2. job analysis
Q.3. market surveys
Q.4. Department Stores

CHAPTER ELEVEN
Q.2. Volume 52, March/April, 1974
      a. John S. Hammond III
Q.3. Volume 91, April 1975
      a. "Black America: Still Waiting for Full Membership"
Q.4. Volume 184, No. 8, Feb. 24, 1975
      b. PPG Industries, Inc.
Q.5. Management Today
Q.6. a. retail trade
      b. May

CHAPTER TWELVE
Q.1. Grand Rapids, Michigan
Q.2. Sierra Leone
      1971
Q.3. c. department stores
Q.4. a. general merchandise
      b. Atlanta, Georgia

CHAPTER THIRTEEN
Q.2. availability of disaster loans
Q.3. the Banking Act
Q.4. Impact of OSHA on Small Business
Q.5. Retail trade — United States — Management

Book No.   15

CHAPTER ONE
Q.2.   a basic architectural course
       a. handbook
Q.3.   health care administration
       a. bibliography
Q.4.   human relations
Q.5.   cigar

CHAPTER TWO
Q.2.   raw material inventory turnover
Q.3.   strikes and boycotts
Q.4.   legal regulations in government buying
Q.5.   personality theory

CHAPTER THREE
Q.3.   cartels
Q.4.   Hawkins v. Bleakly
Q.5.   the decision-making process
       operations research in marketing decisions
Q.6.   blacking

CHAPTER FOUR
Q.2.   Pabco
COMPANY: The Kroger Company
INDUSTRY: Food retailing (Grocery chains)
Q.7.   food industry
Q.8.   grocery

CHAPTER FIVE
Q.2.   a medical expense
       dancing lessons
Q.3.   Eidlitz & Ross, Inc.
Q.4.   I.R.C.
Q.5.   a. Grocery Trade
Q.7.   Grocery and Food Chains
Q.8.   sales
Q.9.   b. Stores, Grocery

CHAPTER SIX
Q.2.   Haiti
Q.3.   Aug. 11, 1978
Q.4.   milk
       a. of evaporated milk in 1974

CHAPTER SEVEN
Q.1.   labor-management
       Monthly Labor Review
Q.2.   a. food stores
Q.3.   food and liquor stores
       a. nonsupervisory employees
Q.4.   figures giving retail sales for grocery stores
       "Income & Trade"
       retail sales—monthly
       a. Nobember, 1977

Q.5.   General
       domestic trade
       a. for total estimated sales (unadjusted) for food stores
Q.6.   grocery chains analysis
Q.7.   1977
       Industry and Commerce
       manufacturing industry plant and equipment book value

CHAPTER EIGHT
Q.1.   Colorado
Q.2.   Lawrence, Kansas
Q.3.   Oneida
Q.4.   Clarksburg, West Virginia
Q.5.   b. Jewel Companies
       profit margins
Q.6.   grocer stores (SIC 5411)
       a. year-to-year percent change in average hourly earnings for food
           retailing

CHAPTER NINE
Q.4.   television advertising
       v. 63, 1977
Q.5.   fiduciaries
Q.6.   P. Kotler
       Harvard Business Review, v. 49, 1971, p. 74
Q.7.   management teams

CHAPTER TEN
Q.2.   logistics
Q.3.   advertising campaigns
Q.4.   Food Industry and Trade

CHAPTER ELEVEN
Q.2.   Volume 52, March/April, 1974
       a. John Kitching
Q.3.   Volume 91, May 1975
       a. "What's Really Wrong at Chrysler"
Q.4.   Volume 184, No. 9, Mar. 3, 1975
       b. Lockheed
Q.5.   *Managerial Planning*
Q.6.   a. grocery trade
       b. August

CHAPTER TWELVE
Q.1.   Duluth, Minnesota
Q.2.   Dahomey
       1971
Q.3.   c. foodstuffs
Q.4.   a. grocery
       b. Denver, Colorado

CHAPTER THIRTEEN
Q.2.   investigating financing devices
Q.3.   checking and savings accounts
Q.4.   *Petroleum Industry Involvement in Alternative Sources of Energy*
Q.5.   Food industry and trade—Technological innovations

Book No. 16

CHAPTER ONE
Q.2. Fundamentals of Electrical Engineering Technology
    a. handbook
Q.3. marketing research
    a. bibliography
Q.4. job descriptions
Q.5. cigarette

CHAPTER TWO
Q.2. standard error of estimate
Q.3. wildcat strikes
Q.4. the negotiation process
Q.5. vocational preferences

CHAPTER THREE
Q.3. monopoly
Q.4. Helvering v. Davis
Q.5. the decision-making process
    waiting line theory (queueing)
Q.6. buzz-word

CHAPTER FOUR
Q.2. Pap-plus plant air package
COMPANY: McDonald's Corporation
INDUSTRY: Food service (restaurants)
Q.7. restaurants and restaurant equipment
Q.8. restaurant

CHAPTER FIVE
Q.2. a medical expense
    diaper service
Q.3. First Nat'l Bank of Sharon v. Heiner
Q.4. I.T.
Q.5. a. Food Service Industry
Q.7. Restaurants and Confectionaries
Q.8. total revenues
Q.9. b. Eating Places

CHAPTER SIX
Q.2. Hong Kong
Q.3. Aug. 15, 1978
Q.4. meats
    a. of steer beef carcass, choice, at Midwest markets in 1974

CHAPTER SEVEN
Q.1. transportation and communication
    Survey of Current Business
Q.2. a. services
Q.3. food and liquor stores
    a. nonsupervisory employees
Q.4. figures giving retail sales for restaurants
    "Income & Trade"
    eating & drinking places
    a. Nov, 1977

Q.5. General
    domestic trade
    a. for total estimated sales (unadjusted) for eating and drinking places
Q.6. restaurant chains industry analysis
Q.7. 1977
    Industry and Commerce
    manufacturing industry purchases of fuel and electric energy quantity and cost, 1974-75

CHAPTER EIGHT
Q.1. Iowa
Q.2. Louisville, Kentucky
Q.3. Outagamie
Q.4. Hinton, West Virginia
Q.5. b. Howard Johnson
    sales record
Q.6. restaurants (SIC 5812)
    a. sales for eating and drinking places (in "Retail Trade" table)

CHAPTER NINE
Q.4. travel market
    v. 63, 1977
Q.5. incentives in industry
Q.6. P. Wright
    Journal of Marketing Research, v. 12, 1975, p. 60
Q.7. managerial effectiveness

CHAPTER TEN
Q.2. management information systems
Q.3. market segmentation
Q.4. Restaurants, Lunchrooms, etc.

CHAPTER ELEVEN
Q.2. Volume 52, May/June, 1974
    a. Ellen C. Hughes
Q.3. Volume 91, May 1975
    a. "I.T.T.'s Disaster in Hartford"
Q.4. Volume 184, No. 10, Mar. 10, 1975
    b. National Steel Corporation
Q.5. *Operational Research Quarterly*
Q.6. a. hotels, restaurants
    b. October

CHAPTER TWELVE
Q.1. Independence, Missouri
Q.2. Mali
    1971
Q.3. c. restaurants
Q.4. a. hotels, motels, restaurants and clubs
    b. Wichita, Kansas

CHAPTER THIRTEEN
Q.2. investigating government business opportunities
Q.3. the Consumer Fraud Act
Q.4. *Petroleum Marketing Practices*
Q.5. Restaurants, lunch rooms, etc.

Book No. 17

CHAPTER ONE
Q.2. an introductory course in costume design
a. encyclopedia
Q.3. management development
a. bibliography
Q.4. job design
Q.5. cleaning

CHAPTER TWO
Q.2. straight line depreciation
Q.3. thefts
Q.4. nondisclosure agreements
Q.5. aptitude

CHAPTER THREE
Q.3. consumer behavior
Q.4. Holden v. Hardy
Q.5. the decision-making process
management information systems
Q.6. conformer

CHAPTER FOUR
Q.2. Port-O-Reel
COMPANY: Goodyear Tire & Rubber Company
INDUSTRY: Tires and rubber goods
Q.7. rubber industry
Q.8. rubber

CHAPTER FIVE
Q.2. a medical expense
dust elimination system
Q.3. Albert J. Goldsmith
Q.4. I. T. Info.
Q.5. a. Rubber Industry
Q.7. Tires, Rubber and Rubber Goods
Q.8. net sales
Q.9. b. Tires and Inner Tubes

CHAPTER SIX
Q.2. Hungary
Q.3. Aug. 20, 1978
Q.4. rubber
a. of spot crude rubber (smoked sheets) in New York in 1974

CHAPTER SEVEN
Q.1. employment, unemployment and wages
Economic Indicators
Q.2. a. rubber, plastics products
Q.3. rubber products manufacturing industry
a. production and related workers
Q.4. figures on exports of motor vehicle tires
"Automotive, Machine Tools, Rubber & Tires"
tires
a. 1974

Q.5. Industry
rubber and rubber products
a. for production of synthetic rubber
Q.6. tires and rubber companies stock price indexes
Q.7. 1977
Industry and Commerce
pollution abatement capital expenditures and operating costs

CHAPTER EIGHT
Q.1. Kentucky
Q.2. Baton Rouge, Louisiana
Q.3. Washington
Q.4. Clay Center, Kansas
Q.5. b. B.F. Goodrich
profit margins
Q.6. tires and tubes (SIC 3011)
a. value added

CHAPTER NINE
Q.4. youth market
v. 63, 1977
Q.5. insurance agencies
Q.6. L.L. Berry
Journal of Retailing, v. 47, 1971, p. 41
Q.7. managerial continuity

CHAPTER TEN
Q.2. market surveys
Q.3. physical distribution of goods
Q.4. Rubber Industry and Trade

CHAPTER ELEVEN
Q.2. Volume 52, May/June, 1974
a. Valentin A. Nazarevsky
Q.3. Volume 91, May 1975
a. "The Old Uranium King Means to be Rich Again"
Q.4. Volume 184, No. 11, Mar. 17, 1975
b. Porex Materials Corporation
Q.5. *Operations Research*
Q.6. a. rubber
b. April

CHAPTER TWELVE
Q.1. Butte, Montana
Q.2. Zambia
1971
Q.3. c. rubber industry-tires
Q.4. a. rubber trade
b. Akron, Ohio

CHAPTER THIRTEEN
Q.2. handling grievances
Q.3. the Consumer Credit Protection Act
Q.4. *Real Estate Tax Shelter Subsidies and Direct Subsidy Alternatives*
Q.5. Tires, Rubber — Noise

CHAPTER ONE
Q.2.   a seminar on agriculture of the future
       a. encyclopedia
Q.3.   industrial research
       a. directory
Q.4.   job enrichment
Q.5.   clothing

CHAPTER TWO
Q.2.   times bond interest earned
Q.3.   tardiness
Q.4.   open-end contracts
Q.5.   laboratory experimentation, procedures

CHAPTER THREE
Q.3.   reward systems and incentives
Q.4.   Kentucky Whip and Collar Co. v. Illinois Central Railway
Q.5.   basic management concepts
       incentive systems
Q.6.   contango facilities

CHAPTER FOUR
Q.2. Powdercraft
COMPANY: U.S. Steel Corporation
INDUSTRY: Steel
Q.7.   metals industry
Q.8.   steel

CHAPTER FIVE
Q.2.   a medical expense
       a fall-out shelter
Q.3.   Abraham Goldstein
Q.4.   L.O.
Q.5.   a. Metals Industry
Q.7.   Steel and Iron
Q.8.   products and services sold
Q.9.   b. Steel pipe and tubes

CHAPTER SIX
Q.2.   Iceland
Q.3.   Sept. 9, 1978
Q.4.   nickel
       a. of nickel (spot cathode sheets) in 1974

CHAPTER SEVEN
Q.1.   chemicals and allied products
       Survey of Current Business
Q.2.   a. primary metal industries
Q.3.   iron and steel foundries
       a. production and related workers
Q.4.   the composite price of finished steel
       "Metals"
       steel prices
       a. 1975

Q.5.   Industry
       metals and manufactures
       a. for production of raw steel
Q.6.   steel making industry analysis
Q.7.   1977
       Labor and Employment
       Mountain-Plains region, collective bargaining expirations, by
          industry group and individual company

CHAPTER EIGHT
Q.1.   Maryland
Q.2.   Portland, Maine
Q.3.   Waukesha
Q.4.   Council Grove, Kansas
Q.5.   b. Steel Company of Canada
           sales record
Q.6.   steel mill products (SIC 3312)
       a. value added for ferrous castings

CHAPTER NINE
Q.4.   old age market
       v. 64, 1978
Q.5.   insurance research
Q.6.   N. Hanna
       Journal of Marketing, v. 39, 1975, p. 63
Q.7.   management theory

CHAPTER TEN
Q.2.   marketing research
Q.3.   ratio analysis
Q.4.   Steel Industry and Trade

CHAPTER ELEVEN
Q.2.   Volume 52, May/June, 1974
       a. Gopal C. Pati
Q.3.   Volume 91, June 1975
       a. "The Slow Road Back to Full Employment"
Q.4.   Volume 184, No. 12, Mar. 24, 1975
       b. Tennant Company
Q.5.   Optimum
Q.6.   a. mines/mining industry
       b. December

CHAPTER TWELVE
Q.1.   Arlington, Virginia
Q.2.   Zaire
       1971
Q.3.   c. steel industry
Q.4.   a. sheet metal working
       b. Warrendale, Pennsylvania

CHAPTER THIRTEEN
Q.2.   investigating job discrimination
Q.3.   containerization
Q.4.   Regulatory Reform in Air Transportation
Q.5.   Steel industry and trade — United States

Book No. 19

CHAPTER ONE
Q.2. a seminar on nutrition and preventive medicine
    a. handbook
Q.3. materials management
    a. bibliography
Q.4. job satisfaction
Q.5. coal

CHAPTER TWO
Q.2. accounts receivable turnover
Q.3. paternalism
Q.4. paints (buying of)
Q.5. multivariate methods and covariation analysis

CHAPTER THREE
Q.3. public relations
Q.4. Lauf v. E.G. Shinner & Co., Inc.
Q.5. industrial engineering
    process analysis
Q.6. cybernetics

CHAPTER FOUR
Q.2. Power-lock
COMPANY: Burlington Industries
INDUSTRY: Textile
Q.7. textiles
Q.8. textile

CHAPTER FIVE
Q.2. a medical expense
    fluoridation
Q.3. Frederick B. Hill, Jr.
Q.4. M.T.
Q.5. a. Wool Industry
Q.7. Textiles — Cotton
Q.8. net sales
Q.9. b. Textile goods

CHAPTER SIX
Q.2. Iraq
Q.3. Sept. 17, 1978
Q.4. cotton
    a. of cotton yard on cones in 1974

CHAPTER SEVEN
Q.1. electric power and gas
    Survey of Current Business
Q.2. a. textile mill products
Q.3. textile and products industry
    a. production and related workers
Q.4. figures giving total U.S. man-made fiber production
    "Textile, Chemical, Paper"
    man-made fibers
    a. 1974

Q.5. Industry
    textile products
    a. for shipments fo carpets, rugs, carpeting
Q.6. textile industry analysis
Q.7. 1977
    Labor and Employment
    Mountain-Plains region employment and occupational changes

CHAPTER EIGHT
Q.1. Michigan
Q.2. Kenosha, Wisconsin
Q.3. Waupaca
Q.4. Dodge City, Kansas
Q.5. b. Lowenstein
    sales record
Q.6. textile mill products (SIC 22)
    a. value added

CHAPTER NINE
Q.4. old age market
    v. 63, 1977
Q.5. International Telephone and Telegraph Corporation
Q.6. E.J. Kelley
    Journal of Marketing, v. 39, 1975, p. 44
Q.7. managerial obsolescence

CHAPTER TEN
Q.2. new business enterprises
Q.3. sales management
Q.4. Textile Industry

CHAPTER ELEVEN
Q.2. Volume 52, May/June, 1974
    a. Esther Peterson
Q.3. Volume 91, June 1975
    a. "Uncloaking the CIA"
Q.4. Volume 184, No. 13, Mar. 31, 1975
    b. Dixie Bearings, Inc.
Q.5. *Personnel*
Q.6. a. textile industry
    b. December

CHAPTER TWELVE
Q.1. Carson City, Nevada
Q.2. Zambia
    1970
Q.3. c. textile industry
Q.4. a. textiles
    b. New York, New York

CHAPTER THIRTEEN
Q.2. handling job performance problems
Q.3. railroads
Q.4. *Regulatory Problems of the Independent Owner-Operated in the
    Nation's Trucking Industry, Part 1*
Q.5. Textile industry — Economic aspects — United States

Book No.   20

CHAPTER ONE
Q.2.   a course in pharmacology
       a. handbook
Q.3.   public relations and communications
       a. bibliography
Q.4.   leadership
Q.5.   coffee

CHAPTER TWO
Q.2.   composite rate of depreciation
Q.3.   featherbedding
Q.4.   plywood (buying of)
Q.5.   psychometric theory and validity

CHAPTER THREE
Q.3.   economies of scale
Q.4.   Leisy v. Hardin
Q.5.   basic management concepts
       scientific management
Q.6.   Delphi approach

CHAPTER FOUR
Q.2.   Jacknife Control
COMPANY: Philip Morris, Inc.
INDUSTRY: Tobacco
Q.7.   tobacco industry
Q.8.   tobacco

CHAPTER FIVE
Q.2.   a medical expense
       scientology counseling
Q.3.   Hotel Management Co. v. Fahs
Q.4.   O.D.
Q.5.   a. Tobacco Industry
Q.7.   Tobacco Products
Q.8.   operating revenues
Q.9.   b. Tobacco and tobacco products, wholesale

CHAPTER SIX
Q.2.   Israel
Q.3.   Sept. 27, 1978
Q.4.   tobacco
       a. of burley tobacco (farm price) in 1974

CHAPTER SEVEN
Q.1.   leather and products
       Survey of Current Business
Q.2.   a. tobacco manufacturers
Q.3.   tobacco manufacturing industry
       a. production and related workers
Q.4.   figures giving exports of leaf tobacco
       "Agricultural Products"
       tobacco exports
       a. 1974

Q.5.   Industry
       food and kindred products: tobacco
       a. for exports of cigarettes
Q.6.   tobacco products, output
Q.7.   1977
       Labor and Employment
       NYC occupational earnings survey of private industry

CHAPTER EIGHT
Q.1.   Missouri
Q.2.   Racine, Wisconsin
Q.3.   Waushara
Q.4.   Emporia, Kansas
Q.5.   b. Reynolds
       profit margins
Q.6.   tobacco products (SIC 2131)
       a. value added

CHAPTER NINE
Q.4.   market research
       v. 63, 1977
Q.5.   investment managers
Q.6.   D.W. Cravens
       Journal of Marketing, v. 36, 1972, p. 31
Q.7.   participative management

CHAPTER TEN
Q.2.   the real estate business
Q.3.   sales forecasting
Q.4.   Tobacco Manufacture and Trade

CHAPTER ELEVEN
Q.2.   Volume 52, May/June, 1974
       a. Wickham Skinner
Q.3.   Volume 91, June 1975
       a. "The Further Misadventures of Harold Geneen"
Q.4.   Volume 184, No. 10, Mar. 10, 1975
       b. National Steel Corporation
Q.5.   *Personnel Administrator*
Q.6.   a. tobacco
       b. April

CHAPTER TWELVE
Q.1.   Atlantic City, New Jersey
Q.2.   Tunisia
       1970
Q.3.   c. tobacco industries
Q.4.   a. tobacco
       b. Washington, D.C.

CHAPTER THIRTEEN
Q.2.   investigating patent laws
Q.3.   monetary policy
Q.4.   *Regulations of Various Federal Regulatory Agencies and Their Effect on Small Business, Part 4*
Q.5.   Tobacco manufacture and trade — United States

8
Answer Sheets

Because the student assignment pages are an integral part of the workbook, the most convenient way to proceed is to have students turn in the entire workbook periodically for the evaluation of assigned work. At any given time, therefore, the instructor is likely to have in hand a number of workbooks with more than one completed assignment to correct. To facilitate grading, the answer sheets are arranged by complete book. No answer has been written for the first question in each chapter, because it is possible for students to provide different yet correct answers. Also, it provides the instructor a means for determining whether each student has an adequate overall understanding of the type of source under discussion.

Although the answers provided on the following pages have been carefully checked and tested, students may interpret the questions differently, or through means not previously used by any other student, uncover a different and yet correct answer. These possibilities should be kept in mind by the instructor while grading the assignments.

CHAPTER ONE
Q.2. a. *Encyclopedia of Philosophy*
b. p. 249
Q.3. a. *Dartnell Public Relations Handbook*
b. p. 144
Q.4. a. *Taylorism at Watertown Arsenal; Scientific Management in Action 1908–1915*
b. p. 1
Q.5. a. Potash Institute of North America
b. p. 26

CHAPTER TWO
Q.2. p. 104, *Accountant's Handbook of Formulas and Tables*
Q.3. a. 48–14
b. James Gardner, "Employee Safety"
c. *Handbook of Modern Personnel Administration*
Q.4. a. 20–25, *Purchasing Handbook*
b. "Governmental Purchasing"
Q.5. a. 1069–1106
b. Abegglen, J.C. *The Japanese Factory*. Glencoe, Ill.: The Free Press, 1958.

CHAPTER THREE
Q.3. a. Atkinson, John W. (1957) 1958 "Motivational Determinants of Risk-taking Behavior." Pages 322–339 in John W. Atkinson (editor), *Motives in Fantasy, Action and Society: A Method of Assessment and Study*. Princeton, N.J.: Van Nostrand.
b. v. 1, p. 33
Q.4. a. 208 U.S. 161 (1908)
b. p. 9, *Roberts' Dictionary of Industrial Relations*
Q.5. a. p. 506
b. "The History of Management Thought"
Q.6. a. commodities
b. p. 11, *International Dictionary of Management*

CHAPTER FOUR
Q.2. a. Arnold Engineering Co.
b. AAAA
Q.3. a. Thornton A. Wilson
b. Aircraft
c. 3721
d. 74,800
Q.4. Advanced Technology Center, Inc.
Q.5 1921
Q.6. a. yes
b. 1943
Q.7. *ABD Directory*
Q.8. a. Academy of Model Aeronautics
b. 12035
c. yes
d. *Model Aviation*

CHAPTER FIVE
Q.2. a. 1566.45
b. yes
c. *New Matters*
Q.3. 5569.04
Q.4. Board of Tax Appeals reports
Q.5. a. Air Systems Encyclopedia
b. Government Data Publications
$49.50 per copy
Q.6. a. Industrial
b. 1934 Delaware
c. Astro Ltd.
Q.7. AAR Corporation
Q.8. $3,918,535
Q.9. a. T-Z Blue Section 5
b. 3724
c. A.B.A. Industries, Inc.
Q.10. a. $1.62 $0.79
b. First National Bank of Boston

CHAPTER SIX
Q.2. a. 145,997 km.
b. *The Statesman's Yearbook*, p. 1107
Q.3. a. PL 95-227 (HR 5322)
b. *Dow Jones-Irwin Business Almanac*
Q.4. a. 12.78c
b. p. 66

CHAPTER SEVEN
Q.1. a. 23842-1
b. 23842-1.3
c. p. 980
Q.2. a. .3%
b. U.S. Internal Revenue Service, Statistics of Income, 1974 *Corporation Income Tax Returns*
Q.3. a. $6.45
b. U.S. Dept. of Labor, Bureau of Labor Statistics
c. p. 50
Q.4. a. 80.0%
b. Federal Reserve Board

Q.5. a. $9,366 million
b. S-40
Q.6. *Security Price Index Record*
Q.7. a. 2506-15.12
b. *Annual Survey of Manufactures*
c. *Manufacturers' Alternative Energy Capabilities (1977-78 Heating Season)*

CHAPTER EIGHT
Q.1. a. *Taxable Sales in California*
b. yes
c. p. 40
Q.2. a. 49,792
b. 7–4
Q.3. a. $10,874,000
b. $1,388,000
c. $57,559,000
Q.4. a. 30,204
b. Piztiz, Martin's, J.C. Penney, Sears, G.C. Murphy, Belk-Hudson, Ike Saks, Rutenberg's Hagedorn
Q.5. a. 7.48%
b. Lockheed
Q.6. a. $6,823 million
b. p. 303

CHAPTER NINE
Q.4. a. "Advertising regulations: special considerations in computing unrelated business income (taxation of tax exempt organizations' advertising income from their publications)." J.F. Peck II *Association Management* 30:61-4+, Ap '78.
b. p. 54
Q.5. ABC may pull the plug next year on fledgling retail hi-fi business. R.P. Zucker. *Merchandising Week* 106:23 N 25 '74.
Q.6. Ford, I.D.
Stability Factors in industrial Marketing Channels.
Q.7. MBO: Appraisal with transactional analysis. H. Weihrich.
Personnel Journal 55:173–175+, Apr. 1976.
Q.8. a. 3721
b. Sikorsky Aircraft — Profile sees huge spending growth in next 6–8 yrs. *Aviation Week* 4/3/78 p. 41.
Q.9. Boeing:
Siemens to acquire 12% holding in Messerschmitt. *Financial Times* 7/12/78 p. 22.

CHAPTER TEN
Q.2. a. *Advertising in America*
b. p. 103
Q.3. a. George J. Abrams. *How I Made a Million Dollars with Ideas*. Chicago: Playboy Press, 1972.
b. *Library of Congress — Books: Subjects*, p. 362
Q.4. Aircraft Industry

CHAPTER ELEVEN
Q.2. a. "Ideas for Action: Drawbacks of continuing corporate growth"
b. Cummins Engine Co., Inc.
Q.3. a. Max Ways
b. Jonathan L. Scott
c. A & P
Q.4. a. Detecting Smog
b. p. 4
c. Covey & Koons, Inc.
Q.5. a. Yes. Essays
b. academic
c. BusI, PAIS, PsyAb, SOCI, WorAb
Q.6. a. *AOPA Pilot*
b. Annual Aircraft Directory

CHAPTER TWELVE
Q.1. a. *The Nugget*
b. 1901
Q.2. a. Pres. Pompidou arrives, Niamey, Niger, for official visit
b. Ja 25, 32:5
Q.3. a. Received $25.4 million Air Force contract for prod . . . .
b. 1/7–2;3
c. State Dept. disclosed that some 18 highly placed consultants were actually . . .
Q.4. a. p. 1060
b. *Aerospace Safety Magazine*

CHAPTER THIRTEEN
Q.2. a. 6.0–6.301
b. *Equal Employment Opportunity Compliance Officer's Handbook*
Q.3. a. H782-46
b. Ways and Means Committee, House
c. 282 p.
Q.4. S241-15
Q.5. a. *An analysis of aerospace/defense economic impact and industrial development opportunities in Huntsville, Alabama*
b. 78-25132
c. United States. Dept. of Defense. Office of Economic Adjustment

Book No.   2

CHAPTER ONE
Q.2. a. *Encyclopedia of Religion and Ethics*
       b. p. 254
Q.3. a. *Information Systems Manager's Handbook*
       b. p. 196
Q.4. a. *Management Services by Accounting Firms*
       b. p. 67
Q.5. a. Asbestos Textile Institute
       b. p. 40

CHAPTER TWO
Q.2. p. 107, *Accountant's Handbook of Formulas and Tables*
Q.3. a. 64-4
       b. Lawrence Steinmetz, "Job Dislocations: Retraining and Relocating
          Employees"
       c. *Handbook of Modern Personnel Administration*
Q.4. a. 20-31, *Purchasing Handbook*
       b. "Governmental Purchasing"
Q.5. a. 1307-1319
       b. Adams, J.S. "Inequity in Social Change." In L. Berkowitz (Ed.),
          Advances in Experimental Social Psychology, Vol. 2. New York:
          Academic Press, 1965, 267-299.

CHAPTER THREE
Q.3. a. Ackoff, Russell L.; and Rivett, Patrick 1963 *A Manager's Guide to
          Operations Research* New York: Wiley.
       b. v. 11, p. 294
Q.4. a. 244 U.S. 590 (1917)
       b. p. 9, *Roberts' Dictionary of Industrial Relations*
Q.5. a. p. 917
       b. "Scientific Management and Railroads"
Q.6. a. computer
       b. p. 11, *International Dictionary of Management*

CHAPTER FOUR
Q.2. a. Pittsburgh Corning Corp.
       b. AAAA
Q.3. a. Roy D. Chapin, Jr.
       b. Passenger automobiles
       c. 3711
       d. 27,000
Q.4. Aftermarket & O.E.M. Divisions
Q.5. 1915
Q.6. a. yes
       b. 1954
Q.7. *American Association of Motor Vehicle Administrators Personnel
          Directory of Member Jurisdictions*
Q.8. a. A.C. Owners Club — American Centre
       b. 12079
       c. yes
       d. *News*

CHAPTER FIVE
Q.2. a. 1566.075
       b. yes
       c. *New Matters*
Q.3. 2310.054
Q.4. U.S. Court of Appeals, 2nd circuit
Q.5. a. Gordon Reports & Autoworld
       b. News Analysis, Inc.
          $52.00 per year
Q.6. a. Industrial
       b. 1916   Maryland
       c. AM General Corporation
Q.7. A-T-O Inc.
Q.8. $2,315,470
Q.9. a. T-Z Blue Section 5
       b. 5012
       c. Genuine Parts Company
Q.10. a. $1.56 $3.18
       b. Marine Midland Bank, N.Y.

CHAPTER SIX
Q.2. a. 16,649 miles
       b. *The Statesman's Yearbook*, p. 1116
Q.3. a. PL 95-233 (S 1360)
       b. *Dow Jones-Irwin Business Almanac*
Q.4. a. $112.68
       b. p. 195

CHAPTER SEVEN
Q.1. a. 6722-1
       b. 6722-1.3
       c. p. 613
Q.2. a. .6%
       b. U.S. Internal Revenue Service Statistics of Income, 1974 *Corporation
          Income Tax Returns*
Q.3. a. $7.08
       b. U.S. Dept of Labor, Bureau of Labor Statistics
       c. p. 50

Q.4. a. 72%
       b. Federal Reserve Board
Q.5. a. 738,000 cars
       b. S-40
Q.6. *Standard & Poor's Industry Surveys*
Q.7. a. 2506-15.9
       b. *Annual Survey of Manufactures*
       c. *Fuels and Electric Energy Consumed. SMSA's by . . .*

CHAPTER EIGHT
Q.1. a. *Sales Tax Statistical Summary*
       b. yes
       c. p. 40
Q.2. a. 11,957
       b. 7-4
Q.3. a. $25,740,000
       b. $2,742,000
       c. $119,188,000
Q.4. a. 12,592
       b. J.C. Penney, Weinstein's, Engle's, G. May & Sons, Top Dollar
Q.5. a. 9.51%
       b. General Motors
Q.6. a. $15,844 million
       b. p. 286

CHAPTER NINE
Q.4. a. "Japan's system of distribution under scrutiny (effects limiting
          penetration by foreign goods)." Naohiro Amaya. *World Economy*
          (London) 1:319-26, Je '78
       b. p. 271
Q.5. Ahead: de-federalized cars? J.M. Callahan. *Automotive Industries*
          152:23-4 Ja 1 '75.
Q.6. Greller, M.M.
          Nature of Subordinate Participation in Appraisal Interview.
Q.7. Management consulting and university business schools. R. McLennan
          Management 23:22+ Aug. '76.
Q.8. a. 3711
       b. Automakers recognize women's market, but efforts aren't carried
          through to dealers. *Advertising Age* 1/23/78 p. 56.
Q.9. American Motors:
          To consolidate car operations at one plant, Kenosha Wisc. *Wall Street
          Journal* 3/28/78 p. 3.

CHAPTER TEN
Q.2. a. *Automation and Technological Change*
       b. p. 107
Q.3. a. Dagget, R.V. *Optimizing Selling Floor Coverage*. New York: National
          Retail Merchants Association, 1973.
       b. *Library of Congress — Books: Subjects*, p. 122
Q.4. *Automobiles — Prices*

CHAPTER ELEVEN
Q.2. a. "New templates for today's organizations"
       b. Claremont Grad. School
Q.3. a. Marilyn Wellemeyer
       b. Jonathan L. Scott
       c. A & P
Q.4. a. Parts Forged or Extruded
       b. p. 60
       c. Ludwig Advertising, Inc.
Q.5. a. Yes. One to several pages, signed
       b. Academic, Special Adult
       c. Busl
Q.6. a. *Automotive Aftermarket News*
       b. News Show Daily

CHAPTER TWELVE
Q.1. a. *Arizona Sun*
       b. 1946
Q.2. a. Nigeria's '71 econ rev (Econ Survey of Africa); '72 econ forecast sees
          oil indus, which is expected to yield Govt. revenue of close to
          $1-billion in '72, as key factor; Nigerian workers illus
       b. Ja 31,44:5
Q.3. a. Produced 213,602 cars in 1976 . . .
       b. 1/4-4;3
       c. General Motors Corp. said it is studying a possible joint venture . . .
Q.4. a. p. 1059
       b. *Auto Merchandising News*

CHAPTER THIRTEEN
Q.2. a. 6.63
       b. *Technical Assistance in Affirmative Action Compliance*
Q.3. a. H180-61
       b. Appropriations Committee, House
       c. 5 p.
Q.4. S382-17
Q.5. a. *The fuel efficiency incentive tax proposal, its impact upon the future of
          the U.S. passenger automobile industry*
       b. 78-2262
       c. United States. International Trade Commission

CHAPTER ONE
Q.2. a. *The Loom of Language*
      b. p. 286
Q.3. a. *The Dun & Bradstreet Handbook of Credits & Collections*
      b. p. 215
Q.4. a. *Interpersonal Competence and Organizational Effectiveness*
      b. p. 76
Q.5. a. Automotive Affiliated Representatives
      b. p. 51

CHAPTER TWO
Q.2. p. 111, *Accountant's Handbook of Formulas and Tables*
Q.3. a. 54-18
      b. James Bambrick, "Collective Bargaining and Union Contracts"
      c. *Handbook of Modern Personnel Administration*
Q.4. a. 22-7, *Purchasing Handbook*
      b. "Purchasing Internationally"
Q.5. a. 1538-1546
      b. Ashour, A.S. "The Contingency Model of Leadership Effectiveness:
          An Evaluation." *Organizational Behavior and Human Performance*,
          1973, 9, 339-355.

CHAPTER THREE
Q.3. a. Arensberg, Conrad M. (1937) 1950 *The Irish Countryman*. Gloucester,
          Mass.: Smith
      b. v. 16, p. 122
Q.4. a. 261 U.S. 525 (1923)
      b. p. 10, *Roberts' Dictionary of Industrial Relations*
Q.5. a. p. 314
      b. "Better Wage Incentives"
Q.6. a. critical path
      b. p. 10, *International Dictionary of Management*

CHAPTER FOUR
Q.2. a. Ball Machinery Co.
      b. AAA
Q.3. a. Zoltan Merszei
      b. Plastics
      c. 3079
      d. 53,200
Q.4. *ACS Laboratory Guide*
Q.5. No
Q.6. a. no
      b. NA
Q.7. *ACS Laboratory Guide*
Q.8. a. Chemical Advertisers Group of New York
      b. 666
      c. no
      d. n.a.

CHAPTER FIVE
Q.2. a. 1566.185
      b. yes
      c. *New Matters*
Q.3. 2993.26
Q.4. Cumulative Bulletin of the IRS
Q.5. a. Chemical Economics Handbook
      b. Stanford Research Institute
          $7,000. initial subscription; $4,000 thereafter.
Q.6. a. Industrial
      b. 1947   Delaware
      c. BIO-Science Enterprises
Q.7. Abbott Laboratories
Q.8. $5,652,070
Q.9. a. T-Z Blue Section 5
      b. 5161
      c. Alabama Oxygen Co.
Q.10. a. $3.30 $1.47
      b. Cleveland Trust Co., Cleveland O.

CHAPTER SIX
Q.2. a. 97,473 km.
      b. *The Statesman's Yearbook*, p. 1144
Q.3. a. PL 95-234 (HR 7442)
      b. *Dow Jones-Irwin Business Almanac*
Q.4. a. $48.24
      b. p. 156

CHAPTER SEVEN
Q.1. a. 2702-1
      b. 2702-1.3
      c. p. 295
Q.2. a. 2.9%
      b. U.S. Internal Revenue Service, Statistics of Income, 1974 *Corporation
          Income Tax Returns*
Q.3. a. $5.91
      b. U.S. Department of Labor, Bureau of Labor Statistics
      c. p. 37
Q.4. a. 8,826,399 thousand pounds
      b. U.S. Tariff Commission

Q.5. a. 92,000 sh. tons
      b. S-25
Q.6. *Standard & Poor's Industry Surveys*
Q.7. a. 2506-3.4
      b. *Current Industrial Reports*
      c. *Shipments of Defense-Oriented Industries, 1976*

CHAPTER EIGHT
Q.1. a. *Retail Sales and Use Tax Annual Report*
      b. yes
      c. p. 40
Q.2. a. 46,458
      b. 7-6
Q.3. a. $4,404,000
      b. $866,000
      c. $23,079,000
Q.4. a. 50,953
      b. Nordstrom, Ward's, J.C. Penney, Sears, Lamonts
Q.5. a. 19.17%
      b. Dow
Q.6. a. $51,407 million
      b. p. 108

CHAPTER NINE
Q.4. a. "Getting a perspective on export performance (export performance in
          18 developing countries)." Bernard Ancel and Paavo Lindholm,
          International Trade Forum 13:9-13+, Jl/S '77.
      b. p. 331
Q.5. Bank operations: more direction from Washington? *Burroughs Clearing
      House* 59:18-19 N '74.
Q.6. Silk, A.J., Urban, G.L.
      Pre-Test Market Evaluation of New Packaged Goods — Model and
      Measurement Methodology.
Q.7. The age discrimination in employment act. B.E. Delury. *Industrial
      Gerontology* 3:37-40 #1 1976.
Q.8. a. 3079
      b. Newly formed Vinyl Metal Ind. Assn. discusses goals, standards &
          memberships, via Vinyl Metal Ind As. *News Release* 8/28/78 p. 1.
Q.9. Dow Chemical Co.:
      Merges corporate & communications functions into new unit. *Chemical
      Marketing Reporter* 5/22/78 p. 53.

CHAPTER TEN
Q.2. a. *Beyond the Conglomerates*
      b. p. 110
Q.3. a. American Institute of Graphic Arts. *AIGA Packaging, 1960*. New York:
          1960.
      b. *Library of Congress — Books: Subjects*, p. 127
Q.4. Chemical Industries

CHAPTER ELEVEN
Q.2. a. "How the multidimensional structure works at Dow Corning"
      b. Dow Corning
Q.3. a. Herbert E. Meyer
      b. Jonathan L. Scott
      c. A & P
Q.4. a. Our Metallurgical Coke
      b. p. 22
      c. The Jaqua Company
Q.5. a. Yes. 4-5, short, unsigned
      b. Academic, Special Adult
      c. Busl, WorAb
Q.6. a. *AIChE Journal*
      b. Editorial Index

CHAPTER TWELVE
Q.1. a. *Review*
      b. 1905
Q.2. a. Mrs. Nixon arrives, Accra, Ghana, second stop in 3-nation African tour;
          greeted by prime Min Busia; illus
      b. Ja 6, 3:3
Q.3. a. Texas Oil & Gas Co. acquired firm's interest in 151 gas, oil wells . . .
      b. 1/7-2;3
      c. Three civil suits filed against Allied Chemical Co . . . .
Q.4. a. p. 1068
      b. *Agrichemical Age*

CHAPTER THIRTEEN
Q.2. a. 8.407
      b. *Technical Information Services for Air Pollution Control*
Q.3. a. H401-9
      b. Government Operations Committee, House
      c. 73 p.
Q.4. S721-13
Q.5. a. *NIOSH health and safety guide for the miscellaneous chemical
          products industry*
      b. 78-1972
      c. National Institute for Occupational Safety and Health. Division of
          Technical Services

Book No.   4

CHAPTER ONE
Q.2. a. *Popular Fallacies: A Book of Common Errors Explained and
         Corrected, with Copious References to Authorities*
       b. p.299
Q.3. a. *The Dartnell Marketing Manager's Handbook*
       b. p. 276
Q.4. a. *Management Strategy and Tactics*
       b. p. 80
Q.5. a. Air Transport Association of America
       b. p. 53

CHAPTER TWO
Q.2. p.96, *Accountant's Handbook of Formulas and Tables*
Q.3. a. 51-3
       b. Ann Davis, "Workmen's Compensation"
       c. *Handbook of Modern Personnel Administration*
Q.4. a. 16-37-39, *Purchasing Handbook*
       b. "Buying Commodities"
Q.5. a. 1553-1585
       b. Allen, T.J., & Cohen, S.I. "Information Flow in Research and Develop-
         ment Laboratories." *Administrative Science Quarterly*, 1969, 14,
         12-20.

CHAPTER THREE
Q.3. a. Bailey, Jack 1955 *The British Co-operative Movement*. London:
         Hutchinson's University Library.
       b. v. 3, p. 395
Q.4. a. 310 U.S. 469 (1940)
       b. p. 30, *Roberts' Dictionary of Industrial Relations*
Q.5. a. p. 760
       b. "Fundamentals of Tool Design"
Q.6. a. market research
       b. p. 16, *International Dictionary of Management*

CHAPTER FOUR
Q.2. a. National Sales Corp.
       b. B
Q.3. a. August A. Busch III
       b. Beer
       c. 2082
       d. 14,044
Q.4. Blitz-Weinhard Co.
Q.5. 1937
Q.6. a. yes
       b. 1957
Q.7   *Alcohol Beverage Retail Licensee's Listing*
Q.8. a. American Society of Brewing Chemists
       b. 4394
       c. yes
       d. *Journal*

CHAPTER FIVE
Q.2. a. 1566.483
       b. no
       c. *New Matters*
Q.3. 1179.04
Q.4. Circuit Court of Appeals, 7th circuit
Q.5. a. Beer Marketer's Insight
       b. Beer Marketer's Insight, Inc.
         $39.00 per year
Q.6. a. Industrial
       b. 1852 Missouri
       c. August A. Busch & Co., Inc.
Q.7. Anheuser-Busch, Inc.
Q.8. $1,441,146
Q.9. a. T-Z Blue Section 5
       b. 5181
       c. TFI Companies, Inc.
Q.10 a. $1.23 $1.46
       b. St. Louis Union Trust Co.

CHAPTER SIX
Q.2. a. 16,695 km.
       b. *The Statesman's Yearbook*, p. 1192
Q.3. a. PL 95-241 (HR 10368)
       b. *Dow Jones-Irwin Business Almanac*
Q.4. a. $4.16
       b. p. 72

CHAPTER SEVEN
Q.1. a. 23842-1
       b. 23843-1.4
       c. p. 980
Q.2. a. 1.8%
       b. U.S. Internal Revenue Service, Statistics of Income, 1974 *Corporation
         Income Tax Returns*
Q.3. a. $4.97
       b. U.S. Department of Labor, Bureau of Labor Statistics
       c. p. 29
Q.4. a. 150.43 million bbls.
       b. U.S. Department of Commerce

Q.5. a. 14.62 million bbls.
       b. S-27
Q.6. *Security Price Index Record*
Q.7. a. 2506-15.11
       b. *Annual Survey of Manufactures*
       c. *Origin of Exports of Manufacturing Establishments*

CHAPTER EIGHT
Q.1. a. *Department of Revenue Annual Report*
       b. yes
       c. p. 40
Q.2. a. 111,163
       b. 7-6
Q.3. a. $86,117,000
       b. $13,343,000
       c. $380,661,000
Q.4. a. 17,242
       b. Nordstrom's, J.C. Penney, Sears, Ward's, Lamonts
Q.5. a. 15.96%
       b. Anheuser-Busch
Q.6. a. $2,266 million
       b. p. 348

CHAPTER NINE
Q.4. a. "Psychographics is still an issue on Madison Avenue: does studying
         consumers' attitudes and 'life styles' help businessmen to sell cars
         and soap and dog food?" Peter W. Bernstein. *Fortune* 97:78-80+
         JA 16 '78.
       b. p. 533
Q.5. American industry has raised $3.4 billion--so far this month. *Economist
         253:99 0 26 '74.*
Q.6. Schramm, L.H.
         Job Rights of Strikers in Public-Sector.
Q.7. Black-white differences in leader behavior related to subordinates'
         reactions. W. S. Parker, Jr. *Journal of Applied Psychology* 61:140-147
         Apr. '76.
Q.8. a. 2082
       b. Erie Brewing--Company History. *Modern Brewing Age* 11/77 p. 26.
Q.9. Anheuser-Busch:
         Profiles company and CEO, August A. Busch, III. *Nation's Business*
         11/78 p. 66.

CHAPTER TEN
Q.2. a. *Economic Forecasting*
       b. p. 114
Q.3. a. American Society of Civil Engineers. Task Committee on Revision of
         Manual 33. *Cost Control and Accounting for Civil Engineers.* New
         York: American Society of Civil Engineers, 1971.
       b. *Library of Congress — Books: Subjects*, p. 164
Q.4. Ale

CHAPTER ELEVEN
Q.2. a. "Control your exposure to foreign exchange"
       b. Chemical Bank
Q.3. a. Lawrence A. Mayer
       b. David S. Lewis
       c. General Dynamics
Q.4. a. Superplastic Aluminum Alloy
       b. p. 64
       c. The Franklin Company
Q.5. a. Yes. 8-9, 1-3 pages, signed
       b. Academic, Special Adult
       c. BusI, EcAb, PAIS, PsyAb, SocAb, SOCi
Q.6. a. *Beer Wholesaler*
       b. Imported Beers: Review & Preview

CHAPTER TWELVE
Q.1. a. *Tribune*
       b. 1907
Q.2. a. Easing of pol tensions between Uganda and Tanzania, which
         threatened to break up East African Econ Community of Kenya,
         Tanzania and Uganda, discussed (Econ Survey of Africa)
       b. Ja 31, 54:1
Q.3. a. Quar. div. $.17, 3/9; 2/9
       b. 1/27-23;2
       c. Adolf Coors Co. boosting price it pays for aluminum beverage
         containers . . .
Q.4. a. p. 1063
       b. *Modern Brewery Age*

CHAPTER THIRTEEN
Q.2. a. 5.666
       b. *Human Elements in Work Accidents*
Q.3. a. S721-21
       b. Small Business, Select Committee on, Senate
       c. 190 p.
Q.4. H503-28
Q.5. a. *Home production of beer and wine*
       b. 78-12286
       c. United States. Congress. House. Committee on Ways and Means

MATERIALS & METHODS FOR
BUSINESS RESEARCH

Answers by Book

Book No. 5

CHAPTER ONE
Q.2. a. *The Flammarion Book of Astronomy*
     b. p. 716
Q.3. a. *Handbook of Marketing Research*
     b. p. 282
Q.4. a. *A Concept of Corporate Planning*
     b. p. 181
Q.5. a. *California Dry Bean Advisory Board*
     b. p. 63

CHAPTER TWO
Q.2. p. 129-130, *Accountant's Handbook of Formulas and Tables*
Q.3. a. 65-11
     b. Aurora Parisi, "Employee Terminations"
     c. *Handbook of Modern Personnel Administration*
Q.4. a. 16-43-49, *Purchasing Handbook*
     b. "Buying Commodities"
Q.5. a. 1643-1659
     b. Abegglen, J.C. *The Japanese Factory: Aspects of its Social Organization.* Glencoe, Ill.: The Free Press, 1958.

CHAPTER THREE
Q.3. a. Dewey, Donald J. 1959 *Monopoly in Economics and Law.* Chicago: Rand McNally.
     b. v.1, p. 356
Q.4. a. 259 U.S. 20 (1922)
     b. p. 44, *Roberts' Dictionary of Industrial Relations*
Q.5. a. p. 298
     b. "Management and the Worker"
Q.6. a. job evaluation
     b. p. 19, *International Dictionary of Management*

CHAPTER FOUR
Q.2. a. Oakite Products
     b. AAAA
Q.3. a. Robert E. Floweree
     b. Plywood
     c. 2436
     d. 37,000
Q.4. Abitibi Corp.
Q.5. 1921
Q.6. a. no
     b. NA
Q.7. *American Institute of Timber Construction-Active Members*
Q.8. a. National Hardwood Lumber Association
     b. 1288
     c. yes
     d. *National Hardwood News*

CHAPTER FIVE
Q.2. a. 1566.19
     b. no
     c. *New Matters*
Q.3. 2609.53
Q.4. Code of Federal Regulations
Q.5. a. Beale's Resource Industry Newsletter
     b. Colin Beale
        $98.00 per year
Q.6. a. Industrial
     b. 1927   Georgia
     c. Ashley, Drew & Northern Railway Co.
Q.7. Aberdeen Mfg. Corporation
Q.8. $3,038,000
Q.9. a. T-Z Blue Section 5
     b. 0821
     c. Union Camp Corp.
Q.10. a. $2.13 $1.81
     b. Bank of America N.T. & S.A.

CHAPTER SIX
Q.2. a. 5,054 km.
     b. *The Statesman's Yearbook*, p. 803
Q.3. a. PL 95-245 (HR 9851)
     b. *Dow Jones-Irwin Business Almanac*
Q.4. a. $267.50
     b. p. 210

CHAPTER SEVEN
Q.1. a. 6722-1
     b. 6722-1.5
     c. p. 613
Q.2. a. .4%
     b. U.S. Internal Revenue Service, Statistics of Income, 1974 *Corporation Income Tax Returns*
Q.3. a. $4.72
     b. U.S. Department of Labor, Bureau of Labor Statistics
     c. p. 33
Q.4. a. 8,178 millions of bd. feet
     b. U.S. Department of Commerce
Q.5. a. 738 million bd. ft
     b. S-31

Q.6. *Standard & Poor's Industry Surveys*
Q.7. a. 2506-3.1
     b. *Current Industrial Reports*
     c. *Manufacturers' Shipments, Inventories, and Orders*

CHAPTER EIGHT
Q.1. a. *Statistical Report of Retail Sales Tax Division*
     b. yes
     c. p. 40
Q.2. a. 33,320
     b. 7-6
Q.3. a. $11,016,000
     b. $858,000
     c. $44,750,000
Q.4. a. 2,800
     b. Behrends, Stevens Women's Wear, Casual Shop, Glacier Apparel
Q.5. a. not available
     b. Georgia Pacific
Q.6. a. $3,754 million
     b. p. 39

CHAPTER NINE
Q.4. a. "Radio's renaissance: now it's giving TV a run for the money; a widening variety of programs, from mystery dramas to shows for minorities, is helping to recreate some of radio's old sparkle—and higher profits as well." *U. S. News and World Report* 84:49-50, Ja 18 '78.
     b. p. 681
Q.5. Book materials, manufacturing capacity may be scarce again by summer. R. C. Matthews. *Publishers' Weekly* 207:38+ Ap. 7 '75.
Q.6. Alexande, G. J.
     Optimal Mixed Security Portfolios with Restricted Borrowing.
Q.7. Psychiatric treatment: a barrier to employment progress. G. A. Melchiode and M. Jacobson. *Journal of Occupational Medicine* 18:98-101. Feb. '76.
Q.8. a. 2436
     b. Willamette Industries—Builds $8 mil, 11 mil sq. ft. new softwood plywood plant, La. *Forest Industries* 12/77 p. 9.
Q.9. Georgia-Pacific:
     Company profile. *Forbes* 3/6/78 p. 58.

CHAPTER TEN
Q.2. a. *Applications of the Sciences in Marketing Management*
     b. p. 126
Q.3. a. American Institute of Certified Public Accountants. Committee on Stockbrokerage Auditing. *Audits of Brokers and Dealers in Securities.* New York: American Institute of Certified Public Accountants, 1973.
     b. *Library of Congress—Books: Subjects*, p. 81
Q.4. Woodworking Industries

CHAPTER ELEVEN
Q.2. a. "Don't overautomate your foreign plant"
     b. Harvard Business School
Q.3. a. Robert Ball
     b. David S. Lewis
     c. General Dynamics
Q.4. a. Improved Satin Finish, Nickel
     b. Inside back cover
     c. Kircher, Helton & Collett, Inc.
Q.5. a. Yes. 8, short notes
     b. Academic, Special Adult
     c. Busl, PerManAb
Q.6. a. *British Columbia Lumberman*
     b. Wood Processing

CHAPTER TWELVE
Q.1. a. *Idaho State Journal*
     b. 1891
Q.2. a. Amer Jewish Com yr-end rept on plight of Jews in Moslem world notes biggest Jewish populations remain in Iran, Morocco, Turkey and Tunisia and that govts have maintained basic human rights and security
     b. Ja 2, 5:1
Q.3. a. Will seek to raise about $200 million of intermediate-maturity funds . . .
     b. 1/4-25;2
     c. Supreme Ct. refused to hear challenge by 11 big forest companies . . .
Q.4. a. p. 1102
     b. *Forest Industries*

CHAPTER THIRTEEN
Q.2. a. 5.660
     b. *Handbook for Analyzing Jobs*
Q.3. a. S721-25
     b. Small Business, Select Committee on, Senate
     c. 65 p.
Q.4. H501-15
Q.5. a. *Lumber prices*
     b. 78-9910
     c. United States. Congress. Senate. Committee on Banking, Housing, and Urban Affairs

Book No. 6

CHAPTER ONE
Q.2. a. *The Encyclopedia of Chemical Process Equipment*
      b. p. 737
Q.3. a. *The Dartnell Sales Manager's Handbook*
      b. p. 287
Q.4. a. *Power and Conflict in Organizations*
      b. p. 81
Q.5. a. Bicycle Institute of America
      b. p. 70

CHAPTER TWO
Q.2. p. 47-49, *Accountant's Handbook of Formulas and Tables*
Q.3. a. 65-3
      b. Aurora Parisi, "Employee Terminations"
      c. *Handbook of Modern Personnel Administration*
Q.4. a. p. 11-22, *Purchasing Handbook*
      b. "Price Evaluation"
Q.5. a. 1403-1412
      b. Abelson, R.P. "A Summary of Hypotheses on Modes of Resolution."
          In R.P. Abelson, E. Aronson, W. J. McGuire, T.M. Newcomb, M.J.
          Rosenberg, & P.H. Tannenbaum (Eds.) *Theories of Cognitive
          Consistency: A Sourcebook.* Chicago: Rand-McNally, 1968.

CHAPTER THREE
Q.3. a. Chamberlin, Edward H. (1933) 1956 *The Theory of Monopolistic
          Competition: A Re-orientation of the Theory of Value.* 7th ed.
          Harvard Economic Studies, Vol. 38. Cambridge, Mass.: Harvard
          Univ. Press.
      b. v.3, p. 186
Q.4. a. 221 U.S. 612 (1911)
      b. p. 44, *Roberts' Dictionary of Industrial Relations*
Q.5. a. p. 287
      b. "Group Dynamics"
Q.6. a. purchased life annuity
      b. p. 20, *International Dictionary of Management*

CHAPTER FOUR
Q.2. a. Unican Security Systems Corp.
      b. AAAA
Q.3. a. Joseph C. Brennan
      b. Packaging materials
      c. 3999
      d. 19,000
Q.4. AD-X Corp.
Q.5. 1910
Q.6. a. yes
      b. not given
Q.7   *Aerosol Age Annual Buyers' Guide*
Q.8. a. Salesmen's Association of Paper and Allied Industries
      b. 2260
      c. no
      d. n.a.

CHAPTER FIVE
Q.2. a. 1566.4645
      b. yes
      c. *New Matters*
Q.3. 5362.0376
Q.4. U. S. Court of Claims
Q.5. a. Paper & Packaging Bulletin
      b. The Economist Intelligence Unit, Ltd.
          $130.00 per year
Q.6. a. Industrial
      b. 1930   Delaware
      c. Hartmann Fibre Limited
Q.7. A-T-O Inc.
Q.8. $887,079
Q.9. a. T-Z Blue Section 5
      b. 2651
      c. APL Corporation
Q.10. a. $3.90 $3.40
      b. Company Office

CHAPTER SIX
Q.2. a. 40,000 km.
      b. *The Statesman's Yearbook*, p. 807
Q.3. a. PL 95-254 (HR 10982)
      b. *Dow Jones-Irwin Business Almanac*
Q.4. a. $225.91
      b. p. 251

CHAPTER SEVEN
Q.1. a. 2702-1
      b. 2702-1.4
      c. p. 295
Q.2. a. .6%
      b. U.S. Internal Revenue Service, Statistics of Income, 1974 *Corporation
          Income Tax Returns*
Q.3. a. $5.47
      b. U.S. Department of Labor, Bureau of Labor Statistics
      c. p. 35

Q.4. a. 95%
      b. American Paper Institute
Q.5. a. 232.1 thousand sh. tons
      b. S-37
Q.6. *Standard & Poor's Industry Surveys*
Q.7. a. 2506-3.7
      b. *Current Industrial Reports*
      c. *Survey of Plant Capacity, 1977*

CHAPTER EIGHT
Q.1. a. *Annual Report of Michigan, Department of Treasury Annual Report*
      b. yes
      c. p. 41
Q.2. a. 30,292
      b. 7-7
Q.3. a. $58,429,000
      b. $7,747,000
      c. $341,299,000
Q.4. a. 4,000
      b. Tongass Trading, Bon Marche, Sears (catalog), Ward's (catalog)
Q.5. a. 13.85%
      b. Maryland Cup
Q.6. a. $2,490 million
      b. p. 59

CHAPTER NINE
Q.4. a. "Motivating superior outside sales personnel (a survey of small
          business)." Eleanor Brantley Schwartz. *Journal of Small Business
          Management* 16:19-26, Ja '78.
      b. p. 714
Q.5. Arthur in Paley-land. *Forbes* 115:20-24 + My 1 '75.
Q.6. Breeden, D.T., Litzenbe, R.H.
          Prices of State-contingent Claims Implicit in Option Fees.
Q.7. Working under ABC's 'merit shop' means going in another gate.
          Carpenter. 96:7 July 1976.
Q.8. a. 3999
      b. Product directory for fire protection & safety devices. *Design
          Professional Product Bulletin Directory* 11/78 p. 38
Q.9. Diamond International Corp.:
          To buy LMF, building supplies retailer. *Paper Trade Journal* 7/15/78 p.
          16.

CHAPTER TEN
Q.2. a. *Management Control Systems*
      b. p. 135
Q.3. a. Achinstein, Asher. *Buying Power of Labor and Post-War Cycles.* New
          York: AMS Press, 1968.
      b. *Library of Congress — Books: Subjects*, p. 142
Q.4. Book Industries and Trade

CHAPTER ELEVEN
Q.2. a. " 'Vaguely right' approach to sales force allocations"
      b. Wharton School, University of Pennsylvania
Q.3. a. Herman Nickel
      b. David S. Lewis
      c. General Dynamics
Q.4. a. Composite Superheater Tubes
      b. p. 53
      c. Fitzgerald Advertising, Inc.
Q.5. a. Yes. 4,150 words
      b. Academic, Special Adult
      c. PAIS, PerManAb, WorAb
Q.6. a. *Aerosol Age*
      b. Buyer's Guide and Directory Issue

CHAPTER TWELVE
Q.1. a. *Democrat*
      b. 1905
Q.2. a. Group of Northport (NY) HS students 'adopts' B M Kamara, pol
          prisoner in Sierra Leone
      b. Ja 14, 35:1
Q.3. a. Names a vice-president
      b. 2/9-31;2
      c. Olinkraft Inc. raised price of paperboard for beverage carriers
Q.4. a. p. 1113
      b. *Good Packaging*

CHAPTER THIRTEEN
Q.2. a. 5.603
      b. *Technical Assistance With Apprenticeship and Training*
Q.3. a. S582-2
      b. Nutrition and Human Needs, Select Committee on Senate
      c. 79 p.
Q.4. S722-7
Q.5. a. *Paper and pulp industries and size reduction machinery*
      b. 78-16940
      c. United States. Defense Logistics Agency

Book No. __7__

CHAPTER ONE
Q.2. a. *Geology and Earth Sciences Sourcebook for Elementary and Secondary Schools*
 b. p. 747
Q.3. a. *Handbook of Advertising Management*
 b. p. 295
Q.4. a. *The Manager's Job*
 b. p. 137
Q.5. a. Industrial Fasteners Institute
 b. p. 75

CHAPTER TWO
Q.2. p. 110, *Accountant's Handbook of Formulas and Tables*
Q.3. a. 49-11
 b. Bernerd Burbank, "Employee Health"
 c. *Handbook of Modern Personnel Administration*
Q.4. a. 7-28-30, *Purchasing Handbook*
 b. "Ethics in Purchasing"
Q.5. a. 1043-1055
 b. Adams, J.S. "Toward an Understanding of Inequity." *Journal of Abnormal and Social Psychology*, 1963, 67, 422-436.

CHAPTER THREE
Q.3. a. Denison, Edward F. 1962 *The Sources of Economic Growth in the United States and the Alternatives Before Us.* New York: Committee for Economic Development.
 b. v. 7, p. 344
Q.4. a. 243 U.S. 426 (1916)
 b. p. 58, *Roberts' Dictionary of Industrial Relations*
Q.5. a. p. 159
 b. "Income Tax Depreciation and Obsolescence; Estimated Useful Lives and Depreciation Rates"
Q.6. a. Common Market
 b. p. 21, *International Dictionary of Management*

CHAPTER FOUR
Q.2. a. Hydraulic Press Brick Co.
 b. AAAA
Q.3. a. J. Fred Haigler
 b. Meat products
 c. 2011
 d. 9,000
Q.4. a. AZL Resources, Inc.
Q.5. 1911
Q.6. a. yes
 b. not given
Q.7. *The Almanac of the Canning, Freezing, Preserving Industries*
Q.8. a. American Stock Yards Association
 b. 1998
 c. no
 d. n.a.

CHAPTER FIVE
Q.2. a. 1566.4647
 b. no
 c. *New Matters*
Q.3. 1531.203
Q.4. Treasury Department Circular
Q.5. a. Food Drug Cosmetic Law Reports
 b. Commerce Clearing House, Inc. $440.00 per year
Q.6. a. Industrial
 b. 1969 Delaware
 c. IBP International, Inc.
Q.7. American Stores, Company
Q.8. $2,077,158
Q.9. a. T-Z Blue Section 5
 b. 2011
 c. AZL Resources, Inc.
Q.10. a. $3.09 $1.51
 b. National Bank of Commerce

CHAPTER SIX
Q.2. a. 6,400 km.
 b. *The Statesman's Yearbook*, p. 253
Q.3. a. PL 95-256 (HR 5385)
 b. *Dow Jones-Irwin Business Almanac*
Q.4. a. 73.12¢
 b. p. 222

CHAPTER SEVEN
Q.1. a. 23842-1
 b. 23842-1.6
 c. p. 981
Q.2. a. 1.8%
 b. U.S. Internal Revenue Service, Statistics of Income, 1974 *Corporation Income Tax Returns*
Q.3. a. $4.97
 b. U.S. Department of Labor, Bureau of Labor Statistics
 c. p. 29

Q.4. a. 50 lbs.
 b. U.S. Department of Agriculture
Q.5. a. 2,018 million lbs.
 b. S-28
Q.6. *Moody's Industrial Manual*
Q.7. a. 9626-1.31
 b. *Reviews of Data on Science Resources.*
 c. *Comparison of National Industrial R & D Estimates with Actual NSF/ Census Data*

CHAPTER EIGHT
Q.1. a. *Report of Sales and Use Tax Collections*
 b. yes
 c. p. 41
Q.2. a. 62,190
 b. 7-9
Q.3. a. $20,520,000
 b. $1,636,000
 c. $80,993,000
Q.4. a. 1,440
 b. Sitka Bazaar, Sitka Cold Storage, Market Center
Q.5. a. 4.17%
 b. Oscar Mayer
Q.6. a. $4,351 million
 b. p. 339

CHAPTER NINE
Q.4. a. "Variable pricing as a promotional tool (use of prices as a promotional tool by a television and appliance chain with 44 stores in several states)." James R. Krum. *Atlanta Economic Review.* 27:47-50, N/D '77.
 b. p. 714
Q.5. At Life Savers, filter leaves improved flow rates by 10%. *Food Processing* 36:74 Mr '75.
Q.6. Robichek, A.A., Eaker, M.R. Foreign-Exchange Hedging and Capital Asset Pricing Model.
Q.7. A powerful new voice in management. T.J. Murray. *Dun's Review* 107:70-71. April 1976.
Q.8. a. 3011
 b. Michelin Tire — Company profile. *New York Times* 1/29/78 p. F1
Q.9. Iowa Beef Processors: Pacific Hldg. to buy 82% it doesn't own for $255 million. *Wall Street Journal* 11/7/78 p. 6.

CHAPTER TEN
Q.2. a. *Scanning the Business Environment*
 b. p. 137
Q.3. a. Dun and Bradstreet, Inc. Business Education Division. *A Handbook for Good Customer Relations.* New York: 1970.
 b. *Library of Congress — Books: Subjects*, p. 295
Q.4. Butchers

CHAPTER ELEVEN
Q.2. a. "Facing up to pollution controls"
 b. McKinsey and Co., Inc.
Q.3. a. Sanford Rose
 b. William J. McCune, Jr.
 c. Polaroid
Q.4. a. A Novel Ignition System
 b. p. 13
 c. Al Paul Lefton Company, Inc.
Q.5. a. Yes. 1, 2 pages, signed
 b. Academic, Special Adult
 c. PerManAb, SOCI, WorAb
Q.6. a. *Canner/Packer*
 b. Transportation & Freezing

CHAPTER TWELVE
Q.1. a. *State Journal-Register*
 b. 1831
Q.2. a. Dahomey's '71 econ rev (Econ Survey of Africa); tourist potential of country, as possible factor in '72 econ forecast, discussed
 b. Ja 31, 51:1
Q.3. a. Amalgamated Meat Cutters and Butchers union to seek pay boosts at . . .
 b. 1/6-22;5
 c. Higher meat-import quotas in 1977 likely if suppliers close loopholes
Q.4. a. p. 1104
 b. *Meat Industry*

CHAPTER THIRTEEN
Q.2. a. 5.704
 b. *A Plant-Wide Productivity Plan in Action; Three Years of Experience with the Scanlon Plan*
Q.3. a. S400-3
 b. Governmental Affairs Committee, Senate
 c. 1760 p.
Q.4. S721-30
Q.5. a. *The future role of cooperatives in the red meats industry*
 b. 78-16520
 c. United States. Dept. of Agriculture. Economics, Statistics and Cooperative Service

CHAPTER ONE
Q.2. a. *A Collector's Guide to Minerals and Gemstones*
      b. p. 754
Q.3. a. *ASPA Handbook of Personnel and Industrial Relations*
      b. p. 307
Q.4. a. *Management Services by Accounting Firms*
      b. p. 67
Q.5. a. Association of American Publishers
      b. p. 78

CHAPTER TWO
Q.2. p. 67-68, *Accountant's Handbook of Formulas and Tables*
Q.3. a. 49-11
      b. Bernerd Burbank, "Employee Health"
      c. *Handbook of Modern Personnel Administration*
Q.4. a. 16-4-75, *Purchasing Handbook*
      b. "Buying Commodities"
Q.5. a. 962-963
      b. Alderfer, C.P. "Convergent and Discriminant Validation of Satisfaction
          and Desire Measures by Interviews and Questionnaires." *Journal of
          Applied Psychology*, 1967, 51, 509-520.

CHAPTER THREE
Q.3. a. Bock, Betty 1960 *Mergers and Markets: An Economic Analysis of
          Case Law.* Studies in Business Economics, No. 69. New York:
          National Industrial Conference Board.
      b. v.10, p. 254
Q.4. a. 375 U.S. 261 (1964)
      b. p. 64, *Roberts' Dictionary of Industrial Relations*
Q.5. a. p. 70
      b. "Three Applications of Break-Even Methods in Economic Analysis"
Q.6. a. stocks
      b. p. 22, *International Dictionary of Management*

CHAPTER FOUR
Q.2. a. Honeywell Information Systems
      b. AAAA
Q.3. a. E. Burke Giblin
      b. Ethical pharmaceuticals & proprietary pharmaceuticals
      c. 2834
      d. 57,500
Q.4. ATI, Inc.
Q.5. no
Q.6. a. yes
      b. 1967
Q.7   *Accredited Colleges of Pharmacy*
Q.8. a. Pharmaceutical Advertising Club
      b. 66
      c. yes
      d. *PACer*

CHAPTER FIVE
Q.2. a. 1566.637
      b. yes
      c. *New Matters*
Q.3. 5943.25
Q.4. Executive Order
Q.5. a. F-D-C Reports — "The Pink Sheet"
      b. F-D-C Reports, Inc.
          $220.00 per year
Q.6. a. Industrial
      b. 1920   Delaware
      c. Adams Dominicana
Q.7. Abbott Laboratories
Q.8. $2,349,198
Q.9. a. T-Z Blue Section 5
      b. 2834
      c. ATI Inc.
Q.10 a. $2.01 $1.78
      b. Irving Trust Co., N.Y.

CHAPTER SIX
Q.2. a. 66,000 km.
      b. *The Statesman's Yearbook*, p. 331
Q.3. a. PL 95-268 (HR 9179)
      b. *Dow Jones-Irwin Business Almanac*
Q.4. a. $8.41
      b. p. 77

CHAPTER SEVEN
Q.1. a. 6722-1
      b. 6722-1.6
      c. p. 613
Q.2. a. 2.9%
      b. U.S. Internal Revenue Service, Statistics of Income, 1974 *Corporation
          Income Tax Returns*
Q.3. a. $5.91
      b. U.S. Department of Labor, Bureau of Labor Statistics
      c. p. 37

Q.4. a. 89 thousand tons
      b. U.S. International Trade Commissioner
Q.5. a. $2,041 million
      b. S-12
Q.6   *Quarterly Financial Report*
Q.7. a. 9626-2.77
      b. *Science Resource Studies Highlights*
      c. *Industrial R & D Spending Reached $26.6 billion in 1976*

CHAPTER EIGHT
Q.1. a. *State of New Mexico . . . Monthly Statement*
      b. yes
      c. p. 41
Q.2. a. 71,136
      b. 7-10
Q.3. a. $50,320,000
      b. $8,299,000
      c. $223,809,000
Q.4. a. N.A.
      b. J.C. Penney
Q.5. a. 19.44%
      b. Warner-Lambert
Q.6. a. $446 million
      b. p. 152

CHAPTER NINE
Q.4. a. "What every marketer should know about women (social changes
          affecting marketing techniques)." Rena Bartos. *Harvard Business
          Review* 56:73-85, My/Je '78.
      b. p. 877
Q.5. Canners cut prices to move inventory. *Industry Week* 185:54-6 My 5 '75.
Q.6. Bloom, D., Twyman, T.
      Impact of Economic-change on Evaluation of Advertising Campaigns.
Q.7. The boom in executive self-interest. *Business Week* p. 16+. May 24,
      1976.
Q.8. a. 2834
      b. Discusses the patient as neglected force in marketing prescription
          drugs. *Medical Marketing & Media* 3/78 p. 47.
Q.9. Warner-Lambert:
      Builds $11 million headquarters expansion, N.J. *Chemical Marketing
      Reporter* 7/17/78 p. 4.

CHAPTER TEN
Q.2. a. *Challenges for Business in the 1970's*
      b. p. 143
Q.3. a. R.V. Daggett. *Optimizing Selling Floor Coverage.* New York: National
          Retail Merchants Association, 1973.
      b. *Library of Congress — Books: Subjects*, p. 295
Q.4. Drugstores

CHAPTER ELEVEN
Q.2. a. "Is your purchasing department a good buy?"
      b. Bureau of Business and Economic Research, Northeastern University
Q.3. a. Rush Loving, Jr.
      b. William J. McCune, Jr.
      c. Polaroid
Q.4. a. A "Revolutionary" Cardiac Pacemaker
      b. 22a
      c. Gimbel Hammon Fairell, Inc.
Q.5. a. Yes. Various number, length 100-200 words, signed
      b. Academic, Special Adult
      c. BusI, PAIS, WorAb
Q.6. a. *American Druggist*
      b. American Druggist Blue Book

CHAPTER TWELVE
Q.1. a. *Post-Tribune*
      b. 1907
Q.2. a. Mali's '71 econ rev (Econ Survey of Africa); Govt's efforts to realign
          econ since Pres Traore's mil regime overthrew former Govt in '68
          discussed
      b. Ja 31, 52:1
Q.3. a. Quar div $.25, 3/10; 2/4
      b. 1/26-22;3
      c. The Zoo story; Why they start putting animals on the pill . . .
Q.4. a. p. 1075
      b. *Pharmaceutical Technology*

CHAPTER THIRTEEN
Q.2. a. 5.661
      b. *Relating General Educational Development to Career Planning*
Q.3. a. H561-22
      b. Merchant Marine and Fisheries Committee, House
      c. 599 p.
Q.4. S722-3
Q.5. a. *Competitive problems in the drug industry*
      b. 78-22557
      c. United States. Congress. Senate. Select Committee on Small
          Business. Subcommittee on Monopoly and Anticompetitive Activities

Book No.   9

CHAPTER ONE

Q.2. a. *Popular Titles and Subtitles of Musical Compositions*
b. p. 420
Q.3. a. *Production Handbook*
b. p. 332
Q.4. a. *People and Productivity*
b. p. 115
Q.5. a. Cigar Box Manufacturers
b. p. 81

CHAPTER TWO

Q.2. p. 116, *Accountant's Handbook of Formulas and Tables*
Q.3. a. 62-4
b. Joseph Augustine, "Personnel Turnover"
c. *Handbook of Modern Personnel Administration*
Q.4. a. 1-22, *Purchasing Handbook*
b. "Purchasing Management"
Q.5. a. 861-885
b. Albrecht, P.A., Glaser, E.M., & Marks, J. "Validation of a Multiple
Assessment Procedure for Managerial Personnel." *Journal of
Applied Psychology*, 1964, 48, 351-360.

CHAPTER THREE

Q.3. a. Folk, George E. 1942 *Patents and Industrial Progress: A Summary,
Analysis, and Evaluation of the Record on Patents of the Temporary
National Economic Committee*. New York: Harper.
b. v.11, p. 471
Q.4. a. 236 U.S. 1 (1915)
b. p. 92, *Roberts' Dictionary of Industrial Relations*
Q.5. a. p. 279
b. "Executive Direction of Projects"
Q.6. a. Acquisition
b. p. 24, *International Dictionary of Management*

CHAPTER FOUR

Q.2. a. West Coast Chain Manufacturing Co.
b. AA
Q.3. a. William C. Messinger
b. Automated unit or packaged handling systems
c. 3568
d. 16,000
Q.4. ACME Chain
Q.5. 1915
Q.6. a. no
b. NA
Q.7. *ABC Directory*
Q.8. a. Construction Equipment Advertisers
b. 44
c. no
d. n.a.

CHAPTER FIVE

Q.2. a. 2019.0675
b. yes
c. *New Matters*
Q.3. 1330.501
Q.4. U.S. District Court
Q.5. a. Comparative Data
b. Equipment Guide-Book Company
Varies: $125.00 - $145.00 per year
Q.6. a. Industrial
b. 1892   Wisconsin
c. Rexnord (Canada) Ltd.
Q.7. A-T-O, Inc.
Q.8. $634,901
Q.9. a. T-Z Blue Section 5
b. 3531
c. A-T-O Inc.
Q.10. a. $2.41 $1.14
b. Northern Trust Co., Chicago, Ill.

CHAPTER SIX

Q.2. a. 17,100 km.
b. *The Statesman's Yearbook*, p. 348
Q.3. a. PL 95-273 (S1617)
b. *Dow Jones-Irwin Business Almanac*
Q.4. a. $112.68
b. p. 195

CHAPTER SEVEN

Q.1. a. 2702-1
b. 2702-1.5
c. p. 295
Q.2. a. .7%
b. U.S. Internal Revenue Service, Statistics of Income, 1974 *Corporation
Income Tax Returns*
Q.3. a. $5.78
b. U.S. Department of Labor, Bureau of Labor Statistics
c. p. 47

Q.4. a. 281.3 thousand
b. U.S. Department of Commerce
Q.5. a. $308 million
b. S-34
Q.6 *Standard & Poor's Industry Surveys*
Q.7 a. 9626-1.30
b. *Reviews of Data on Science Resource*
c. *Scientific and Technical Personnel in Private Industry, 1960-70 and
1975*

CHAPTER EIGHT

Q.1. a. *Statistics of Taxation*
b. yes
c. p. 41
Q.2. a. 27,356
b. 7-10
Q.3. a. $62,458,000
b. $8,342,000
c. $328,131,000
Q.4. a. 4,300
b. J.C. Penney, Sears, Henry's, Cornet
Q.5. a. 16.09%
b. Caterpillar
Q.6. a. $4,645 million
b. p. 215

CHAPTER NINE

Q.4. a. "The effect of documented versus undocumented advertising claims."
Michael J. Etzel and E. Leon Knight, Jr. *Journal of Consumer Affairs*
10:233-8 Winter '76.
b. p. 55
Q.5. Cigaret makers broaden brand placement payment. *Vending Times*
14:1+ D '74.
Q.6. Lahti, R. E.
Managerial Performance and Appraisal.
Q.7. Using rational behavior training to improve managerial skills. D.S.
Goodman. *Personnel Administrator*. 21:36-40. Jan. 1976.
Q.8. a. 3568
b. Product directory for mechanical and fluid power transmission. *Design
Professional Product Bulletin Directory* 11/78 p. 55.
Q.9. Rexnord: Buys High Strength Adhesives. *Paper Trade Journal* 1/15/78
p. 55.

CHAPTER TEN

Q.2. a. *Accountants, Data Processing Services*
b. p. 150
Q.3. a. Russell Lincoln Ackoff. *A Concept of Corporate Planning*. New York:
Wiley-Interscience, 1969 or 1970.
b. *Library of Congress — Books: Subjects*, p. 493
Q.4. Earthmoving Machinery

CHAPTER ELEVEN

Q.2. a. "Business and the changing society"
b. Harvard Business School
Q.3. a. Deborah DeWitt Malley
b. William J. McCune, Jr.
c. Polaroid
Q.4. a. Environmentally Safe Substitute for Phosphorous
b. p. 19
c. Watts, Lamb, Kenyon & Herrick, Inc.
Q.5. a. Yes. 6, 3-4 pages, signed
b. General Adult, Academic, Special Adult
c. SOCI, WorAb
Q.6. a. *Apartment Construction News*
b. Financial Resources Directory

CHAPTER TWELVE

Q.1. a. *Gazette*
b. 1883
Q.2. a. Pres Mobutu renames several wellknown places in Zaire; Kinshasa
Prov to be known as Shaba; Stanley Pool renamed Malebo Pool;
Mt. Stanley renamed Mt. Ngaliema
b. Ja 2, 8:1
Q.3. a. Expects increased incoming orders to boost earnings, . . .
b. 1/27-21;6
c. Sears, Roebuck & Co. must pay total of $10.1 million to eight San
Francisco couples who brought consumer fraud suit . . .
Q.4. a. p. 1073
b. *Construction Bulletin*

CHAPTER THIRTEEN

Q.2. a. 4.306
b. *Current Population Reports*
Q.3. a. S402-1
b. Governmental Affairs Committee, Senate
c. 1760 p.
Q.4. S362-26
Q.5. a. *NCF equipment management manual*
b. 78-226
c. United States. Naval Facilities Engineering Command

Book No. __10__

CHAPTER ONE

Q.2. a. *Dictionary of French Literature*
      b. p. 351
Q.3. a. Handbook of Industrial Research Management
      b. p. 338
Q.4. a. *Improving the Performance of the Experienced Manager*
      b. p. 144
Q.5. a. American Society of Brewing Chemists
      b. p. 83

CHAPTER TWO

Q.2. p. 1, *Accountant's Handbook of Formulas and Tables*
Q.3. a. 49-12
      b. Bernerd Burbank, "Employee Health"
      c. *Handbook of Modern Personnel Administration*
Q.4. a. 2-20-22, *Purchasing Handbook*
      b. "The Purchasing Organization"
Q.5. a. 384-392
      b. Alutto, J.A. "Some Dynamics of Questionnaire Completion and
          Return among Professional and Mangerial Personnel: The Relative
          Impacts of Reception at Work Site or Place of Residence." *Journal
          of Applied Psychology*, 1970, 54, 430-432.

CHAPTER THREE

Q.3. a. Bergson, Abram; and Kuznets, Simon (editors) 1963 *Economic
          Trends in the Soviet Union*. Cambridge, Mass.: Harvard Univ. Press.
      b. v. 12, p. 535
Q.4. a. 249 U.S. 265 (1919)
      b. p. 109, *Roberts' Dictionary of Industrial Relations*
Q.5. a. p. 838
      b. "Purchasing Handbook"
Q.6. a. workers' participation
      b. p. 29, *International Dictionary of Management*

CHAPTER FOUR

Q.2. a. Porter, H.K., Inc.
      b. AAAA
Q.3. a. W.H. Krome George
      b. Primary and fabricated aluminum
      c. 3353
      d. 45,200
Q.4. Alcan Aluminum Corp.
Q.5. 1918
Q.6. a. yes
      b. 1942
Q.7. *American Bureau of Metal Statistics Yearbook*
Q.8. a. Aluminum Association
      b. 2044
      c. yes
      d. *World Aluminum Abstracts*

CHAPTER FIVE

Q.2. a. 2019.068
      b. yes
      c. *New Matters*
Q.3. 1330.3863
Q.4. Excess Profits Tax Council ruling
Q.5. a. Aluminum Statistical Review
      b. Aluminum Association, Inc.
          $1.00 per copy
Q.6. a. Industrial
      b. 1888 Pennsylvania
      c. Adam metal Supply, Inc.
Q.7. Alcan Aluminum Ltd.
Q.8. $2,924,400
Q.9. a. T-Z Blue Section 5
      b. 1051
      c. Alcan Aluminum Limited
Q.10. a. $4.14 $3.09
      b. Mellon Bank, N.A.

CHAPTER SIX

Q.2. a. 51,253 km
      b. *The Statesman's Yearbook*, p. 354
Q.3. a. PL 95-279 (HR6782)
      b. *Dow Jones-Irwin Business Almanac*
Q.4. a. $5-$15 per ton
      b. p. 75

CHAPTER SEVEN

Q.1. a. 23842-1
      b. 23842-1.5
      c. p. 980
Q.2. a. .2%
      b. U.S. Internal Revenue Service, Statistics of Income, 1974 *Corporation
          Income Tax Returns*
Q.3. a. $5.30
      b. U.S. Department of Labor, Bureau of Labor Statistics
      c. p. 45
Q.4. a. 3,879 thousand short tons
      b. U.S. Bureau of Mines

Q.5. a. 399 thousand sh. tons
      b. S-33
Q.6. *Security Price Index Record*
Q.7. a. 226-2.7
      b. *Comments of the Council on Wage and Price Stability*
      c. *Toxic Substances Control*

CHAPTER EIGHT

Q.1. a. *Oklahoma Sales Tax Statistical Report*
      b. yes
      c. p. 41
Q.2. a. 21,097
      b. 7-12
Q.3. a. $28,419,000
      b. $1,867,000
      c. $116,150,000
Q.4. a. 10,000
      b. J.C. Penney, Western Auto, Sam Hills, Solt-Lauritsen, Pennington,
          Cornet, Sears
Q.5. a. 12.20%
      b. Reynolds Metals
Q.6. a. $1,466 million
      b. p. 195

CHAPTER NINE

Q.4. a. "Distribution and the structure of retail trade in a Philippines commercial
          town setting [Dagupan]." Norbert Dannhaeuser. *Economic
          Development and Cultural Change* 25:471-503, Ap '77.
      b. p. 295
Q.5. AT&T carriers agree on distribution rate cut. *Electronic News* 20:25 Mr 17
      '75.
Q.6. Pollay, R.W.
      Wanted — History of Advertising.
Q.7. Sex effects in evaluating leaders K.M. Bartol and D.A. Butterfield.
      Journal of Applied Psychology 61:446-454 #4 1976.
Q.8. a. 3353
      b. Discusses need for product development programs in aluminum
          machining techniques. *American Metal Market* 9/11/78 p. 30.
Q.9. Aluminum Co. of America:
      Forms Alcoa Recycling from aluminum can recycling division.
      Beverage Industry 9/22/78 p. 2.

CHAPTER TEN

Q.2. a. *Developing Executive Leaders*
      b. p. 155
Q.3. a. American Business Communication Association. *ABCA Membership
          Directory*. Urbana, Ill.: 1971.
      b. *Library of Congress — Books: Subjects*, p. 58
Q.4. Aluminum Foil

CHAPTER ELEVEN

Q.2. a. "Research and pseudo-research in marketing"
      b. Lee Creative Research
Q.3. a. Walter Guzzardi, Jr.
      b. William J. McCune, Jr.
      c. Polaroid
Q.4. a. To Weigh Axle Loads More Accurately
      b. p. 1
      c. Griswold-Eshleman Company
Q.5. a. Yes, 10, essay length, signed
      b. Academic, Special Adult
      c. WorAb
Q.6. a. *Brick and Clay Record*
      b. Refractories Issue

CHAPTER TWELVE

Q.1. a. *Kansan*
      b. 1921
Q.2. a. SW Kapwepwe, former Vice Pres of Zambia, who heads United
          Progressive Party in opposition to Pres Kaunda, is beaten by crowd,
          Lusaka; most other leaders of Progressive Party were arrested 3
          mos ago but have not been brought to trial
      b. Ja 13,16:3
Q.3. a. Names a vice president, purchasing transportation
      b. 1/4-21;1
      c. Anaconda Co. and Reynolds Metals Co. have settled 1975 lawsuit . . .
Q.4. a. p. 1108
      b. *Light Metal Age*

CHAPTER THIRTEEN

Q.2. a. 4.350-4.366
      b. *Disclosure and Corporate Ownership*
Q.3. a. S241-2
      b. Banking, Housing and Urban Affairs Committee, Senate
      c. 614 p.
Q.4. 5263-13
Q.5. a. *Effects of pollution abatement on international trade*
      b. 78-19632
      c. United States. Bureau of Domestic Commerce. Office of Business
          and Legislative Issues

CHAPTER ONE
Q.2. a. *Biology Data Book*
      b. p. 720
Q.3. a. Purchasing Handbook
      b. p. 341
Q.4. a. *Duties and Problems of Chief Financial Executives*
      b. p. 360
Q.5. a. Building and Construction Trades Department
      b. p. 87

CHAPTER TWO
Q.2. p. 107–109, *Accountant's Handbook of Formulas and Tables*
Q.3. a. 49-9
      b. Bernerd Burbank, "Employee Health"
      c. *Handbook of Modern Personnel Administration*
Q.4. a. 11-6, *Purchasing Handbook*
      b. "Price Evaluation"
Q.5. a. 379-384
      b. Alutto, J.A. "Some Dynamics of Questionnaire Completion and Return among Professional and Managerial Personnel: The Relative Impacts of Reception at Work Site or Place of Residence." *Journal of Applied Psychology*, 1970, 54, 430-432.

CHAPTER THREE
Q.3. a. Bernstein, Marver H. 1955 *Regulating Business by Independent Commission*. Princeton Univ. Press.
      b. v. 13, p. 396
Q.4. a. 272 U.S. 306 (1926)
      b. p. 109, *Roberts' Dictionary of Industrial Relations*
Q.5. a. p. 753
      b. "Manufacturing Analysis"
Q.6. a. sales promotion
      b. p. 31, *International Dictionary of Management*

CHAPTER FOUR
Q.2. a. Wisner Manufacturing Corp.
      b. AAA
Q.3. a. Frank T. Cary
      b. Business machines, electronic data processing systems
      c. 3573
      d. 310,155
Q.4. AEL Industries, Inc.
Q.5. No
Q.6. a. yes
      b. 1948
Q.7. *Annotated Bibliography of Electronic Data Processing*
Q.8. a. Computer Aided Manufacturing International
      b. 916
      c. yes
      d. *CAM-i News Alert*

CHAPTER FIVE
Q.2. a. 2019.355
      b. yes
      c. *New Matters*
Q.3. 666.35
Q.4. Federal Register
Q.5. a. Autotransaction Industry Report
      b. International Data Corporation $85.00 per year
Q.6. a. Industrial
      b. 1911 New York
      c. Information Satellite Corporation
Q.7. Adacorp, Inc.
Q.8. $16,304,333
Q.9. a. T-Z Blue Section 5
      b. 3573
      c. AEL Industries Inc.
Q.10. a. $3.99 $2.70
      b. Company Office, N.Y., N.Y.

CHAPTER SIX
Q.2. a. 9,536 km.
      b. *The Statesman's Yearbook*, p. 365
Q.3. a. PL 95-283 (HR 8331)
      b. *Dow Jones-Irwin Business Almanac*
Q.4. a. $183.9
      b. p. 268

CHAPTER SEVEN
Q.1. a. 6722-1
      b. 6722-1.7
      c. p. 613
Q.2. a. 1.0%
      b. U.S. Internal Revenue Service, Statistics of Income, 1974 *Corporation Income Tax Returns*

Q.3. a. $5.78
      b. U.S. Department of Labor, Bureau of Labor Statistics
      c. p. 47
Q.4. a. 182.4%
      b. Federal Reserve Board
Q.5. a. 165.8
      b. S-4
Q.6. *Moody's Industrial Manual*
Q.7. a. 2506-3.4
      b. *Current Industrial Reports*
      c. *Shipments of Defense-Oriented Industries, 1975*

CHAPTER EIGHT
Q.1. a. *Sales Tax Collections by City or Town and County*
      b. yes
      c. p. 41
Q.2. a. 17,560
      b. 7-15
Q.3. a. $5,079,000
      b. $45,000
      c. $19,987,000
Q.4. a. 28,200
      b. Boston Store, Woolco, Fed. Mart, TG&Y Family Center, Smitty's
Q.5. a. 29.97%
      b. International Business Machines Corp.
Q.6. a. $6,108 million
      b. p. 264

CHAPTER NINE
Q.4. a. "Merchandising legislation in Louisiana." Fred R. Endsley and Lucien R. Laborde, Jr. *Louisiana Business Review* 41:2-4+ Jl '77.
      b. p. 602
Q.5. Copper, aluminum concerns call for federal cooperation in meeting the industry's needs. *Chemical Marketing Reporter* 206:7+ Jl 29 '74.
Q.6. Monroe, K.B. and Dellabit, A.J. Models for Pricing Decisions.
Q.7. Where are the managers for 1980? L.A. Wangler. *Journal of College Placement* 36:34-37 #3 1976.
Q.8. a. 3573
      b. National Atlantic Ind. — Relocates headquarters and facilities to 66,000 sq. ft. plant, NY. *Mini-Micro Systems* 7/78 p. 22.
Q.9. International Business Machines: Company profile. *Barron's National Business & Financial Weekly* 1/9/78 p. 9.

CHAPTER TEN
Q.2. a. *Franchising and the Total Distribution System*
      b. p. 162
Q.3. a. James Brennan. *The Conscious Communicator*. Reading, Mass.: Addison-Wesley, 1974.
      b. *Library of Congress — Books: Subjects*, p. 63
Q.4. Computers

CHAPTER ELEVEN
Q.2. a. "How to reach the young consumer"
      b. Mailbag International
Q.3. a. Thomas Griffith
      b. William Henry Krome George
      c. Aluminum Company of America
Q.4. a. Front Wheel Bearing
      b. p. 39
      c. Wunderman, Ricotta & Kline, Inc.
Q.5. a. Yes. Various number/length
      b. General Audience, Academic, Special Audience
      c. PerManAb, WorAb
Q.6. a. *Automation*
      b. Production Equipment Issue

CHAPTER TWELVE
Q.1. a. *News*
      b. 1834
Q.2. a. '70 econ rev, '71 outlook; illus
      b. Ja 29,54:4
Q.3. a. Received $131.9 million Navy contract for sonar sets
      b. 1/7-2;3
      c. Talcott National Corp. unit concluded sale of its computer leasing unit to EFM Computer Leasing Inc. for $16.6 million cash
Q.4. a. p. 1059
      b. *Digital Design*

CHAPTER THIRTEEN
Q.2. a. 4.365
      b. *Situation Reports — Consumerism*
Q.3. a. S402-1
      b. Governmental Affairs Committee, Senate
      c. 1760 p.
Q.4. S261-44
Q.5. a. *County market survey: computers and related equipment, Japan*
      b. 78-19969
      c. United States. Bureau of International Commerce.

Book No. 12

CHAPTER ONE
Q.2. a. *Dictionary of Spanish Literature*
      b. p. 359
Q.3. a. *Handbook of Sampling for Auditing and Accounting*
      b. p. 185
Q.4. a. *Systematic Corporate Planning*
      b. p. 182
Q.5. a. Candy, Chocolate and Confectionary Institute
      b. p. 109

CHAPTER TWO
Q.2. p. 100-101, *Accountant's Handbook of Formulas and Tables*
Q.3. a. 49-12
      b. Bernerd Burbank, "Employee Health"
      c. *Handbook of Modern Personnel Administration*
Q.4. a. 5-5, 6, *Purchasing Handbook*
      b. "The Purchase Order"
Q.5. a. 777-822
      b. Abrahams, N.M. & Alf. E. Jr. "Pratfalls in Moderator Research."
         Journal of Applied Psychology, 1972, 56, 245-251.

CHAPTER THREE
Q.3. a. Burns, E.M. 1933 "Minimum Wage." Volume 10, pages 491-495 in
         Encyclopaedia of the Social Sciences. New York: Macmillan.
      b. v. 16, p. 423
Q.4. a. 273 U.S. 657 (1927)
      b. p. 109, *Roberts' Dictionary of Industrial Relations*
Q.5. a. p. 116
      b. "The Management Function: A Positive Approach to Labor Relations"
Q.6. a. flexible working hours
      b. p. 32, *International Dictionary of Management*

CHAPTER FOUR
Q.2. a. Ling Products, Inc.
      b. AA
Q.3. a. R.O. Anderson
      b. Exploration
      c. 2911
      d. 28,000
Q.4. ATC Petroleum
Q.5. 1917
Q.6. a. yes
      b. not given
Q.7. *Alaska Petroleum and Industrial Directory*
Q.8. a. Independent Petroleum Association of America
      b. 2353
      c. yes
      d. *Petroleum Independent*

CHAPTER FIVE
Q.2. a. 2019.10
      b. yes
      c. *New Matters*
Q.3. 3041.049
Q.4. Federal Rules Decision
Q.5. a. NPN Bulletin
      b. McGraw-Hill, Inc.
         $195.00 per year
Q.6. a. Industrial
      b. 1870 Pennsylvania
      c. ARCO Carribean, Inc.
Q.7. Abella Resources Ltd.
Q.8. $8,462,524
Q.9. a. T-Z Blue Section 5
      b. 1381
      c. Ada Resources Inc.
Q.10. a. $3.97 $2.38
      b. Security Pac. N.B., L.A., Cal.

CHAPTER SIX
Q.2. a. 27,013 km.
      b. *The Statesman's Yearbook*, p. 371
Q.3. a. PL 95-333 (HR 13385)
      b. *Dow Jones-Irwin Business Almanac*
Q.4. a. $211.8
      b. p. 263

CHAPTER SEVEN
Q.1. a. 2702-1
      b. 2702-1.8
      c. p. 296
Q.2. a. .1%
      b. U.S. Internal Revenue Service, Statistics of Income, 1974 *Corporation
         Income Tax Returns*
Q.3. a. $7.21
      b. U.S. Department of Labor, Bureau of Labor Statistics
      c. p. 38
Q.4. a. 32,893 wells
      b. Oil & Gas Journal; World Oil

Q.5. a. 90%
      b. S-35
Q.6   *Moody's Transportation Manual*
Q.7. a. 9306-3.14
      b. *Federal Energy News*
      c. *Final Industrial Energy Efficiency Improvement Targets Set by FEA*

CHAPTER EIGHT
Q.1. a. *Comparative Statement of Collected Revenues*
      b. yes
      c. p. 42
Q.2. a. 47,973
      b. 7-16
Q.3. a. $706,237,000
      b. $97,612,000
      c. $3,787,192,000
Q.4. a. 12,815
      b. M.M. Cohn, Sterling, El Dorado House, B.W. Reeves, J.A. West
Q.5. a. 21.49%
      b. Sun
Q.6. a. 523 billion of ton-miles
      b. p. 441

CHAPTER NINE
Q.4. a. "The effects of commercial clutter on radio news." Joseph R. Dominick.
         Journal of Broadcasting 20:169-76, Spring '76.
      b. p. 759
Q.5. Data base file system by Inforex. *Electronic News* 19:90 S 9 '74.
Q.6. Mallen, B.
         Channel Power — Form Economic Exploitation.
Q.7. Behavioral considerations in management information systems change.
         K.G. Jin *Dissertation Abstracts International* 37:441A, July, 1976.
Q.8. a. 2911
      b. Texaco — Tries demarketing to improve profitability *Wall Street Journal*
         3/16/78 p. 16.
Q.9. Atlantic Richfield:
         Speaks loud and clear on public issues. *International Management*
         4/78 p. 22.

CHAPTER TEN
Q.2. a. *Panic in the Boardroom*
      b. p. 169
Q.3. a. *Allocating Field Sales Resources; a Symposium*. New York:
         National Industrial Conference Board, 1970.
      b. *Library of Congress — Books: Subjects*, p. 573
Q.4. Automobiles — Service Stations

CHAPTER ELEVEN
Q.2. a. "The territorial hunger of our major banks"
      b. Rutgers University, Stonier Graduate School of Banking
Q.3. a. David Bell
      b. William Henry Krome George
      c. Aluminum Company of America
Q.4. a. Steel (Manganese) Alloy that Resists Wear
      b. p. 14
      c. Marsteller, Inc.
Q.5. a. Yes. 8, 150 words, signed
      b. General Audience, Academic
      c. WorAb
Q.6. a. *AAPG Bulletin*
      b. Membership Directory

CHAPTER TWELVE
Q.1. a. *Banner*
      b. 1897
Q.2. a. Govt, in further swing to left, issues order nationalizing all private bldgs
         worth over $14,300; move linked to Pres Nyerere anxiety over
         Uganda coup; map
      b. My 16,14:1
Q.3. a. Completed $536 million acquisition of Anaconda Co.
      b. 1/13-2;2
      c. National bargaining committee of 60,000 member Oil, Chemical and
         Atomic Workers union will meet Jan. 4 . . .
Q.4. a. p. 1114
      b. *The Oil Can*

CHAPTER THIRTEEN
Q.2. a. 6.50
      b. *Directory of Data Sources on Racial and Ethnic Minorities*
Q.3. a. S402-1
      b. Governmental Affairs Committee, Senate
      c. 1760 p.
Q.4. H721-12
Q.5. a. *OPEC's proposal to peg the price of oil exports to special drawing
         rights*
      b. 78-975
      c. United States. Congress. House. Committee on Banking, Finance,
         and Urban Affairs. Subcommittee on Economic Stabilization

CHAPTER ONE

Q.2. a. *American Institute of Physics Handbook*
      b. p. 766
Q.3. a. *The Director's Handbook*
      b. p. 149
Q.4. a. *Corporate Excellence Diagnosis*
      b. p. 68
Q.5. a. Portland Cement Association
      b. p. 117

CHAPTER TWO

Q.2. p. 100, *Accountant's Handbook of Formulas and Tables*
Q.3. a. 65-8
      b. Aurora Parisi, "Employee Terminations"
      c. *Handbook of Modern Personnel Administration*
Q.4. a. 10-7, 8, *Purchasing Handbook*
      b. "Price Considerations"
Q.5. a. 748-751
      b. Acker, S.R. & Perlson, N.R. "Can We Sharpen our Management of
          Human Resources?" *Behavioral Sciences Applications*, Corporate
          Personnel Department, Olin Corporation, 1971.

CHAPTER THREE

Q.3. a. Almond, Gabriel A.; and Verba, Sidney 1963 *The Civic Culture:
          Political Attitudes and Democracy in Five Nations*. Princeton Univ.
          Press.
      b. v. 2, p. 217
Q.4. a. 254 U.S. 443 (1921)
      b. p. 111, *Roberts' Dictionary of Industrial Relations*
Q.5. a. p. 401
      b. "Arbitration and Collective Bargaining"
Q.6. a. stock exchange
      b. p. 35, *International Dictionary of Management*

CHAPTER FOUR

Q.2. a. Gateway Safety Products Co.
      b. AAAA
Q.3. a. C. Raymond Dahl
      b. Paper
      c. 2621
      d. 32,000
Q.4. A.G.P. Industries, Inc.
Q.5. 1921
Q.6. a. yes
      b. 1950
Q.7. *Annual Review Number with Mill and Personnel Directory*
Q.8. a. Salesmen's Association of Paper and Allied Industries
      b. 2260
      c. no
      d. n.a.

CHAPTER FIVE

Q.2. a. 2019.114
      b. no
      c. *New Matters*
Q.3. 4729.657
Q.4. Chief Counsel's memorandum
Q.5. a. Paper & Packaging Bulletin
      b. The Economist Intelligence Unit, Ltd.
          $130.00 per year
Q.6. a. Industrial
      b. 1924   Nevada
      c. Forest Terminals Corp.
Q.7. Boise Cascade Corporation
Q.8. $2,125,977
Q.9. a. T-Z Blue Section 5
      b. 2647
      c. American Hospital Supply Corporation
Q.10. a. $3.88 $4.26
      b. Bank of California, N.A.

CHAPTER SIX

Q.2. a. 73,677 km.
      b. *The Statesman's Yearbook*, p. 387
Q.3. a. PL 95-334 (HR 11504)
      b. *Dow Jones-Irwin Business Almanac*
Q.4. a. $179.04
      b. p. 251

CHAPTER SEVEN

Q.1. a. 23842-1
      b. 23842-1.1
      c. p. 980
Q.2. a. .6%
      b. U.S. Internal Revenue Service, Statistics of Income, 1974 *Corporation
          Income Tax Returns*
Q.3. a. $5.47
      b. U.S. Department of Labor, Bureau of Labor Statistics
      c. p. 35
Q.4. a. 2,368 thousand tons
      b. American Paper Institute

Q.5. a. 3,878,000 sh. tons
      b. S-36
Q.6. *Security Price Index Record*
Q.7. a. 2506-3.1
      b. *Current Industrial Reports*
      c. *Manufacturers' Shipments, Inventories, and Orders*

CHAPTER EIGHT

Q.1. a. *Annual Report of the Tax Commission*
      b. yes
      c. p. 42
Q.2. a. 23,769
      b. 7-17
Q.3. a. $19,337,000
      b. $2,250,000
      c. $87,342,000
Q.4. a. 24,800
      b. A.W. Cox, Mont. Ward, J.C. Penney, Leggetts, Thornton's, Ammar
          Bros., K-Mart
Q.5. a. 15.69%
      b. Crown Zellerbach
Q.6. a. $8,243 million
      b. p. 54

CHAPTER NINE

Q.4. a. "The reliability and forecasting value of advance estimates of retail
          sales." Dan M. Bechter. *Federal Reserve Kansas City* p. 17-22,
          Ap '77.
      b. p. 778
Q.5. Dyes: Upbeat outlook. *Chemical Marketing Reporter* 206.5+ D 23 '74.
Q.6. Rosenblo., B.
      Motivating Independent Distribution Channel Members.
Q.7. Applying management principles to the occupational health unit.
      J.S. Goodwin & S.O. Horner *Occupational Health Nursing* 24:13-15
      Jun. 1, 1975.
Q.8. a. 2621
      b. Crown Zellerbach— Reduces fires to 4 per year with paper machine
          water washdown, Wash. *Pulp & Paper* 3/78 p. 126.
Q.9. Crown Zellerbach:
      Reorganizes Containers Group into two divisions, Gaylord
      Containerboard. *Boxboard Cointainers* 2/78 p. 9.

CHAPTER TEN

Q.2. a. *The International Money Game*
      b. p.177
Q.3. a. Ronald D. Michman. *Marketing Channels*. Columbus, Ohio: Grid, Inc.,
          1974.
      b. *Library of Congress — Books: Subjects*, p. 573
Q.4. Book Industries and Trade

CHAPTER ELEVEN

Q.2. a. "Once upon a seesaw"
      b. Harvard Business School
Q.3. a. Walter Guzzardi, Jr.
      b. William Henry Krome George
      c. Aluminum Company of America
Q.4. a. A New Type of Plywood
      b. p. 34-43
      c. Ries Cappiello Colwell, Inc.
Q.5. a. Yes. 1, 500 words, signed
      b. General Audience, Academic
      c. Busl, PerManAb, PsyAb, WorAb
Q.6. a. *American Paper Industry*
      b. PIMA Directory & Paper and Pulp Mill Catalog

CHAPTER TWELVE

Q.1. a. News
      b. 1880
Q.2. a. Pres Bourguiba enters Walter Reed Hosp, Washington; failing health
          noted; illus of seaside mausoleum built for Bourguiba at his
          instructions
      b. Ja 7,7:4
Q.3. a. Earned $3.82 to $3.87 a share in 1976 and 'fully expects' to improve
          on that in 1977 . . .
      b. 1/20-26;5
      c. St. Regis Paper Co. said it would have $13.4 million water treatment
          plant at its kraft mill in Tacoma, Washington completed by July . . .
Q.4. a. p. 1113
      b. *Paper Age*

CHAPTER THIRTEEN

Q.2. a. 7.452
      b. *Patent, Copyright, and Trademark Protection Overseas*
Q.3. a. H502-42
      b. Interstate and Foreign Commerce Committee, House
      c. 872 p.
Q.4. H721-16
Q.5. a. *Petroleum refining, industrial chemical, drug, and paper and allied
          products industries*
      b. 78-15717
      c. United States. Bureau of Labor Statistics

Book No. 14

CHAPTER ONE
Q.2. a. *Handbook of Engineering Fundamentals*
    b. p. 775
Q.3. a. *Office Administration Handbook*
    b. p. 202
Q.4. a. *Management and the Social Sciences: An Essay*
    b. p. 84
Q.5. a. American Cocoa Research Industry
    b. p. 131

CHAPTER TWO
Q.2. p. 99-100, *Accountant's Handbook of Formulas and Tables*
Q.3. a. 36-1
    b. John Shea, "Holidays, Vacations, Accidents, Sickness, Long-term
        Disability and Other Time Off the Job"
    c. *Handbook of Modern Personnel Administration*
Q.4. a. 16-44,45, *Purchasing Handbook*
    b. "Buying Commodities"
Q.5. a. 17-39
    b. Ashby, W.R. *Design for a Brain*. London: Chapman and Hall, 1952.

CHAPTER THREE
Q.3. a. Bergson, Abram; and Kuznets, Simon (editors) 1963 *Economic
        Trends in the Soviet Union*. Cambridge, Mass.: Harvard Univ. Press.
    b. v. 2, p. 301
Q.4. a. 325 U.S. 711
    b. p. 115, *Roberts' Dictionary of Industrial Relations*
Q.5. a. p. 137
    b. "The Creative Person and the Creative Process"
Q.6. a. sales promotion
    b. p. 37, *International Dictionary of Management*

CHAPTER FOUR
Q.2. a. Buckeye Rubber Products, Inc.
    b. AAAA
Q.3. a. Ralph Lazarus
    b. Not given
    c. 5311
    d. 76,000
Q.4. Abraham & Straus
Q.5. 1914
Q.6. a. yes
    b. 1951
Q.7. *Annual Study on the State of the Discount Industry*
Q.8. a. Retail Advertising Conference
    b. 73
    c. no
    d. n.a.

CHAPTER FIVE
Q.2. a. 2019.15
    b. yes
    c. *New Matters*
Q.3. 4137.135
Q.4. *Weekly Internal Revenue Bulletin*
Q.5. a. Barometer of Small Business
    b. Accounting Corp. of America
        $12.50 per year
Q.6. a. Industrial
    b. 1929   Delaware
    c. no
Q.7. Alexander's Inc.
Q.8. $3,712,864
Q.9. a. T-Z Blue Section 5
    b. 5331
    c. Arlen Realty & Development Corp.
Q.10. a. $3.50 $2.57
    b. Manufacturers Hanover Tr. Co., N.Y.

CHAPTER SIX
Q.2. a. 17,195 km.
    b. *The Statesman's Yearbook*, p. 416
Q.3. a. PL 95-339 (HR 12426)
    b. *Dow Jones-Irwin Business Almanac*
Q.4. a. 205.8¢
    b. p. 378

CHAPTER SEVEN
Q.1. a. 2702-1
    b. 2702-1.7
    c. p. 296
Q.2. a. 2.5%
    b. U.S. Internal Revenue Service, Statistics of Income, 1974 *Corporation
        Income Tax Returns*
Q.3. a. $3.41
    b. U.S. Department of Labor, Bureau of Labor Statistics
    c. p. 57

Q.4. a. 11.09 billion dollars
    b. U.S. Dept. of Commerce
Q.5. a. $6,468 million
    b. S-12
Q.6. *Standard & Poor's Trade & Securities Statistics*
Q.7. a. 2506-3.7
    b. *Current Industrial Reports*
    c. *Survey of Plant Capacity, 1976*

CHAPTER EIGHT
Q.1. a. *Taxable Sales in California*
    b. yes
    c. p. 40
Q.2. a. 13,549
    b. 7-21
Q.3. a. $13,444,000
    b. $1,388,000
    c. $46,686,000
Q.4. a. 7,954
    b. Wards, E.M. Payne, K-Mart, J.C. Penney, Hill's
Q.5. a. 9.01%
    b. Federated Department Stores, Inc.
Q.6. a. 6.3%
    b. p. 464

CHAPTER NINE
Q.4. a. "Retail promotions as a function of trade promotions: a descriptive
        analysis (examines temporary sales promotions in a large regional
        supermarket chain over a six-month period)." Michel Chevalier and
        Ronald C. Curhan. *Sloan Management Review* 18:19-32, Fall '76
    b. p. 797
Q.5. Arbitrator, blacks and discipline. K. Jennings. *Personnel Journal*
    54:32-37+, Ja '75
Q.6. Cummins, J.D.
    Economics of Scale in Independent Insurance Agencies.
Q.7. Understanding the attitudes of today's employees. J.F. Mee. *Nation's
    Business* 64:22-24+, Aug. '76.
Q.8. a. 5311
    b. Woolworth (FW) — Company profile *Financial World* 1/1/78 p. 30.
Q.9. Federated Dept. Stores, Inc.:
    Questionable marketing strategies of some divisions undermine
    company's profit. *Chain Store Age* 6/78 p. 41.

CHAPTER TEN
Q.2. a. *Work Sampling*
    b. p. 183
Q.3. a. Advertising Research Foundation. *Are there Consumer Types?*
    New York: 1964.
    b. *Library of Congress — Books: Subjects*, p. 536
Q.4. Chain Stores

CHAPTER ELEVEN
Q.2. a. "Do's and don'ts of computer models for planning"
    b. Harvard Business School
Q.3. a. Juan Cameron
    b. William Henry Krome George
    c. Aluminum Company of America
Q.4. a. Significant Air Compression Advancement
    b. p. 20d
    c. Howard Swink Advertising Agency, Inc.
Q.5. a. Yes. 1-2 pages, signed
    b. Academic, Special Audience
    c. WorAb
Q.6. a. *Chain Store Age — Executives Edition*
    b. Shopping Center Report

CHAPTER TWELVE
Q.1. a. *Press*
    b. 1890
Q.2. a. '70 econ rev, '71 outlook
    b. Ja 29,48:5
Q.3. a. Elected a director
    b. 1/26-21;4
    c. Crowley, Milner & Co. will close its aging main store in downtown
        Detroit July 2, laying off about 150 employees
Q.4. a. p. 1088
    b. *Shopping Center World*

CHAPTER THIRTEEN
Q.2. a. 2.2
    b. *Economic Injury Disaster Loans*
Q.3. a. S241-11
    b. Banking, Housing and Urban Affairs Committee, Senate
    c. 1140 p.
Q.4. H721-13
Q.5. a. *Checklist for going into business*
    b. 78-9527
    c. United States. Small Business Administration

Book No. __15__

CHAPTER ONE

Q.2. a. *Handbook of Architectural Practice*
      b. p. 388
Q.3. a. *Administrator's Collection*
      b. p. 175
Q.4. a. *The Applicability of Organizational Sociology*
      b. p. 75
Q.5. a. Cigar Institute of America
      b. p. 132

CHAPTER TWO

Q.2. p. 108-109, *Accountant's Handbook of Formulas and Tables*
Q.3. a. 50-17
      b. Peter Davis, "Federal and State Labor Laws"
      c. *Handbook of Modern Personnel Administration*
Q.4. a. 20-25 *Purchasing Handbook*
      b. "Governmental Purchasing"
Q.5. a. 571-598
      b. Adorno, T.W., Frenkel-Brunswik, E., Levinson, D.J. & Sanford, R.N.
          The Authoritarian Personality. New York: Harper & Row, 1950.

CHAPTER THREE

Q.3. a. Brady, Robert A. 1943 *Business as a System of Power*. New York:
          Columbia Univ. Press.
      b. v. 2, p. 325
Q.4. a. 243 U.S. 210 (1917)
      b. p. 179, *Roberts' Dictionary of Industrial Relations*
Q.5. a. p. 650
      b. "Operations Research in Making Marketing Decisions"
Q.6. a. industrial action
      b. p. 39, *International Dictionary of Management*

CHAPTER FOUR

Q.2. a. Pabco Fluid Power Company
      b. AAA
Q.3. a. James P. Herring
      b. Chain Food Stores
      c. 5411
      d. 80,000
Q.4. a. A.G. Co., Inc.
Q.5. 1914
Q.6. a. yes
      b. 1960
Q.7. *The Almanac of the Canning, Freezing, Preserving Industries*
Q.8. a. Grocery Manufacturers of America
      b. 1162
      c. no
      d. n.a.

CHAPTER FIVE

Q.2. a. 2019.18
      b. no
      c. *New Matters*
Q.3. 1372.2822
Q.4. Internal Revenue Code
Q.5. a. Food Industry Newsletter
      b. Profit Press, Inc.
          $47.00 per year
Q.6. a. Industrial
      b. 1902 Ohio
      c. Wesco Foods Co.
Q.7. Albertson's Inc.
Q.8. $6,091,149
Q.9. a. T-Z Blue Section 5
      b. 5411
      c. Albertson's Inc.
Q.10. a. $1.79 $1.11
      b. First National Bank, Cincinnati, Ohio

CHAPTER SIX

Q.2. a. 4,000 km.
      b. *The Statesman's Yearbook*, p. 575
Q.3. a. PL 95-342 (S920)
      b. *Dow Jones-Irwin Business Almanac*
Q.4. a. $11.76
      b. p. 230

CHAPTER SEVEN

Q.1. a. 6722-1
      b. 6722-1.8
      c. p. 613
Q.2. a. .9%
      b. U.S. Internal Revenue Service Statistics of Income, 1974 *Corporation
          Income Tax Returns*
Q.3. a. $4.41
      b. U.S. Department of Labor, Bureau of Labor Statistics
      c. p. 57
Q.4. a. 12.64 billion dollars
      b. U.S. Dept. of Commerce

Q.5. a. $14,942 million
      b. S-12
Q.6. Standard & Poor's Industry Surveys
Q.7. a. 2506-13.2
      b. *Annual Survey of Manufactures, 1974*
      c. *Expenditures for New Plant and Equipment and Book Value of Fixed
          Assets and Rental Payments for Building and Equipment*

CHAPTER EIGHT

Q.1. a. *Sales Tax Statistical Summary*
      b. yes
      c. p. 40
Q.2. a. 6,564
      b. 7-22
Q.3. a. $29,103,000
      b. $2,336,000
      c. $136,608,000
Q.4. a. 28,119
      b. J.C. Penney, Stone & Thomas, Sears, Watson's
Q.5. a. 2.53%
      b. Jewel Cos.
Q.6. a. 9.6%
      b. p. 470

CHAPTER NINE

Q.4. a. "Purging Madison Avenue from Canadian television II (an update
          on legal and political actions arising from Canadian efforts to reduce
          the amount of United States advertising on Canadian cable
          television and the flow of Canadian advertising dollars to United
          States stations)." Caroline D. Asher *Law and Policy in International
          Business* 9:1009-27 no. 3 '77.
      b. p. 863
Q.5. Contemporary view of liability for breach of trust. R.D. Niles. *Trusts and
      Estates* 114:12-16+ Ja; 82-5+ F '75.
Q.6. Barry, T.E. and Wooton, L.M.
      Forecasting Consumer Values.
Q.7. Communicating with researchers. R. Bennett *Industrial Training
      International* 11:71-74 1976.
Q.8. a. 5411
      b. Somers (Johnny) — Company history *Progressive Grocer* 6/78 p. 57
Q.9. The Kroger Co.:
      To sell Top Value Enterprises to Baldwin-United. *Wall Street Journal*
      12/11/78 p. 27.

CHAPTER TEN

Q.2. a. *Business Logistics*
      b. p. 188
Q.3. a. John R.G. Jenkins. *Planning the Advertising Campaign*. New York:
          Macmillan, 1971.
      b. *Library of Congress — Books: Subjects*, p. 390
Q.4. Farm Produce

CHAPTER ELEVEN

Q.2. a. "Winning and losing with European acquisitions"
      b. John Kitching Associates
Q.3. a. Peter Vanderwicken
      b. Perry Mendel
      c. Kinder-Care
Q.4. a. Flat Screen Video System
      b. p. 39
      c. McCann-Erickson, Inc.
Q.5. a. Yes. 1-2 pages, signed
      b. Academic, Special Audience
      c. PAIS
Q.6. a. *Canadian Grocer*
      b. Survey of Chains and Groups

CHAPTER TWELVE

Q.1. a. *Herald & News Tribune*
      b. 1969
Q.2. a. '70 econ rev, '71 outlook
      b. Ja 29,55:5
Q.3. a. Quar div $.36, 3/1; 1/28
      b. 1/17-17;2
      c. FDA announced that beginning in March all food additives will
          undergo tests for safety
Q.4. a. p. 1089
      b. *Rocky Mountain Food Dealer*

CHAPTER THIRTEEN

Q.2. a. 2.17
      b. *Starting a Small Business Investment Company*
Q.3. a. S241-37
      b. Banking, Housing and Urban Affairs Committee, Senate
      c. 429 p.
Q.4. S312-13
Q.5. a. *Technology applied to the food industry*
      b. 78-15815
      c. National Commission on productivity and Work Quality

Book No. 16

CHAPTER ONE

Q.2. a. *American Electricians' Handbooks; A Reference Book for the Practical Electrical Man*
    b. p. 789
Q.3. a. *A Basic Bibliography on Marketing Research*
    b. p. 283
Q.4. a. *Organization: The Framework of Management*
    b. p. 126
Q.5. a. Retail Tobacco Dealers of America
    b. p. 133

CHAPTER TWO

Q.2. p. 46-47, *Accountant's Handbook of Formulas and Tables*
Q.3. a. 54-31
    b. James Bambrick, "Collective Bargaining and Union Contracts"
    c. *Handbook of Modern Personnel Administration*
Q.4. a. 11-8-10, *Purchasing Handbook*
    b. "Price Evaluation"
Q.5. a. 521-561
    b. Adkins, W.R. "Life Skills: Structured Counseling for the Disadvantaged." *Personnel and Guidance Journal*, 1970, 49, 108-116.

CHAPTER THREE

Q.3. a. Bain, Joe S. 1956 *Barriers to New Competition: Their Character and Consequences in Manufacturing Industries.* Cambridge, Mass.: Harvard Univ. Press.
    b. v. 10, p. 467
Q.4. a. 301 U.S. 619 (1937)
    b. p. 183, *Roberts' Dictionary of Industrial Relations*
Q.5. a. p. 1097
    b. "On a Congestion Problem in an Aircraft Factory"
Q.6. a. accountable management
    b. p. 51, *International Dictionary of Management*

CHAPTER FOUR

Q.2. a. Elliott Company
    b. AAAA
Q.3. a. R.A. Kroc
    b. Operation of fast food restaurants
    c. 5812
    d. 1,945
Q.4. The AAV Companies
Q.5. No
Q.6. a. yes
    b. 1955
Q.7. *Bibliography of Hotel & Restaurant Administration and Related Subjects*
Q.8. a. Chinese American Restaurant Association
    b. 1138
    c. no
    d. n.a.

CHAPTER FIVE

Q.2. a. 2019.71
    b. no
    c. *New Matters*
Q.3. 1571.87
Q.4. Income Tax Ruling
Q.5. a. Foodservice Training & Management Education Report
    b. Restaurant-Hotel Aids, Inc.
       $14.00 per year
Q.6. a. Industrial
    b. 1965 Delaware
    c. Yes. Not listed
Q.7. American Agronomics Corp.
Q.8. $1,175,881
Q.9. a. T-Z Blue Section 5
    b. 5812
    c. The AAV Companies
Q.10. a. $2.72 $1.31
     b. American National Bank & Trust Co., Chicago, Ill.

CHAPTER SIX

Q.2. a. 1,110 km.
    b. *The Statesman's Yearbook*, p. 585
Q.3. a. PL 95-345 (HR 7581)
    b. *Dow Jones-Irwin Business Almanac*
Q.4. a. 73.12¢
    b. p. 222

CHAPTER SEVEN

Q.1. a. 2702-1
    b. 2702-1.9
    c. p. 296
Q.2. a. 1.3%
    b. U.S. Internal Revenue Service Statistics of Income, 1974 *Corporation Income Tax Returns*
    c. p. 57
Q.3. a. $4.41
    b. U.S. Department of Labor, Bureau of Labor Statistics.
    c. p. 57
Q.4. a. 5486 million dollars
    b. U.S. Dept. of Commerce
Q.5. a. $6,134 million
    b. S-12

Q.6. *Standard & Poor's Industry Surveys*
Q.7. a. 2506-14.6
    b. *Annual Survey of Manufactures, 1975*
    c. *Fuels and Electric Energy Consumed*

CHAPTER EIGHT

Q.1. a. *Retail Sales and Use Tax Annual Report*
    b. yes
    c. p. 40
Q.2. a. 100,602
    b. 7-25
Q.3. a. $62,776,000
    b. $8,533,000
    c. $440,595,000
Q.4. a. 5,300
    b. A.W. Cox, G.C. Murphy, Davis, Tots & Teens, Grace Ann Fabrics, Dollar General
Q.5. a. 24.09%
    b. McDonald's
Q.6. a. $58,008 million
    b. p. 464

CHAPTER NINE

Q.4. a. "Methodology for short-range travel demand predictions: analysis of carpooling incentives (Great Britain). Moshe Ben-Akiva and Terry J. Atherton. *Journey of Transport Economics and Policy* 11:224-61, S '77.
    b. p. 881.
Q.5. Confessions of a premium incentive travel packager. R.A. Bechard. *Insurance* 75:31-2 Jl '74.
Q.6. Andrease, A.R.
    Ghetto Marketing Life-Cycle — Case of Underachievement.
Q.7. The relationships between the leadership effectiveness of first-line supervisors and measures of authoritarianism, creativity, general intelligence, and leadership style. R.J. Deveau. *Dissertation Abstracts International* 37:1360A-61A, Sep. '76.
Q.8. a. 5812
    b. Discusses fast-food marketing *Advertising Age* 8/7/78 p. 42.
Q.9. McDonald's Corporation:
    To keep headquarters at Oak Brook, Ill. *Wall Street Journal* 4/27/78 p. 3.

CHAPTER TEN

Q.2. a. *A Handbook of Systems Analysis*
    b. p. 200
Q.3. a. Edgar A. Pessemier. *Profiles of Market Segments and Product Competitive Structures.* West Lafayette, Ind.: Krannert Graduate School of Industrial Administration, Purdue University, 1973.
    b. *Library of Congress — Books: Subjects*, p. 536
Q.4. Hotels, Taverns, etc.

CHAPTER ELEVEN

Q.2. a. "'Shelf sitters' re-examined"
    b. Harvard Business Review
Q.3. a. Carol J. Loomis
    b. Perry Mendel
    c. Kinder-Care
Q.4. a. Non-Coking Coal
    b. p. 12
    c. Campbell-Ewald Company
Q.5. a. Yes. 10, 1 page, signed
    b. Academic, Special Audience
    c. ApMech, Busl, BritTech, Engl, SOCI
Q.6. a. *Canadian Hotel & Restaurant*
    b. Sources Directory

CHAPTER TWELVE

Q.1. a. *Examiner*
    b. 1898
Q.2. a. Mali acceptance of aid from US, USSR and Communist China discussed as part of its new policy of trying to maintain friendship with East and West; illus
    b. Je 20,2:3
Q.3. a. Heard on the Street: Price competition among restaurant chains keeps growing long-term industry factor
    b. 1/11-47;3
    c. Brewing Boycott: Rising coffee prices beginning to stir consumer protests, . . .
Q.4. a. p. 1093
    b. *Kansas Restaurant*

CHAPTER THIRTEEN

Q.2. a. 1.100-1.105
    b. *Government Business Opportunities*
Q.3. a. H501-26
    b. Interstate and Foreign Commerce Committee, House
    c. 112 p.
Q.4. H501-18
Q.5. a. *Energy audit workbook for restaurants*
    b. 78-25429
    c. United States. Dept. of Energy. Office of Conservation and Solar Applications. Office of State Grant Programs

CHAPTER ONE

Q.2. a. *Esquire's Encyclopedia of 20th Century Men's Fashions*
      b. p. 395
Q.3. a. *Executive and Management Development for Business and
          Government: A Source Book*
      b. p. 311
Q.4. a. *Integrating the Individual and the Organization*
      b. p. 75
Q.5. a. International Fabricare Institute
      b. p. 141

CHAPTER TWO

Q.2. p. 75, *Accountant's Handbook of Formulas and Tables*
Q.3. a. 66-8
      b. Robert Sand, "The Role of Legal Counsel"
      c. *Handbook of Modern Personnel Administration*
Q.4. a. 19-38, *Purchasing Handbook*
      b. "Purchasing Construction Contracts"
Q.5. a. 473-516
      b. Altman, I. "Aspects of the Criterion Problem in Small Group Research:
          The Analysis of Group Tasks." *Acta Psychologica*, 1966, 25,
          199-221.

CHAPTER THREE

Q.3. a. Bell, Daniel 1959 *The End of Ideology*. Glencoe, Ill.: Free Press.
      b. v. 3, p. 353
Q.4. a. 169 U.S. 336 (1898)
      b. p. 185, *Roberts' Dictionary of Industrial Relations*
Q.5. a. p. 496
      b. "Cost/Benefit Analysis of Information Systems"
Q.6. a. work group
      b. p. 81, *International Dictionary of Management*

CHAPTER FOUR

Q.2. a. Industrial Electric Reels, Inc.
      b. A
Q.3. a. Charles J. Pilliod, Jr.
      b. Tires
      c. 3011
      d. 152,000
Q.4. AMF Voit, Inc.
Q.5. 1918
Q.6. a. no
      b. NA
Q.7. *Materials & Compounding Materials and Machinery for Rubber*
Q.8. a. Rubber Association of America (formerly) or Rubber Manufacturers
          Association
      b. 2630
      c. yes
      d. *Rubber Highlights*

CHAPTER FIVE

Q.2. a. 2019.36
      b. no
      c. *New Matters*
Q.3. 4717.485
Q.4. Income Tax Information Release
Q.5. a. Rubber Trends
      b. The Economist Intelligence Unit, Ltd.
          $130.00
Q.6. a. Industrial
      b. 1898   Ohio
      c. Cosmoflex Inc.
Q.7. Abbott Laboratories
Q.8. $5,791,494
Q.9. a. T-Z Blue Section 5
      b. 3011
      c. Alliance Tire & Rubber Co., Ltd.
Q.10. a. $1.69 $2.53
      b. National City Bank, Cleveland, Ohio

CHAPTER SIX

Q.2. a. 29,895 km.
      b. *The Statesman's Yearbook*, p. 593
Q.3. a. PL 95-351 (HR 2777)
      b. *Dow Jones-Irwin Business Almanac*
Q.4. a. 39.8¢
      b. p. 293

CHAPTER SEVEN

Q.1. a. 23842-1 or 242-4
      b. 23842-1.2 or 242-4.2
      c. p. 980 or p. 10
Q.2. a. 1.0%
      b. U.S. Internal Revenue Service Statistics of Income, 1974 *Corporation
          Income Tax Returns*
Q.3. a. $4.65
      b. U.S. Department of Labor, Bureau of Labor Statistics
      c. p. 39

Q.4. a. 8,724 thousand casings
      b. Rubber Manufacturers Association
Q.5. a. 207.37 thousand metric tons
      b. S-37
Q.6. *Security Price Index Record*
Q.7. a. 2506-3.6
      b. *Current Industrial Reports*
      c. *Pollution Abatement Costs and Expenditures, 1976*

CHAPTER EIGHT

Q.1. a. *Department of Revenue Annual Report*
      b. yes
      c. p. 40
Q.2. a. 41,754
      b. 7-27
Q.3. a. $48,752,000
      b. $4,903,000
      c. $195,563,000
Q.4. a. 2,125
      b. Browne's, J.C. Penney, J.M. McDonald
Q.5. a. 9.00%
      b. Goodyear
Q.6. a. $3,534 million
      b. p. 164

CHAPTER NINE

Q.4. a. "Packaging for the young consumer: a descriptive study." James U.
          McNeal. *Akron Business and Economic Review* 7:5-11, Winter '76.
      b. p. 984
Q.5. Agency co. fight against direct writers most successful in New England:
      Survey *National Underwriter Property and Casualty Insurance Edition*
      78:1+ Ag 16 '74.
Q.6. Goldman, A.
      Confined Shopping Behavior among Low Income Consumers—
      Empirical-Test.
Q.7. "Acquired Rights" in West Germany. *European Industrial Relations
      Review* 27:12-13 Mar '76.
Q.8. a. 3011
      b. Michelin Tire—Company profile *New York Times* 1/29/78 p. F1.
Q.9. Goodyear Tire & Rubber Co.:
      Reorganizes chemical division into elastomers and plastic products
      areas. *Rubber & Plastics News* 6/26/78 p. 11.

CHAPTER TEN

Q.2. a. *Marketing Management & Administrative Action*
      b. p. 202
Q.3. a. Kenneth B. Ackerman. *Understanding Today's Distribution Center*.
          Washington, D.C.: Traffic Service Corp., 1972.
      b. *Library of Congress—Books: Subjects*, p. 121
Q.4. Rubber, Artificial

CHAPTER ELEVEN

Q.2. a. "A Soviet economist looks at U.S. Business"
      b. Institute of World Economy and International Relations
Q.3. a. Arthur M. Louis
      b. Perry Mendel
      c. Kinder-Care
Q.4. a. Zinc-Nickel Oxide Battery
      b. p. 15
      c. Lowe & Stevens, Inc.
Q.5. a. Yes. 5, 1 page
      b. Academic, Special Audience
      c. ASTI, ApMech, BusI, ChemAb, Engl, MathR, PsyAb, SOCI
Q.6. a. *Modern Tire Dealer*
      b. Annual Product Catalog

CHAPTER TWELVE

Q.1. a. *Montana Standard*
      b. 1876
Q.2. a. '70 econ rev; '71 outlook; illus
      b. Ja 29,64:1
Q.3. a. Moved on Oct 1 to end prorated refunds on auto tires that get cut, . . .
      b. 1/16-1;5
      c. Goodyear Tire & Rubber Co. moved on Oct. 1, 1976 to end prorated
          refunds on auto tires that get cut, . . .
Q.4. a. p. 1125
      b. *Rubber Chemistry and Technology*

CHAPTER THIRTEEN

Q.2. a. 5.853
      b. *Arbitration of a Grievance*
Q.3. a. S241-2
      b. Banking, Housing and Urban Affairs Committee, Senate
      c. 614 p.
Q.4. J932-52
Q.5. a. *Noise and traction characteristics of bias-ply and radial tires for
          heavy duty trucks*
      b. 78-5273
      c. United States. Dept. of Transportation. Office of Noise Abatement

Book No. 18

CHAPTER ONE

Q.2. a. *Cyclopedia of American Agriculture; A Popular Survey of Agricultural Conditions, Practices, and Ideals in the United States and Canada*
b. p. 824
Q.3. a. *Directory*
b. p. 340
Q.4. a. *Management and the Social Sciences*
b. p. 84
Q.5. a. American Apparel Manufacturers Association
b. p. 143

CHAPTER TWO

Q.2. p. 114, *Accountant's Handbook of Formulas and Tables*
Q.3. a. 65-4
b. Aurora Parisi, "Employee Terminations"
c. *Handbook of Modern Personnel Administration*
Q.4. a. 20-39, *Purchasing Handbook*
b. "Governmental Purchasing"
Q.5. a. 442-451
b. Abelson, R.P. "Simulation of Social Behavior." In G. Lindzey & E. Aronson (Eds.) Handbook of Social Psychology, Vol. 2. (2nd ed.) Reading, Mass.: Addison-Wesley, 1968, 274-356.

CHAPTER THREE

Q.3. a. Abruzzi, Adam 1956 *Work, Workers, and Work Measurement.* New York: Columbia Univ. Press.
b. v. 7, p. 251
Q.4. a. 299 U.S. 334 (1937)
b. p. 243, *Roberts' Dictionary of Industrial Relations*
Q.5. a. p. 314
b. "Better Wage Incentives"
Q.6. a. stock exchange
b. p. 84, *International Dictionary of Management*

CHAPTER FOUR

Q.2. a. Powdercraft Corp.
b. AAA
Q.3. a. Edgar B. Speer
b. Every variety of steel form and composition
c. 3312
d. 165,845
Q.4. A & A Associates, Inc.
Q.5. 1916
Q.6. a. yes
b. 1938
Q.7. *American Bureau of Metal Statistics Yearbook*
Q.8. a. American Institute for Imported Steel
b. 2047
c. no
d. n.a.

CHAPTER FIVE

Q.2. a. 2019.41
b. no
c. *New Matters*
Q.3. 5322.5218
Q.4. Law Opinion
Q.5. a. Metals Sourcebook
b. McGraw-Hill, Inc.
$140.00 per year
Q.6. a. Industrial
b. 1965   Delaware
c. Alside, Inc.
Q.7. Algoma Steel Corporation, Ltd.
Q.8. $8,604,200
Q.9. a. T-Z Blue Section 5
b. 3317
c. Ameron, Inc.
Q.10. a. $5.03 $4.01
b. Company Office

CHAPTER SIX

Q.2. a. 11,000-12,000 km.
b. *The Statesman's Yearbook*, p. 600
Q.3. a. PL 95-361 (S 2543)
b. *Dow Jones-Irwin Business Almanac*
Q.4. a. 173.5¢
b. p. 234

CHAPTER SEVEN

Q.1. a. 2702-1
b. 2702-1.10
c. p. 296
Q.2. a. .2%
b. U.S. Internal Revenue Service Statistics of Income, 1974 *Corporation Income Tax Returns*
Q.3. a. $6.10
b. U.S. Department of Labor, Bureau of Labor Statistics
c. p. 45
Q.4. a. 12.02¢ per pound
b. *Iron Age*

Q.5. a. 11,467 thousand sh. tons
b. S-32
Q.6. *Standard & Poor's Industry Surveys*
Q.7. a. 6976-1.19
b. *Mountain-Plains Regional Reports*
c. *Collective Bargaining Calendar for the Mountain Plains Region*

CHAPTER EIGHT

Q.1. a. *Statistical Report of Retail Sales Tax Division*
b. yes
c. p. 40
Q.2. a. 27,715
h. 7-28
Q.3. a. $181,151,000
b. $19,332,000
c. $883,099,000
Q.4. a. 1,173
b. J.C. Penney, Leader
Q.5. a. 8.64%
b. Steel Company of Canada
Q.6. a. $5,497 million
b. p. 179

CHAPTER NINE

Q.4. a. "Exploring the gray market segment: cultivating retirement-age consumers could benefit alert retailers, but significant results would be likely only in unusual situations." Betsy D. Gelb, *MSU Business Topics* 26:41-6, Spring '78.
b. p. 602
Q.5. Operations research in the insurance industry: A survey of applications. W.S. Jewell. *Operations Research* 22:918-28 S '74.
Q.6. Hollande, S.C.
Merchandising Shortages and Retail Policies.
Q.7. Integrating management theory into action programs. E.A. Winning. *Personnel* 53:21-29 May-June 1976.
Q.8. a. 3312
b. Blast furnaces & steel mills expend for new plant & equipment data, 1978. *U.S. Department of Commerce News* 3/9/78 p. 6
Q.9. U.S. Steel Corporation:
Merges Southern steel division into Eastern steel division. *American Metal Market* 2/2/78 p. 2.

CHAPTER TEN

Q.2. a. *Marketing and Market Research*
b. p. 207
Q.3. a. Automotive Service Industry Association. Warehouse Distributors Division. *Cost of Doing Business Analysis for ASIA Automotive Warehouse Distributors.* Chicago: Automotive Service Industry Association, 1970.
b. *Library of Congress — Books: Subjects*, p. 328
Q.4. Iron and Steel Workers

CHAPTER ELEVEN

Q.2. a. "Business can make ex-convicts productive"
b. Indiana University, Northwest
Q.3. a. Lewis Beman
b. Wallace W. Booth
c. United Brands
Q.4. a. Weight Reductions
b. p. 78
c. Colle & McVoy Advertising Agency, Inc.
Q.5. a. Yes. 2-500 words, signed
b. General Audience
c. CanI, IntPolSc
Q.6. a. *Brick and Clay Record*
b. International Review

CHAPTER TWELVE

Q.1. a. *Northern Virginia Sun*
b. 1939
Q.2. a. Belgian Congo changes name to Zaire Repub; new name is taken from original name of Congo River, which in Zaire will be called Zaire River
b. O 28,2:4
Q.3. a. Toned down its estimate on how good 1977 will be for the steel industry
b. 1/7-4;3
c. Co-Steel International Ltd. will build $95 million steel production plant at Perth Amboy, N.J . . . .
Q.4. a. p. 1127
b. *Iron & Steelmaker*

CHAPTER THIRTEEN

Q.2. a. 6.9
b. "Job Discrimination and Affirmative Action"
Q.3. a. H641-16
b. Public Works and Transportation Committee, House
c. 770 p.
Q.4. S261-22
Q.5. a. *Administration's comprehensive program for the steel industry*
b. 78-24665
c. United States. Congress. House. Committee on Ways and Means. Subcommittee on Trade

CHAPTER ONE
Q.2. a. *CRC Handbook of Food Additives*
      b. p. 816
Q.3. a. *A Bibliography of Purchasing Literature*
      b. p. 342
Q.4. a. *The Social Psychology of Work*
      b. p. 102
Q.5. a. Coal Mining Institute of America
      b. p. 144

CHAPTER TWO
Q.2. p. 109-110, *Accountant's Handbook of Formulas and Tables*
Q.3. a. 2-1
      b. Saul Gellerman, "Motivation and Performance"
      c. *Handbook of Modern Personnel Administration*
Q.4. a. 16-51, 52 *Purchasing Handbook*
      b. "Buying Commodities"
Q.5. a. 327-328
      b. Armstrong, J.S. & Soelberg, P. "On the Interpretation of Factor
         Analysis." *Psychological Bulletin*, 1968, 70, 361-364.

CHAPTER THREE
Q.3. a. Barnouw, Erik 1956 *Mass Communication— Television, Radio, Film,
         Press: The Media and Their Practice in the United States of
         America.* New York: Rinehart.
      b. v.13, p. 216
Q.4. a. 303 U.S. 323 (1938)
      b. p. 280, *Roberts' Dictionary of Industrial Relations*
Q.5. a. p. 753
      b. "Manufacturing Analysis"
Q.6. a. feedback concept
      b. p. 97, *International Dictionary of Management*

CHAPTER FOUR
Q.2. a. Merit Abrasive Products, Inc.
      b. AAA
Q.3. a. William A. Klopman
      b. Textiles
      c. 2211
      d. 67,000
Q.4. ABC Draperies, Inc.
Q.5. NO
Q.6. a. no
      b. NA
Q.7. *American producers of Man-made Fibers*
Q.8. a. Amatex Export Trade Association
      b. 2802
      c. no
      d. n.a.

CHAPTER FIVE
Q.2. a. 2019.442
      b. yes
      c. *New Matters*
Q.3. 2377.3245
Q.4. Miscellaneous Tax Ruling
Q.5. a. World Wool Digest
      b. International Wool Secretariat
         $8.50 per year
Q.6. a. Industrial
      b. 1937   Delaware
      c. Goodall Sanford Inc.
Q.7. Anderson Clayton & Co.
Q.8. $2,284,626
Q.9. a. T-Z Blue Section 5
      b. 2299
      c. Aberdeen Mfg. Corp.
Q.10. a. $3.75 $3.05
      b. Chase Manhattan Bank, N.Y.

CHAPTER SIX
Q.2. a. 5,824 miles
      b. *The Statesman's Yearbook*, p. 693
Q.3. a. PL. 95-369 (HR 10899)
      b. *Dow Jones-Irwin Business Almanac*
Q.4. a. 121.1¢
      b. p. 135

CHAPTER SEVEN
Q.1. a. 2702-1
      b. 2702-1.11
      c. p. 296
Q.2. a. .7%
      b. U.S. Internal Revenue Service Statistics of Income, 1974 *Corporation
         Income Tax Returns*
Q.3. a. $3.69 or $3.40
      b. U.S. Department of Labor, Bureau of Labor Statistics
      c. p. 31 or p. 32

Q.4. a. 8,105 million lbs.
      b. *Textile Organon*
Q.5. a. 269.8 million sq. yds.
      b. S-39
Q.6. *Standard & Poor's Industry Surveys*
Q.7. a. 6976-1.20
      b. *Mountain-Plains Regional Reports*
      c. *Occupational Employment Projections to 1985*

CHAPTER EIGHT
Q.1. a. *Annual Report of Michigan, Department of Treasury Annual Report*
      b. yes
      c. p. 41
Q.2. a. 15,079
      b. 7-71
Q.3. a. $27,621,000
      b. $1,648,000
      c. $127,651,000
Q.4. a. 6,212
      b. Eckles, McDonalds, J.C. Penney, Wards
Q.5. a. 11.09%
      b. Lowenstein
Q.6. a. $14,495 million
      b. p. 362

CHAPTER NINE
Q.4. a. "Gray power: next challenge to business? Will retirement-age
         consumers be the next group to increase demands on business?
         Betsy D. Gelb. *Business Horizons*. 20:38-45, Ap '77.
      b. p. 669
Q.5. Brazil; ITT bows to local control. *Business Week* p. 35+ Mr 31 '75.
Q.6. Shama, A.
      Management and Consumers in an Era of Stagflation.
Q.7. An empirical investigation of "plateaued" managers. R.G. Nehrbass.
      Dissertation Abstracts International 36:7521A-2A May '76.
Q.8. a. 2211
      b. Carolina Mills— Plans to modernize plant for cotton flannel in North
         Carolina. *America's Textiles Reporter Bulletin* 8/78 p. 4.
Q.9. Burlington Industries:
      Discusses methods of treating cotton dust problem via steam and
      additives. *Daily News Record* 10/9/78 p. 18.

CHAPTER TEN
Q.2. a. *Entrepreneurship*
      b. p. 216
Q.3. a. *Allocating Field Sales Resources; A Symposium.* New York:
         National Industrial Conference Board, 1970.
      b. *Library of Congress— Books: Subjects*, p. 520
Q.4. Bleaching

CHAPTER ELEVEN
Q.2. a. "Consumerism as a retailer's asset"
      b. Giant Food
Q.3. a. Charles J.V. Murphy
      b. Wallace W. Booth
      c. United Brands
Q.4. a. Fire and Corrosion Protection
      b. p. 2
      c. Covey & Koons, Inc.
Q.5. a. Yes. 5-10, notes
      b. Academic, Special Audience
      c. Busl, PerManAb, PsychAb
Q.6. a. *American Dyestuff Reporter*
      b. New Product Review

CHAPTER TWELVE
Q.1. a. *Nevada Appeal*
      b. 1865
Q.2. a. Copper indus nationalized
      b. Ja 2,4:3
Q.3. a. Names president of Burlington Hosiery Co. unit
      b. 1/6-18;2
      c. Allied Chemical Co. raised prices an average 14% on several of its
         fine nylon apparel yarns
Q.4. a. p. 1131
      b. *American Dyestuff Reporter*

CHAPTER THIRTEEN
Q.2. a. 5.809
      b. *Solving Job Performance Problems*
Q.3. a. H782-48
      b. Ways and Means Committee, House
      c. 81 p.
Q.4. H721-3
Q.5. a. *Economic analysis of pretreatment standards for the textile industry*
      b. 78-6561
      c. United States. Environmental Protection Agency. Office of Analysis
         and Evaluation

Book No.   20

CHAPTER ONE
Q.2. a. *AMA Drug Evaluations*
    b. p. 818
Q.3. a. *Basic Books in the Mass Media*
    b. p. 145
Q.4. a. *Behavior in Organizations: A Multi-dimensional View*
    b. p. 76
Q.5. a. Green Coffee Association of New Orleans
    b. p. 148

CHAPTER TWO
Q.2. p. 79-80, *Accountant's Handbook of Formulas and Tables*
Q.3. a. 50-17
    b. Peter Davis, "Federal and State Labor Laws"
    c. *Handbook of Modern Personnel Administration*
Q.4. a. 16-43, *Purchasing Handbook*
    b. "Buying Commodities"
Q.5. a. 202-213
    b. American Psychological Association. *Technical Recommendations for Psychological Tests and Diagnostic Techniques.* Washington, D.C.: American Psychological Association, 1954.

CHAPTER THREE
Q.3. a. Bain, Joe S. 1952 *Price Theory.* Rev. & enl. ed. New York: Holt.
    b. v. 4, p. 495
Q.4. a. 135 U.S. 100 (1890)
    b. p. 287, *Roberts' Dictionary of Industrial Relations*
Q.5. a. p. 917
    b. "Scientific Management and Railroads"
Q.6. a. brainstorming
    b. p. 102, *International Dictionary of Management*

CHAPTER FOUR
Q.2. a. Breeze Corporations, Inc.
    b. AAAA
Q.3. a. George Weissman
    b. cigarettes
    c. 2111
    d. 53,000
Q.4. American Brands, Inc.
Q.5. 1919
Q.6. a. no
    b. NA
Q.7. *Costa's World Tobacco Directory*
Q.8. a. Tobacco Associates
    b. 2870
    c. yes
    d. *Tobacco Associates Annual Report*

CHAPTER FIVE
Q.2. a. 2019.7866
    b. no
    c. *New Matters*
Q.3. 1131.0259
Q.4. Office decision
Q.5. a. Federal Excise Tax Reports
    b. Commerce Clearing House, Inc.
      $72.00 per year
Q.6. a. Industrial
    b. 1919   Virginia
    c. Abdulla of Bond Street Ltd.
Q.7. American Brands, Inc.
Q.8. $4,293,782
Q.9. a. T-Z Blue Section 5
    b. 5194
    c. Culbro Corp.
Q.10. a. $0.54 $0.33
    b. Morgan Guaranty Trust Co., N.Y.

CHAPTER SIX
Q.2. a. 10,657 km.
    b. *The Statesman's Yearbook*, p. 716
Q.3. a. PL 95-387 (S-1103)
    b. *Dow Jones-Irwin Business Almanac*
Q.4. a. 113.7¢
    b. p. 349

CHAPTER SEVEN
Q.1. a. 2702-1
    b. 2702-1.13
    c. p. 296
Q.2. a. 3.7%
    b. U.S. Internal Revenue Service Statistics of Income, 1974 *Corporation Income Tax Returns*
Q.3. a. $4.99
    b. U.S. Department of Labor, Bureau of Labor Statistics
    c. p. 30
Q.4. a. 65.14 million lbs.
    b. U.S. Department of Commerce

Q.5. a. 7,823 millions of cigarettes
    b. S-30
Q.6. *Standard & Poor's Trade & Securities Statistics*
Q.7. a. 6926-1.53
    b. *Middle-Atlantic Regional Reports*
    c. *Wages in New York City, May 1976*

CHAPTER EIGHT
Q.1. a. *Report of Sales and Use Tax Collections*
    b. yes
    c. p. 41
Q.2. a. 23,454
    b. 7-71
Q.3. a. $8,754,000
    b. $863,000
    c. $43,038,000
Q.4. a. 12,827
    b. Newman's, Wards, J.C. Penney
Q.5. a. 19.67%
    b. Reynolds
Q.6. a. $4,128 million
    b. p. 358

CHAPTER NINE
Q.4. a. "Gaining valuable market research information through (small business) arrangements with universities." Stephen W. Brown. *Journal of Small Business Management.* 15:34-40, Ap '77.
    b. p. 589
Q.5. Evaluating your outside investment manager. R.S. Driscoll. *Financial Executive* 43:10-13 Ja '75.
Q.6. Spiro, R.L., Perreaul, W.D.
    Factors Influencing Sales Call Frequency of Industrial Salespersons.
Q.7. Relationships between goal clarity, participation in goal setting, and personality characteristics on job satisfaction in scientific organization. R.D. Arvey, et al. *Journal of Applied Psychology* 61:103-105 #1 1976.
Q.8. a. 2111
    b. Philip Morris—Company profile. *Forbes* 7/10/78 p. 29.
Q.9. Company profile, *Forbes* 7/10/78 p. 29.

CHAPTER TEN
Q.2. a. *Modern Real Estate Practice*
    b. p. 244
Q.3. a. William L. Berry. *Selecting Exponential Smoothing Constants.* Lafayette, Ind.: Herman C. Krannert Graduate School of Industrial Administration, Purdue University, 1972.
    b. *Library of Congress—Books: Subjects*, p. 519
Q.4. Cigarette Manufacture and Trade

CHAPTER ELEVEN
Q.2. a. "The focused factory"
    b. Harvard Business School
Q.3. a. Carol J. Loomis
    b. Wallace W. Booth
    c. United Brands
Q.4. a. Non-Coking Coal
    b. p. 12
    c. Campbell-Ewald Company
Q.5. a. Yes, 1-500 words, signed
    b. Academic, Special Audience
    c. PerManAb, WorAb
Q.6. a. *Tobacco International*
    b. Dixie Directory

CHAPTER TWELVE
Q.1. a. *Press*
    b. 1895
Q.2. a. '69 econ rev; outlook bright despite widespread damage from Oct floods
    b. Ja 30,56:1
Q.3. a. Agreed to let Soviets produce and market Marlboro cigarets starting later in 1977.
    b. 1/18-23;2
    c. Marlboro cigarets are going to the Soviet Union, but the Marlboro man will probably have to stay home
Q.4. a. p. 1131
    b. *The Tobacco Observer*

CHAPTER THIRTEEN
Q.2. a. 1.64
    b. *Patents*
Q.3. a. S382-9
    b. Foreign Relations Committee, Senate
    c. 32 p.
Q.4. H721-1
Q.5. a. *Leasing of flue-cured tobacco marketing quotas*
    b. 78-16167
    c. United States. Congress. House. Committee on Agriculture. Subcommittee on Tobacco

Materials & Methods
for
Business Research
Workbook

TABLE OF CONTENTS

ACKNOWLEDGEMENTS

The technique of using a workbook to teach bibliographic skills was first developed by Miriam Dudley of UCLA. There is no more apt beginning for those who build upon the method than to acknowledge her work. In deciding on the materials to include in this workbook, their classification, and the sorts of things to say about each, the authors have benefited from close consideration of Business Information Sources by Lorna Daniells, How to Use the Business Library by H. Webster Johnson, Sources of Business Information by Edwin T. Coman, Sources of Information in the Social Sciences edited by Carl White, and Literature and Bibliography of the Social Sciences by Thelma Friedes. The flow charts in Chapter Fourteen were adapted from Thomas Kirk, "Problems in Library Instruction in Four-Year Colleges" in Educating the Library User (New York: Bowker) edited by John Lubans, pages 93-95.

The development of a teaching resource such as this work-book requires the efforts of many people. First, the authors are greatly indebted to Carla Stoffle, series editor, for her guidance and encouragement throughout the writing of the material. A special thanks is given to Gail Kummings for her careful editing. For their assistance in the preparation of this workbook, the authors are grateful to several members of the University of Wisconsin-Parkside's Library/Learning Center staff. Among them, Shirley Mandernack, Diane Smith

and Ann Kuffel deserve special thanks. The authors are also
indebted to the Council on Library Resources and National
Endowment for the Humanities for the College Library Program
Grant which provided resources to make the development of this
workbook possible. Finally, the students of three successive
years in the Library Research Methods and Materials in Business Management at UW-Parkside deserve acknowledgement. Each
year the classes absorbed the material and tested the exercises. Their reactions in turn served as indicators for extensive revisions of the workbook.

INTRODUCTION

The ability to locate information in an organized and efficient manner is an important asset for students. The more they know about the materials and methods necessary for effective information gathering, the more productive and less time-consuming will they find their research and independent study time. In addition, effective library research skills will enable students after they leave school to perform more effectively in the business world through the use of information sources available at most libraries.

This workbook focuses on methods of information gathering and types of information sources appropriate for research and independent study in business. The specific objectives of the workbook are: to introduce basic types of information sources that business students should be able to use, to familiarize students with several examples of each type of source, and to prepare students to use those information sources efficiently and effectively in independent study and research. Upon completion of the assignments in this workbook, students should be able to:

--identify and use content reference works in business
(dictionaries, encyclopedias, handbooks, yearbooks
and services)

--identify and use specialized finding aids (bibliographies,
guides, periodical indexes and abstracts)

--locate and use government publications

--locate sources of statistical data

--locate articles and book reviews in business periodicals and newspapers

--identify sources of information found outside of a library

--utilize specific research techniques and search strategies for efficient and effective information gathering

--cite periodicals, books, and documents according to standard bibliographic form.

The value of the above objectives to business students is clear if one looks at their application. With the materials explained in this workbook, students assigned a paper or needing information about, for example, buyer behavior in the tobacco industry should quickly and easily be able to find: a concise definition and discussion of the concept of "buyer behavior" as used in marketing research; lists of articles and books written about the topic; discussions of the effects of adverse publicity and government regulation on cigarette smokers; government documents reporting the results of research on the topic; reviews of books useful in selecting a balanced coverage; statistics about the performance of the cigarette industry over a period of time and about cigarette consumption in various geographic regions and by selected demographic groups; and sources outside the library which could be contacted directly for additional information, if needed.

This workbook is divided into fourteen chapters and an appendix. In each of the first thirteen chapters, a category or
type of bibliographic tool is described, its utility for business students is explained, and standard examples of the type
are described individually. In the assignments accompanying
the chapters, students are asked to use these standard sources
to locate information. Each brief assignment translates the
discussion in a chapter into practical experience, demonstrating the ease with which sources can be located and information secured. Since finding information about companies and
industries is such a common information need of business students, tools that are especially appropriate to this purpose
are emphasized by including questions on them in a special
section of many assignments. Students are each assigned one
company and the industry of which it is a part to follow
through this series of questions, in order to clarify what
each source can contribute to building a comprehensive profile of a particular company and/or industry.

The first chapter of the workbook deals with works which
introduce reference materials. In Chapters Two through Eight,
substantive reference works are discussed; these are sources
of either statistical or narrative information useful in
business research and include such works as subject encyclopedias, yearbooks, and loose-leaf services. Chapters Nine
and Ten introduce finding aids; these reference aids, such as
bibliographies and periodical indexes, identify books and
periodical articles on business topics. In Chapters Eleven

and Twelve, scholarly and trade journals, professional business periodicals, and newspapers are discussed. Government
publications and the finding aids essential to their use in
research are the subject of Chapter Thirteen. The focus of
the last chapter is on research and study techniques and
strategies which put the various types of sources discussed
in previous chapters within the context of an individual research project. An Appendix lists additional examples of
each of the types of sources discussed in Chapters One through
Fourteen.

The intention behind this workbook is not to present an
exhaustive treatment of its subject matter. Rather, the
bibliographic examples have been selected according to the
following criteria: they are all in the English language;
they are generally available in medium size college libraries;
they are important examples of the types of sources most useful to business students; and they are drawn from several
functional areas of business, including marketing, finance,
management, accounting and operations research.

Too often, learning bibliographic skills is an unneces-
sarily haphazard and time-consuming process that leaves students unfamiliar with many types of sources that would increase the ease and productivity of their study hours. It
is hoped that this workbook will offer those who use it a
more thorough and less frustrating introduction to bibliographic sources useful to the study of business research.

NOTE TO THE STUDENT

In order to carry out research efficiently, you must be
familiar with the library's major services and collections,
its classification system for books and periodicals, and the
arrangement of the card catalogue. If you have questions
about these matters consult either the printed descriptive
materials available in the library or a reference librarian
before you begin to use this workbook.

A few simple procedures, if followed as you use this
workbook, will maximize its benefits to you and minimize the
time you spend on the exercises. Be sure to read the text
material carefully, especially the source annotations, before
turning to the assignment sheet for each chapter. Read the
entire assignment sheet before attempting to do any of the
questions, and make a preliminary decision about which source
discussed in the chapter is appropriate for each question.
When using a source for the first time, examine its table of
contents, the explanatory material in its preface and/or introduction, and the index, if there is one, to determine how
the source can be used most efficiently.

There are no "trick" questions in the assignments. If
you spend more than ten to fifteen minutes on an individual
question, your approach to the problem may be incorrect. Ask
a reference librarian for advice. You should also seek help
from a reference librarian when you cannot find a source

where it should be shelved or on a nearby table in the reference area.

Finally, because each of the chapters in this workbook has a very specific focus, it is important to read the Introduction carefully. Besides imparting an initial sense of the content of the workbook, it should convey an idea of the overall research ability to which each of the chapters contributes.

Chapter 1

GUIDES TO THE LITERATURE

Objective 1:   After reading this chapter, the student will
                describe a situation in which a guide would
                be useful.
Objective 2:   Given a subject field other than business,
                the student will use a comprehensive guide
                to identify an appropriate example of a
                specified type of reference source (a guide,
                encyclopedia, bibliography, etc.).
Objective 3:   Given a business topic, the student will use
                a guide to business literature to identify
                a specified reference work of a specified
                type.
Objective 4:   Given a topic in a functional area of busi-
                ness, the student will use a guide to identify
                a specified work on the topic.
Objective 5:   Given an industry, the student will use a
                guide to identify a trade association related
                to that industry.

Guides to the literature introduce various types of publications available in a given subject field or fields. The
purpose of a guide is to identify sources that will enable
students successfully to undertake information searches on
individual topics. Most searches start with some type of
reference work, and there are guides which concentrate almost
exclusively on these. The chief function of some of these
reference works, such as periodical indexes and bibliographies,
is to lead researchers on to other sources. It is useful to
think of such reference works as finding aids, in order to
distinguish between them and content reference works such as
handbooks, subject dictionaries, and loose-leaf services.

Some guides include discussions of various types of

primary research materials such as government and trade publications; a few include lists of important book-length studies, textbooks, and in some cases even journal articles on topics in a subject field. The uses of each of these types of publications will be discussed in subsequent chapters of this workbook. The point to be made here is that whenever it seems necessary to use a particular type of reference tool, lists of suitable titles may be found in an appropriate guide.

Students unfamiliar with a particular subject discipline can identify its reference publications by consulting a guide which attempts coverage of a wide spectrum of the fields of knowledge. The standard general guide is:

Sheehy, Eugene P. Guide to Reference Books. 9th ed. Chicago: American Library Association, 1976.

The primary purpose of this volume is to list and evaluate reference sources. Individual books are grouped under the headings: General Reference Works, the Humanities, Social Sciences, History and Area Studies, Pure and Applied Sciences. Within each group, titles are subdivided by subject, and then by specific type of material (encyclopedia, dictionary, bibliography, etc.). There is an index of authors, titles, and specific topics.

In business, as in most academic disciplines, there are specialized guides to the literature pertinent to various aspects of the field. To find information on a familiar or unfamiliar area in business, therefore, students can begin by consulting one of these specialized guides to business literature. Such specialized guides give titles of appropriate content reference works and finding aids used to identify books, articles and statistical sources. Most guides to business literature also identify textbooks, book-length studies of individual topics, and pamphlets.

A comprehensive and current guide that covers the entire field of business is:

Daniells, Lorna M. Business Information Sources. Berkeley, Calif.: University of California Pr., 1976.

> The first part of this guide discusses basic business reference sources, such as bibliographies, indexes and abstracts, and is arranged by type of source. The second part lists the most important sources under each functional area of business. Sources in the second part are not limited to reference works, but include basic textbooks and collections of readings. The author/title/subject index is quite detailed.

Another useful though very different type of guide is:

Wasserman, Paul, et al. Encyclopedia of Business Information Sources. Detroit: Gale Research, 1976.

> This guide provides a detailed listing of information sources on business activities, products, industries, and countries. It is arranged alphabetically by topic. Under each topic, relevant information sources such as reference works, periodicals, trade associations, and statistical sources are listed.

Using these general business guides students will be able to find still more specialized guides to such functional areas of business as accounting and marketing. Many of these guides contain supplementary information, such as lists of professional and trade organizations, that can be useful in the information gathering process.

An example of one of these specialized guides is:

Bakewell, K. G. B., ed. <u>Management Principles and
Practices: A Guide to Information Sources</u>. Detroit:
Gale Research, 1977.

     This guide attempts to identify the most important
books, periodicals and other sources when appropriate
on all aspects of management. Its twenty-one sections
cover management in general, automation and computers,
planning, communication and other relevant areas in
the behavioral sciences. Such specific functional
areas as research and development, marketing, production, and personnel are highlighted. There is a
detailed table of contents, as well as proper name,
title and subject indexes. The indexes refer to
entry numbers rather than to page numbers.

Another type of guide with which users of this manual will

become familiar is one which focuses on publications of a par-

ticular type, such as directories, periodicals, newspapers, etc.

Examples of this type of guide will be pointed out in subse-

quent chapters.

Chapter 1

GUIDES TO THE LITERATURE

Assignment

1. Describe a situation in which you as a business student would use a guide to the literature.

2. In order to fulfill your pre-business curriculum requirements, you are taking _____
_____
as one of your electives. The instructor has asked each student to select an independent study project. In defining your project, you feel you should consult specialized reference sources in the subject field. To identify these, you consult Sheehy's Guide to Reference Books.

   a. What is the title of the first _____
   _____
   listed for your subject field?
   Note: *"Sheehy" is international in scope; thus it will list reference sources in foreign languages as well as in English. Choose the first title written in the English language to answer this question.*

   b. On what page did you find this information?

3. You are enrolled in Introduction to Business and your instructor has asked you to write a short paper on a topic in an area of business in which you are considering specializing. You choose as your topic _____.
_____
Using Daniells' Business Information Sources,

   a. What is the title of the first _____
   _____ listed for your subject?

b. On what page did you find this information?

4. In your Process of Management course you decide to write
your assigned research paper on _____
_____.
You would like to start your search by identifying basic
reference sources in this area, so you consult Bakewell's
Management Principles and Practices: a Guide to Information Sources.

a. Using the subject index, find the title of the first
source listed on your topic.

b. On what page did you find this information?

5. You have been assigned a case study involving the _____
_____
industry. To complete one aspect of the case you need to
find out if there are any trade associations which are
potential sources of information about the industry. You
consult the Encyclopedia of Business Information Sources.

a. What is the name of the first trade association or
professional society listed?

b. On what page did you find this information?

Chapter 2

HANDBOOKS

Objective 1:   After reading this chapter, the student will
               describe a situation in which a business
               student would use a handbook.
Objective 2:   Given an operation in accounting, the student
               will use a handbook to locate an appropriate
               formula.
Objective 3:   Given a business topic, the student will
               select an appropriate handbook, will identify
               a relevant article, and will provide specified
               information about the article.

A handbook is a compact fact book designed for quick
reference. A handbook usually deals with one broad subject
area, and it emphasizes generally accepted data rather than
recent findings. In the latter respect, handbooks differ
from yearbooks, discussed in Chapter Six, although these
reference tools overlap in the types of information included
and in their utility for researchers.

The handbook format is well-suited to provide a type of
information business executives need: concise explanations
of accepted practices, procedures, and concepts in a given
functional area. The large number of handbooks available may
serve as some measure of their popularity. For most clearly
defined business functions, such as marketing, one can find
several, and they tend to be revised and up-dated frequently.
Many business handbooks are supplemented with such reference
extras as statistical tables, bibliographies, glossaries,
directories, and sample forms. Examples of handbooks useful

to business students are:

Famularo, Joseph S. Handbook of Modern Personnel
Administration. New York: McGraw-Hill, 1972.

   This work covers methods and techniques of personnel
administration. Chapters, arranged under 18 headings,
were written by authorities in the field. Bibliographies
follow each chapter. The subject index at the end refers
readers to both a chapter (bold type) and a page within
that chapter.

Aljian, George W. Purchasing Handbook. 3rd ed.
New York: McGraw-Hill, 1973.

   This handbook is intended to be a practical reference volume for individuals directly or indirectly
involved with procurement and materials management.
Topics ranging from ethics in purchasing to forms and
records are covered in 32 sections. Special features
include a glossary and conversion tables. The subject index at the end refers to section and page
numbers.

Dunnette, Marvin D., ed. Handbook of Industrial and
Organizational Psychology. Chicago: Rand McNally, 1976.

   Of special interest to students as well as prac-
titioners, this volume is a handy reference for those
needing an explanation of the various theoretical concepts and techniques relevant to industrial and organizational psychology. Methodologies are emphasized
in Section II. Each of the 37 chapters includes a bibliography of suggested readings. Name and subject indexes are at the end.

A second type of handbook used in some fields is a simple

compendium of brief definitions, formulas, tables, charts,

forms, and/or illustrations. An example of this type is:

Lipkin, Lawrence, Irwin K. Feinstein, and Lucile Derrick.
Accountant's Handbook of Formulas and Tables. 2nd ed.
Englewood Cliffs, N. J.: Prentice-Hall, 1973.

   This compilation includes formulas for simple and
compound interest, annuities, depreciation, and finance,
each illustrated with a simple problem and its solution.

An index provides access to the formulas by topic.

Some handbooks are truly manuals, with an even more practical, or "how to," purpose and format. An example is Lawson's How to Develop a Personnel Policy Manual (see Appendix for complete citation) which gives detailed procedures for establishing general personnel policies. Recent business school graduates might rely on this type of handbook as a general guide to assist them with various aspects of a new job.

Standard textbooks in many areas of business are often used in place of, or in addition to, handbooks. They are similar types of works in that both emphasize generally accepted data in a form convenient for persons trying to get an overview of a particular field. Daniells' Business Information Sources (see Chapter One) includes many references to textbooks for specific subject fields.

Chapter 2

HANDBOOKS

Assignment

1. Describe a situation in which a business student would
    use a handbook.

2. In your accounting class, the instructor discussed a
    formula on _____.
    You feel that if you could find a similar formula, it
    would give you further insight. Using a source discussed
    in this chapter, locate an example of such a formula.
    Identify the title and page of the source where you found
    this information.

3. You are working on a case study in your personnel manage-
    ment class. The instructor has assigned to each student
    a personnel problem common to the everyday work environ-
    ment. Your assignment deals with _____

    _____.
    One of the first steps you take in your search for a
    solution is to consult a handbook discussed in this
    chapter.

    a. In what section and on what page can information
        about your specific problem be found?

    b. Who is the author and what is the title of the
        chapter that includes a discussion of your assigned
        problem?

    c. What source did you consult?

4. You are taking a course in marketing, and group reports have been assigned. Your group needs some practical information on materials procurement, specifically concerning

    _____ .
    You consult a handbook discussed in this chapter.

    a. What is the source, the section, and the page number(s) where you found information about this topic?

    b. What is the title of the section in which you found the information?

5. You recently covered the topic _____

    _____
    in your industrial psychology class, and would like to do some extra reading before your examination. Because you are pressed for time, a concise statement as well as a few suggestions for further reading on the topic would serve your purpose. Using a specialized source for this field discussed in this chapter,

    a. On what page will you find an essay that covers this topic?

    b. What is the complete citation for the first publication in the bibliography?

Chapter 3

SUBJECT DICTIONARIES AND ENCYCLOPEDIAS

Objective 1:   After reading this chapter, the student will
               describe situations in which a subject dic-
               tionary or a subject encyclopedia would be
               useful in business research or study.
Objective 2:   Given a research topic, the student will lo-
               cate an essay in a subject encyclopedia which
               provides background information on that topic
               and will identify a specified publication in
               the bibliography.
Objective 3:   Given a topic, the student will locate a short
               summary of that topic in an encyclopedic dic-
               tionary and will identify a source of further
               information.
Objective 4:   Given an unfamiliar term, concept, or name,
               the student will use a business dictionary to
               find a definition or identification of the
               term and will identify a specified term which
               is cross referenced.

The primary purpose of a dictionary is to indicate the
meanings of words. The words included and the extent to which
the definitions are exhaustive depend upon the type of dictionary. There are basically four types--dictionaries which
are of a general nature (abridged and unabridged); those which
focus on specific aspects of language (synonyms, slang, etymol-
ogy); those which translate words from one language to another;
and those which concentrate on individual subject areas. The
focus of this discussion is on the fourth type, subject dictionaries.

Almost every academic discipline can be said to have its
own specialized "language." It is the function of a subject
dictionary to explain briefly the words, whether terms or

names, that make up a particular subject's specialized jargon.

Subject dictionaries, therefore, list terms unfamiliar in

common usage, as well as rather ordinary terms which, within

the context of a subject discipline, have taken on highly

specialized and technical meanings. A subject dictionary

useful to business students is:

> Johannsen, Hano, and G. Terry Page. International
> Dictionary of Management: A Practical Guide.
> Boston: Houghton Mifflin, 1975.
>
>   Terms and concepts included were selected from
> the field of management and from related areas of
> business. Many associations, institutions, and
> trade unions are identified and described. Terms
> for which there are cross references are italicized.

Subject dictionaries are also available for most other

functional areas of business, such as marketing, accounting,

finance, and data processing. Also useful are dictionaries

for related subject areas with which business students must

become familiar. A Dictionary of Statistical Terms could

prove useful both to the business executive trying to decipher

a statistical report and to the student taking a course in busi-

ness statistics. Students learning to find their way through

the financial page of the Wall Street Journal may find the

McGraw-Hill Dictionary of Modern Economics to be of real

help (see Appendix for complete citations). Other subject

dictionaries may be identified by consulting a guide such as

Daniells' Business Information Sources (see Chapter One).

While dictionaries contain brief definitions of terms,

encyclopedias contain summary essays on individual topics. There are two types of encyclopedias: general encyclopedias, which are wide-ranging in coverage; and subject encyclopedias, which focus on topics within an individual subject discipline or group of related disciplines.

The essays in subject encyclopedias are accompanied by bibliographies listing major studies of the topic, and by cross reference listings of other essays in the encyclopedia which may contain useful additional information. Students can therefore profitably use an essay in a subject encyclopedia in several ways: as an initial introduction to a topic about which they know very little, as a means of rounding out and placing in a wider context reading they are doing about an individual topic, or as the starting point for research they intend to do on an aspect of a topic. The student engaged in research may find an essay on the topic useful in clarifying and defining the research project, and the bibliography accompanying the essay can provide valuable leads for further reading.

Business students will find this subject encyclopedia to be useful:

International Encyclopedia of the Social Sciences.
New York: Macmillan, 1968. 17 vols.

This seventeen volume set contains articles covering the subject matter of--and some of the most important contributors to the development of--anthropology, economics, geography, history, law, political science, psychiatry, psychology, sociology, and statistics. Individual topics are often treated in more

than one essay, each approaching the topic from the
perspective of a different social science. Although
the encyclopedia is arranged alphabetically, the index
in the last volume should be consulted in order to
find material on a specific topic. The essays themselves are carefully cross-referenced, and the bibliographies accompanying the articles, although dated,
remain useful.

Actually, the distinction that has been made so far between subject dictionaries and encyclopedias is often less
than clear-cut. There are many works in the business fields
which offer more depth than a dictionary, yet less than an
encyclopedia. Explanations of terms and concepts may be
several pages long; cross references and bibliographic sources
often are provided. Such works, sometimes called "encyclopedic dictionaries," can prove useful to students in many of
the ways described earlier in this chapter.

Examples of such encyclopedic dictionaries useful to
students of business are:

Roberts, Harold S. Roberts' Dictionary of Industrial
Relations. rev. ed. Washington, D. C.: Bureau of
National Affairs, 1971.

The definitions given here for specialized terms
and phrases found in the literature of labor-management
relations range in length from one sentence to a page.
Also included are summaries of important cases and
identifications of international unions. Many source
references to books, periodicals, loose-leaf reporting
services and court and legislative reports are provided. A list of abbreviations used for some sources
is given in the "Guide to Users" section found at the
front of the volume.

Heyel, Carl, ed. <u>Encyclopedia of Management</u>. 2nd ed.
New York: Von Nostrand Reinhold, 1973.

    This work attempts to cover all aspects of manage-
ment. Essays, written by recognized authorities, range
in length from about half a page to over ten pages. Information and references provided at the end of most
essays include the names of professional associations
and societies, periodicals, important textbooks, and
journal articles. Essays are arranged alphabetically
by title and there is also an index. Both approaches
should be used, since many topics to which substantial
essays are devoted are not listed by subject in the
index.

Chapter 3

SUBJECT DICTIONARIES AND ENCYCLOPEDIAS

Assignment

1. Describe a situation in which a business student would use a subject dictionary.

2. Describe a situation in which a business student would use a subject encyclopedia.

3. During the first weeks of an independent reading course, you must select a general subject area and compile a reading list of books and articles. You have several subjects in mind, and to learn enough about each of them to make a selection, you turn to the International Encyclopedia of the Social Sciences. One of the subjects you are considering is _____.

    a. What is the first book entry (written in the English language) which appears in the bibliography following the essay? (Supply the complete citation: author, title, place of publication, publisher and date of publication.)

    b. In what volume and on what page did you find this information?

4. While doing assigned reading for your management and
    labor relations course, you come across a reference to

    _____,
    a case with which you are unfamiliar. Using an appro-
    priate dictionary discussed in this chapter, you look
    up the case.

    a. What is the citation for this case given under
        "Source References"?

    b. What is the source and page number where you found
        this information?

5. For your Process of Management course, you must write a
    research paper on some aspect of _____

    _____.
    You decide to write on _____

    _____.
    To begin your research you want to locate some general
    information about the topic as well as references to
    further information. Consulting the Encyclopedia of
    Management,

    a. On what page does an essay on your topic begin?

    b. What is the title of the first book or periodical
        article given in the "Information References" for
        the essay?

6. In a reading assignment for an introductory management
    course, you come across the term _____

    _____,
    which is unfamiliar to you. You consult a dictionary
    discussed in this chapter for a brief, factual definition
    to aid you.

    a. What is the first term used in the definition for
        which there is a cross reference?

    b. In what source and on what page did you find this
        information?

Chapter 4

DIRECTORIES

Objective 1:   After reading this chapter, the student will
               describe a situation in which a directory
               would be useful to a person in business.
Objective 2:   Given a trade name, the student will use the
               Thomas Register of American Manufacturers to
               locate the company which owns that name and
               will supply specified information about the
               company.

Given the name of a company and the industry to which it be-
longs, the student will:

Objective 3:   use a directory of companies described in this
               chapter to determine specified items of in-
               formation concerning that company.
Objective 4:   use a biographical dictionary described in
               this chapter to locate information on a
               company leader.
Objective 5:   use a guide to directories described in this
               chapter to locate information sources for
               that industry.
Objective 6:   use a directory of associations to locate a
               trade association relevant to that industry
               and to identify a publication of that associa-
               tion.

     Directories supply basic information about organizations

and people. The amount of information included in a partic-

ular directory varies greatly. Directories of companies, for

example, may provide only an address, but often provide infor-

mation on size, officers, subsidiaries, and products, as well.

Another important function of directories is to lead research-

ers to sources of information outside of the library. This

function is important, given the fact that no library, no

matter how large or well equipped, can supply the very current

information required by much business research. When neces-

sary, therefore, researchers use directories to locate outside resources, such as trade or professional organizations,
chambers of commerce, or government agencies.

In this chapter we will be discussing directories of
companies, of trade and professional groups, and of individuals, and examples of each type will be described. Since
thousands of directories are published in the United States
alone, however, it is important to realize that guides to
directories are available which can lead researchers to an
appropriate directory, should those cited in this chapter
fail to have the information desired. Actually, two of the
sources discussed in Chapter One, Daniells' Business Information Sources and the Encyclopedia of Business Information
Sources, make a point of listing available directories, so
they are good places to check first. A specialized source
for locating United States directories is:

> Klein, Bernard, ed. Guide to American Directories.
> 10th ed. Rye, N. Y.: B. Klein Publications, 1978.
>
> This work lists over 5,200 industrial, profes-
> sional, and trade directories, describing and giving
> the price of each. It is arranged by subject, with
> subject access through the table of contents. The
> index lists directories by title.

Directories of Companies

Company directories are usually limited in scope either
to a particular geographical area or to an industry. One of
the directories most relied upon for basic information about
large U. S. companies is:

Standard & Poor's Corporation. Standard & Poor's
Register of Corporations, Directors & Executives.
New York: 1928-.

     This publication is in three volumes. Volume one
lists approximately 37,000 United States and Canadian
corporations; entries include location and telephone
numbers, officers, products, sales, number of employees,
and SIC (Standard Industrial Classification) numbers.
Volume two lists directors and executives, giving
limited biographical data for each. Volume three includes a geographic index, SIC index, new additions,
and obituaries.

A similar tool which can be used if a company in the

United States is not listed in the above work is the Million

Dollar Directory published by Dun & Bradstreet.

It should be noted that all of the above directories give

SIC (Standard Industrial Classification) numbers for indivi-

dual companies and also include an index of companies by SIC

number. Established by the government, SIC codes classify

business establishments by type of product and are used in

many business reference sources, so it is important that

students become familiar with them. The classification sys-

tem is described briefly in Chapter Seven. Both the Standard

& Poor's and Dun & Bradstreet directories described above

include brief introductions to this classification system, and

it is recommended that students read one of these explanations

before attempting the exercises for this chapter. Learning

to use these SIC indexes will aid students in satisfying a

common information need--finding the major competitors of a

particular company. Businesses find these lists useful in

planning marketing campaigns as well as in identifying purchasing sources for needed products.

Many directories of companies are restricted to manufacturing firms. A comprehensive United States directory of
this type which often lists companies not found in the directories discussed above is:

> Thomas Register of American Manufacturers. New York:
> Thomas Publishing Co., 1905-.
>
> Volumes 1-7 are an index to manufacturers by
> product; volume 8 lists manufacturers by company
> name and includes information similar to that found
> in Standard & Poor's Register. An index of trade
> names in volume 7 is a particularly useful feature.
> Volumes 9-12 are a compilation of manufacturers'
> catalogs.

Other directories of manufacturing firms are available
for virtually every state and for most foreign countries.
Examples are the Classified Directory of Wisconsin Manufacturers, which is issued annually by the Wisconsin Manufacturers Association, and Kelly's Manufacturers and Merchants
Directory, published in England but having world-wide scope
(see Appendix for complete citations).

Directories which focus on a single industry are also
numerous. It is safe to say that most industries of any size
are served by one or more, published either by trade journals,
trade associations or commercial publishers. Thomas Grocery
Register is an example of a directory for a specific industry
(see Appendix for complete citation).

Directories of Associations

When persons in business find it necessary to go to an outside source for information, it is likely that that source will be a trade or professional association. These groups gather from their members and compile a wealth of statistical data, only a fraction of which is likely to be collected by an individual library. A direct inquiry made to such as association may turn up information difficult to find elsewhere. A comprehensive directory which lists United States associations of all types and includes information on their publications is:

Encyclopedia of Associations. Detroit: Gale Research, 1956-.

> This biennial publication is issued in two volumes, with periodic loose-leaf supplements. Associations are listed in volume one and include trade associations, societies, federations, chambers of commerce, unions and other non-profit groups. Entries are grouped by field (agriculture, business, education, etc.) and indexed by name and key word. Information supplied for each group includes purpose, activities, number of members, publications, etc. Volume two offers a geographic index and list of executives.

Directories of Individuals

In business reading and research, students often encounter references to individuals about whom they would like some background information. A directory of directors such as that found in Standard & Poor's Register of Corporations, Directors and Executives supplies information of a very limited sort for officers and directors of many larger corporations. Much more extensive information of both a personal and career nature is available in the type of work called a "biographical dictionary." Works such as Who's Who in America are examples of this type of publication with which students are probably already familiar. A specialized Who's Who of special interest to business researchers is:

Who's Who in Finance and Industry. Chicago: Marquis, 1936-.

This biennial publication provides brief biographies of financial and industrial leaders. Over 18,000 individuals are listed.

Chapter 4

DIRECTORIES

Assignment

1. Describe a situation in which a person in business would consult a directory.

2. You are employed in the purchasing department of a manufacturing firm. You remember having seen a product at a trade convention which you now realize would be useful to your company. Unfortunately, you can remember only the trade name, _____, not the manufacturer or distributor. You consult a directory of manufacturers described in this chapter which includes an index by trade names.

   a. What is the name of the company which owns this trade name? *Note: Company name follows short phrase describing product.*

   b. You would like additional information about the company so you consult the "Company Names" volume of this directory. What code letters are used to estimate the minimum total tangible assets of the company? *Note: Read "How to Use this Volume" at front of volume first.*

FINDING INFORMATION ABOUT
COMPANIES AND INDUSTRIES

The need to locate information about two groups--companies and industries--is a most persistent one for business students. Many of the sources in this chapter and in those following are very well suited, or even designed, to meet this need. In order to demonstrate the way in which these sources may be used together to furnish a profile of particular companies and industries, each student will be assigned one company and one industry to follow through the next eight chapters. Those questions which are part of this special project will appear last in each assignment, under the heading: *"FINDING INFOR-MATION ABOUT COMPANIES AND INDUSTRIES."* For the purposes of this assignment, it will be assumed that students are involved in an assignment which requires them to do an in-depth analysis of a particular company and its industry and that they are interested in finding out everything they possibly can about both.

Your company is _____.
It is part of the _____ industry.

3. Locate your company in Standard & Poor's Register of Corporations, Directors and Executives.

    a. Who heads this company? (Use first officer listed, whether called president, chairman, etc.)

    b. What is the principal product or line of business? (Give first listed.)

    c. What is its principal SIC number (first listed)?

    d. Approximately how many employees does it have? *Note: If separate information is given for the parent company and subsidiaries or divisions, give figures for parent company.*

4. Using the SIC index in Standard & Poor's Register, look up the SIC number you found in Question 3 to find a list of the major competitors of your company. What is the first company listed? (If your company is listed first, give next one.)

5. Wanting to find some information on the head of your company, you look in volume two of Standard & Poor's Register. Is this person listed? If so, what date of birth is given?

6. You would really like to find more information on the head of your company so you check to see if he/she is listed in Who's Who in Finance and Industry. (Use the 1977-78 edition.)

   a. Is this person listed?

   b. If listed, when did this person start working for your company? (If date is not given, state "not given.")

7. You want to get an idea of what information sources are used within your industry, so you consult the table of contents of Guide to American Directories under the heading _____ to find directories which might be used to locate sources of supply for needed products and services, develop mailing lists, etc. What is the title of the first directory listed?

8. You know that trade associations are excellent sources of information about a particular industry, so you consult the index to the 14th edition of the Encyclopedia of Associations in order to find those relevant to your industry.

   a. What is the first association listed in which _____ is either the first word of the title or the "keyword" supplied. ("Keywords" are those which are in parentheses.)

   b. To what entry number are you referred?

   c. Locate and examine the entry. Are any publications listed for this association?

   d. If so, what is the title of the first one listed?

Chapter 5

SERVICES

Objective 1:   After reading this chapter, the student will
                describe a situation in which a business stu-
                dent would use a service.
Objective 2:   Given a topic, citation, and abbreviation, the
                student will use the Standard Federal Tax
                Reporter to locate specified information.
Objective 3:   Given the name of an industry, the student
                will identify an appropriate service that
                provides information related to that in-
                dustry.
Objective 4:   Given the name of a company, the student will
                use an appropriate investment service listed
                in this chapter to locate specified infor-
                mation.

A service is basically a publication which contains up-
to-date reports and/or statistics on a given subject. They
are revised frequently, sometimes on a daily basis, to insure continuous coverage, with many appearing in loose-leaf
format in order to facilitate the incorporation of new data.
Services are both numerous and popular in the business world,
since persons in business need to be informed in depth on
certain topics but often have little time to spend doing
research.

Investment services and topical law reporters are two
types of services widely known and used by executives. Investment services provide a great deal of financial information
about particular companies and industries, while topical law
reporters cover the governmental rules and regulations which
govern the environment in which these companies operate. Examples of both types will be discussed in this chapter. Serv-

ices are available for many other facets of business activity as well. Persons wanting to check the existence of a service for a given subject area may consult:

> Grant, Mary M. and Norma Cote, eds. <u>Directory of Business and Financial Services</u>. 7th ed. New York: Special Libraries Association, 1976.
>
> This guide to business, economic and financial services describes 1,051 publications issued by 421 different publishers. Coverage, frequency, price and publisher's address are given for each listing. The guide is arranged alphabetically by title and has an index by publisher, as well as a detailed subject index. Indexes refer users to entry numbers rather than to page numbers.

One way to begin research on a company is by examining some of its financial statistics. From the historical data and analytical comments provided in basic investment services, it is usually possible to determine the company's line of business, how it has performed in the past and how it is performing now. Two major investment services are:

> Moody's Investors Service. <u>Moody's Manuals</u>. New York: 1900-.
>
> Six of Moody's financial manuals comprise this set:
>
> <u>Moody's Transportation Manual</u>
> <u>Moody's Public Utilities Manual</u>
> <u>Moody's Bank and Finance Manual</u>
> <u>Moody's Industrial Manual</u>
> <u>Moody's OTC Industrial Manual</u>
> <u>Moody's Municipal and Government Manual</u>
>
> These manuals provide corporate news and financial information on American, Canadian, and other foreign companies listed on United States stock exchanges. News reports, appearing in loose-leaf format are generally issued twice-weekly and cover corporate news releases. The annual bound volumes typically include for each

company a brief history, subsidiaries, plants, officers
and directors, products and detailed financial data
such as the latest annual income statement and balance
sheet, with comparative figures for previous years.
Each manual also has a center blue section containing
special features pertinent to each subject area, such
as industry-wide statistics and lists of largest companies arranged by broad industry groupings. Those un-
sure of which of the manuals contains information on a
particular company may consult the accompanying pam-
phlet, Moody's Complete Corporate Index.

Standard & Poor's Corporation. Standard Corporation
Records. New York: 1925-.

S & P is very similar to Moody's Manuals in the
coverage it offers. The principal differences lie in
the following areas. Unlike Moody's, S & P covers
companies having unlisted securities. The Daily News
section, published every week day, covers current
corporate developments, and it is cumulated and incorporated into the other six sections three times
a month. Indexes in the front of each section refer
users to the main entry for each company as well as
to updated information. Companies not found in the
first index (yellow section) may be subsidiaries and
should be checked in the second (blue section) to
find their parent company. Special features include
lists of companies arranged by four-digit SIC numbers.

Another popular investment service which is comprehensive
in scope is the Value Line Investment Survey (see Appendix
for complete citation). Investors find its analyses and reports on the prospects of individual companies to be particularly useful. Although the above services are designed to
satisfy the needs of the serious investor, business students
use them to find detailed financial information on individual
companies. It is important to note that they list only pub-
licly held firms. It is often very difficult, if not im-
possible, to obtain such financial information for firms under
private ownership. If such companies issue an annual report

and a copy is available, researchers may find this to be their
best source.

A handy and more concise tool than the above services
which also includes useful price charts is:

Moody's Investors Service. Moody's Handbook of Common
Stocks. New York: 1900-.

 This source, which appears quarterly, covers over
1,000 selected common stocks, listed alphabetically.
Each company page contains a ten-year statistical history plus a fifteen-year price chart and Moody's comments
on company background, recent developments and investment quality. There is a cross-index by industry.

Additional services are available to cover virtually all
facets of the securities market, from stock and bond prices
and indexes to earnings and dividends. Advisory services,
such as Standard & Poor's The Outlook, focus on company prospects, actually giving purchase recommendations for individual
stocks. A few of the major services covering the securities
market are listed in the Appendix. Standard & Poor's Security
Price Index Record, which is part of their comprehensive
Statistical Service, is described in Chapter Seven. A comprehensive investment service which analyzes and reports on
36 basic industries, Standard & Poor's Industry Surveys, is
discussed in Chapter Eight.

Topical Law Reporters

Topical law reporters are published to help executives,
accountants, lawyers and others keep abreast of the latest
laws and regulations affecting business operations. These

reporters bring together in a single compilation federal and state statutes, cases, administrative regulations, rulings and decisions. Many services also insert editorial comments and explanations. Being able to find all of this information together in one place greatly simplifies the job of researching a particular topic.

Three publishers dominate this field: Commerce Clearing House, Prentice-Hall, and the Bureau of National Affairs. While the latter is particularly strong in the area of labor law, all three publish roughly comparable services in a variety of legal subject areas, from federal and state taxes to consumer and environmental law. A few of these are listed in the Appendix.

The fact that these tools are designed to simplify research may not be apparent to students using them for the first time. The arrangement and even the vocabulary will probably be unfamiliar, and some perseverance may be necessary before students fully appreciate the convenience offered by these publications. Since law reporters are very similar in their basic arrangement, once the first is mastered, others should seem routine.

A service which thoroughly covers the field of federal taxation and which will serve to illustrate a few of the features common to many services is:

Commerce Clearing House. Standard Federal Tax Reporter. Chicago: 1913-. 15 vols.

COMPILATIONS:

The heart of the Tax Reporter lies in the basic income tax "Compilations." For example, in the 1980 edition these comprised volumes one through nine. They consist of the Internal Revenue Code broken down into sections and subsections, each immediately followed by the pertinent income tax regulations issued by the Commissioner of Internal Revenue, and by digests of court decisions and of rulings made by the Internal Revenue Service. These digests are referred to in the Compilations as "annotations." Editorial features added by CCH, such as explanations, comments and examples often follow. This coordination of different sources allows the researcher to find most of the information needed on a given topic in one place.

The Compilations follow the organization of the Internal Revenue Code: each section of the Code and of the corresponding Regulations section follow in numerical order. However, each item in the Compilations has been assigned its own paragraph (¶) number by CCH, and it is to these numbers that all indexes refer.

INDEX:

The subject indexes to the Compilations are located in the Index volume. The Topical Index is detailed, making it possible to pinpoint the location of specific tax rules. The Rapid Finder Index provides a broad subject approach to general areas.

A short glossary of abbreviations appearing in source citations can be found in the Index volume at the end of the first section, "How to Use this Reporter."

NEW MATTERS:

The section labeled "New Matters" immediately follows and updates the Compilations. It contains new developments, received in weekly reports. The Cumulative Index, which follows, provides a bridge between the Compilations and these current developments. Persons using a particular paragraph number in the Compilations should check that paragraph number in the Cumulative Index to see if there is recent information about their topic. If such exists, they will be referred to a paragraph number in "New Matters."

CITATOR:

The Citator volume contains the Citator Table. This is a "case name" index. It contains references to Tax Court, the Supreme Court, Board of Tax Appeals and other court decisions. Cases are listed alpha-

betically and the location of their annotation in the
Compilations is given. References, as always, are to
paragraph numbers, located at the bottom outside corner
of each page.

Special Information Sources for Companies

The sources covered in this chapter and in the preceding
chapter on directories are those which are used perhaps more
often than any others to obtain data about a company. Periodicals and newspapers (to be discussed in Chapters 11 and 12)
are also very useful for obtaining this type of information.
Other valuable sources available in some libraries of which
students should be cognizant are:

Annual Reports: issued by companies to stock-

holders, these reports provide information on recent

developments and current financial data. On some

university campuses, the placement office may have

a larger collection of these reports than the library.

10-K Reports: required by law to be filed with

the Securities and Exchange Commission on an annual

basis by all firms offering stock to the public.

These reports are superb sources of information about

a company's financial affairs for those who want to

do in-depth research and who need detailed accounts

of business activity. Some libraries subscribe to a

service which makes these available on microfiche.

Brokerage House Reports: generally prepared by

financial analysts in the research departments of

individual brokerage houses and not usually made available to the public at large. However, the Wall Street Transcript, published on a weekly basis and available in many libraries, (see Appendix for complete citation), provides the text from selected reports.

Chapter 5

SERVICES

Assignment

1. Describe a situation in which a service would be useful
    to you as a business student.

2. You are preparing to file your income taxes and need to
    determine if you can claim a deduction for _____
    _____
    specifically concerning _____
    _____

    a. Using the topical index for the Standard Federal Tax
        Reporter, what is the paragraph number of an an-
        notation relevant to your case?

    b. Find this paragraph in the proper volume of the
        Compilations. Based on the precedent that seems
        to have been established, is it likely that your
        deduction will be allowed?

    c. You now want to check to see if there have been
        any current developments that might affect your
        situation. What is the title of the volume that
        gives this type of information?

3. In preparing an assignment for your tax class you come
    across a reference to a tax case: _____
    _____
    To find out where this case is annotated in the Com-
    pilations of the Reporter, you use the Citator Table.
    To what paragraph number are you referred?

4. In researching a topic in the <u>Standard Federal Tax Reporter</u>, you come across a citation to a source which contains the following abbreviation _____.
Since you are unfamiliar with it, you look it up in the "How to Use this Reporter" section of the Index volume. What does it stand for?

FINDING INFORMATION ABOUT
COMPANIES AND INDUSTRIES

5. Using Grant's <u>Directory of Business and Financial Services</u>, identify a service that provides information on your industry.

   a. What is the title of the first service listed for this industry under the heading _____
   _____?

   b. What is the publisher of this service and how much does it cost?

6. Using <u>Moody's Complete Corporate Index</u>, identify the <u>Manual</u> that contains data on your company.

   a. ☐ Bank and Finance

      ☐ Industrial

      ☐ OTC Industrial

      ☐ Public Utility

      ☐ Transportation

   b. Using this <u>Manual</u>, find the main entry for your company. In what year and state was this company incorporated?

      Year _____   State _____

   c. Does your company have subsidiaries? If they are listed, give the name and location of the first.

7. You want to find a selective list of companies that belong to your industry. Using Volume I of Moody's <u>Industrial Manual</u>, turn to the blue pages located in the center of the volume. Find the "Classification of Companies by Industries and Products" section and identify the first company listed under _____.

8. In order to supplement the data found in <u>Moody's Manuals</u>, you consult Standard & Poor's <u>Corporation Records</u>. After identifying the correct volume (alphabetically by name of company), turn to the yellow index pages at the front of the volume and identify the main entry for your company (listed in bold face print). Locate the subheading "Earnings and Finances" and give the _____ _____ of your company for 1976.

9. You would like to identify a listing of companies belonging to your industry that is more specific than the one provided in Moody's. To do this, consult page 2 of the index section (yellow pages) of Standard & Poor's <u>Corporation Records</u>.

   a. According to the "General Index," where can you find an "Index of Leading Companies by Industries?"

   b. Using the above information, find the four-digit SIC number for the _____ industry.

   c. Using the SIC number, turn to the section immediately following, entitled "SIC Codes of Companies Described in <u>Standard Corporation Records</u>," and identify the first company listed under the above code.

10. To add another dimension to this profile of your company, you are interested in locating data on its stocks. Using Moody's Handbook of Common Stocks,

    a. What were the earnings per share for stocks in

       1976? _____ 1973? _____

    b. Who are the transfer agents for your company?

Chapter 6

YEARBOOKS AND ALMANACS

Objective 1:   After reading this chapter, the student will
               describe a situation in which a yearbook or
               almanac would be an appropriate source of in-
               formation in business research.
Objective 2:   Given a topic, the student will use an appro-
               priate yearbook to locate specified data.
Objective 3:   Given a topic, the student will use an almanac
               to locate specified information.

While in many cases they contain a good deal of back-

ground information, yearbooks are fact books which focus on

the developments of a given year. Unlike the handbooks dis-

cussed in Chapter Two, they emphasize current information. Like

handbooks, yearbooks may present only statistics, information

in narrative form, or a combination of the two. Many con-

tain a great deal of information similar to that found in

a directory.

Persons in business are likely to be interested in year-

books of several types. Those which concentrate on a par-

ticular country or countries often give a good picture of

the manufacturing, trade, and other commercial activities with-

in that country. Many also include information on laws af-

fecting trade. Such yearbooks are published by most of the

countries of the world (see Appendix for examples). A year-

book covering all countries of the world is:

Statesman's Yearbook; Statistical and Historical
Annual of the States of the World. New York:
St. Martin's Pr., 1864-.

    The Statesman's Yearbook combines information
from official and unofficial sources on all countries
of the world. It is divided into two major parts:
international organizations and countries. Information for many countries is broken down by states,
provinces, territories, etc. For each country there
is information on its economy, industries, commerce,
transportation system, energy and resources, etc.
There are two indexes: one by place and organizations, the other by-products.

Other yearbooks are available which focus on more spe-

cialized topics. An example of particular interest to those

in manufacturing is:

Commodity Year Book. New York: Commodity Research
Bureau, 1939-.

    This statistical yearbook provides data on produc-
tion, prices, stocks, exports, and imports for over
100 commodities. Editorial comments on new developments affecting individual commodities are included.
Information on a particular commodity can be found by
using the table of contents.

Almanacs are also annual compendia of statistics and

information in narrative form but usually treat topics more

superficially than do yearbooks. This is a reflection of

the specific purpose of the almanac, which is to present in-

formation about an exceptionally broad range of topics. Stu-

dents are probably already somewhat familiar with general

almanacs such as the World Almanac and Book of Facts. These

works are so packed full of facts on diverse topics that they

should never be overlooked by those trying to locate a particular piece of information. A more specialized almanac of

particular interest to persons in business is:

> Levine, Sumner N., ed. <u>Dow Jones-Irwin Business Al-
> manac</u>. Homewood, Ill.: Dow Jones-Irwin, 1976-.
>
> This detailed and comprehensive work contains
> statistical information on various aspects of busi-
> ness, finance, investments, and economics. Featured
> topics include the stock market, labor, commodities,
> business and legislation. A fairly extensive sub-
> ject index is located at the end of the volume.

Business students will find both yearbooks and almanacs

to be useful sources of information on recent trends and de-

velopments. Students should be aware, however, that a dis-

tinction is traditionally observed regarding their utility in

the preparation of written reports. Reliable yearbooks are

credible sources for citation in research papers when a more

original source is not available. (For example, a table in

<u>Commodity Year Book</u> citing statistics from the United States

Bureau of the Census may be used if the census volume is not

available.) On the other hand, the nature and purpose of

almanacs render them inappropriate for citation in most cases.

Business students will find that the above distinction

has been largely ignored in the case of many specialized

business publications. Trade and professional associations

often produce annual publications variously and apparently

arbitrarily called factbooks, sourcebooks, annuals, yearbooks,

almanacs, etc. Most are valuable sources of statistical

and directory type information for particular industries and trades. By whatever name they are called, data found in these publications are usually reliable and may be cited in research papers and reports. Such publications of trade associations may be identified through the <u>Encyclopedia of Associations</u>, as was done in the assignment for Chapter Four. Daniells' <u>Business Information Sources</u> and the <u>Encyclopedia of Business Information Sources</u> also cite many publications of this type.

Chapter 6

YEARBOOKS AND ALMANACS

Assignment

1. Describe a situation in which a yearbook or almanac
    would be an appropriate source of information in
    business research.

2. You are taking a seminar in international business and,
    as part of a case study, need to develop a profile of

    _____
    as a potential customer of an American automobile firm.
    Using the 1978-79 edition of a yearbook described in
    this chapter,

    a. What figures are given for the total miles (or
        kilometers) of highways and roads in this country?

    b. What is the title and page of the source where you
        found this information?

3. Your business law class has been discussing major legis-
    lation enacted during 1978 that had an impact on various
    segments of the business community. You need to identify
    a law which was signed on _____
    which created a great deal of concern among business people.
    Using the 1979 edition of a source discussed in this chapter,

    a. Give the public law number of legislation passed on
        the above date that concerned a specific segment of
        the business community.

    b. What is the title of the source where you found this
        information?

FINDING INFORMATION ABOUT
COMPANIES AND INDUSTRIES

4. Changes in the supply and prices of basic commodities affect every industry. To examine the commodity picture as it affects your industry you consult the <u>Commodity Year Book</u> to find price data on _____.

   a. What was the average price _____
   _____
   _____?

   b. On what page did you find this information _____?

Chapter 7

COMPREHENSIVE STATISTICAL SOURCES

Objective 1: Given the name of a periodical and a topic,
              the student will use ASI to determine if
              data on that topic are included in the
              periodical.
Objective 2: Given an industry, the student will locate
              statistics covering that industry using
              comprehensive statistical sources discussed
              in this chapter.
Objective 3: Given an industry, the student will use a
              guide to statistics to identify a publica-
              tion which includes data on that industry.

Familiarity with sources of statistical data is a neces-
sity for persons in the field of business. When called upon
to submit a report, make a decision, or offer a recommenda-
tion, the business executive wants to be able to support his
or her opinions and actions with facts and figures. Investors, as a group, are particularly avid seekers of information concerning the performance and prospects of a particular
company or industry, and the large number of investment
sources available, including the sources described in the
preceding chapter, reflects this interest. Business students
should be no less concerned about finding documentation to
support a term paper thesis, report, or a case study.

Understanding this need for data, government agencies,
trade associations, and commercial publishers, as well as
businesses themselves produce a constant flow of statistical
information. It comes to libraries in many forms: as loose-

leaf services, charting services, statistical yearbooks, industrial "factbooks," statistical periodicals, large census volumes, and as special issues of periodicals, to name only a few. Many of these types of statistical sources have already been discussed in preceding chapters. The purpose of this chapter is to introduce students to several basic sources which are good places to look first, to guides to statistics, and to a few specialized materials such as census publications which contain valuable statistics.

Statistical Classification Schemes

In using many statistical sources, students will encounter references to "SIC numbers" and "SMSA's." Both are classification schemes developed by the U. S. government to handle certain types of statistical data: the first is used to classify industries; the second, geographic areas.

Students were introduced briefly to the Standard Industrial Classification (SIC) System in Chapter Four, "Directories." This system classifies establishments by the type of activity in which they are engaged and covers the entire field of economic activities, subdivided as follows:

Industrial Division	Title	Major Groups
A	Agriculture, forestry and fisheries	01-09
B	Mining	10-14
C	Contract construction	15-17
D	Manufacturing	20-39
E	Transportation, communications, electric, gas, and sanitary services	40-49
F	Wholesale and retail trade	50-59
G	Finance, insurance and real estate	60-67
H	Services	70-89
I	Public administration	91-97
J	Nonclassifiable establishments	99

Below the 2-digit "major group," the SIC provides for 3-digit "industry groups" and finally for 4-digit "industries." To illustrate:

Division D - Manufacturing

Major group:	20	Food and kindred products
Industry group:	202	Dairy products
Industry:	2023	Condensed and evaporated milk

This classification scheme has been widely adopted within and without the government, making it possible to compare data collected by federal and state agencies, trade associations, and private research organizations. One of the uses to which the SIC scheme lends itself is in the identification of the leading companies in a particular industry. Students needing to determine precisely which types of business establishments are included within each number should consult a handbook published by the government for this purpose, the Standard Industrial Classification Manual (see Appendix for complete citation).

In addition to legally constituted geographic units
(states, cities, and counties), economic and social data are
often gathered and presented for Standard Metropolitan Statistical Areas (SMSA's). These are areas in and around cities
which function economically and socially as a unit. They
generally consist of one whole county or more. An explanation of SMSA's and a recent list of these areas can be found
in an appendix of <u>Statistical Abstract of the United States</u>,
described below.

Basic Sources

Various agencies of the U. S. government, of course,
publish a wide variety of statistical works in various formats. Since the following yearbook summarizes a good deal of
this output and serves as a guide to much of the rest, it is
a good place to check first:

> <u>Statistical Abstract of the United States</u>.
> Washington, D. C.: Government Printing Office,
> 1879- .
>
> Published annually, this work is a reliable source
> for statistics on the economy, business, population,
> and politics. Emphasis is on information of national
> scope, but there are also tables for regions, states,
> and some local areas. To locate statistics on a
> specific topic, researchers may use the subject index;
> for broader subjects, the table of contents is more
> useful. The introductory text to each section, the
> source notes for each table, and the bibliography of
> sources are extremely useful guides to other sources.

The following two sources are published commercially and
are noteworthy both for their currency and their completeness:

Handbook of Basic Economic Statistics. Economic
Statistics Bureau of Washington, D. C., 1947-.

       Published annually with monthly supplements,
the Handbook is a convenient compilation of data
originally collected and released in many forms
by the U. S. government. Annual historical data
for each series are given, if available, starting
with 1913. Statistics for recent years are broken
down on a monthly or quarterly basis. Monthly
features include a "National Summary of Business
Conditions" and an "Economic Highlights Section."
An index provides topical access.

Standard & Poor's Corporation. Standard & Poor's
Statistical Service. New York: 1970-. (Formerly
Standard & Poor's Trade and Securities Statistics.)

       This service consists of three parts. The first
part, "Current Statistics," updates the second, "Basic
Statistics." Areas covered by separate pamphlets are
Banking and Finance; Production and Labor; Price In-
dexes (Commodities); Income and Trade; Building and
Building Materials; Railroads and Communications;
Electric Power and Fuels; Metals; Autos, Rubber and
Tires; Textiles, Chemicals, Paper; and Agricultural
Products. The third part, the "Security Price Index
Record," appears on a yearly basis. An index intro-
duces each section.

Guides to Statistics

Of course, researchers will often need to go beyond

these basic sources to find needed statistics. Since the

U. S. government is the most important primary source and its

major publications tend to be available in most college and

university libraries, students beginning a search should find

out what data it has published on their topics. For this pur-

pose, the American Statistics Index (ASI) greatly simplifies

the task of determining which agency has published statis-

tics on a particular topic and in precisely which document,

report, bulletin, periodical issue, census volume, and even
on which table and page they appear.

> American Statistics Index. Washington, D. C.:
> Congressional Information Service, 1973-.
>
> This commercially produced abstract is an im-
> portant source for identifying statistical publi-
> cations published by the United States government.
> It indexes and abstracts statistics on numerous
> topics from the publications of many government
> agencies, describes these publications, and makes
> the material available on microfiche.
>
> This source is issued monthly in two sections--
> indexes and abstracts--and is cumulated annually.
> The index volume contains four separate indexes
> that list publications by subject and name; by
> geographic, economic, and demographic categories;
> by title; and by agency report numbers. The ab-
> stract volume gives brief descriptions of the pub-
> lications and their content.

More comprehensive guides provide access to statistics
published by a variety of sources. Actually, two of the
business guides introduced in Chapter One, Daniells' Business
Information Sources and the Encyclopedia of Business Information Sources, are excellent places to turn for direction.
Daniells devotes several chapters to statistical sources and
includes specialized sources throughout the book. The detailed index to this guide provides an effective topical
approach.

A more specialized guide directs users to very specific
statistical series found in thirty of the most widely used
loose-leaf services and statistical yearbooks:

Balachandran, M. <u>A Guide to Trade and Securities</u>
<u>Statistics</u>. Ann Arbor, Mich.: Pierian Pr., 1977.

     Composite statistical data available in thirty
publications are analyzed on an item by item basis,
using a subject/keyword approach. Sources are listed
and described at the front of the volume.

Census Materials

Most persons are familiar with the Bureau of the Census

in its role as gatherer and compiler of the Census of Popula-

tion, taken every ten years. Many may not realize the ex-

tent of its activities as a compiler and publisher of econo-

mic censuses. Taken every five years, in years ending in

2 and 7, these include the Censuses of <u>Construction Industries</u>,

<u>Manufactures</u>, <u>Mineral Industries</u>, <u>Retail Trade</u>, <u>Selected Ser-</u>

<u>vice Industries</u>, <u>Transportation</u>, and <u>Wholesale Trade</u>. The

Bureau of the Census distributes a <u>Catalog of Publications</u>

which describes these and its other series (see Appendix for

complete citation); they are also thoroughly indexed and

abstracted in the <u>American Statistics Index</u> (ASI), described

above.

It is important to note that, although the censuses are

published relatively infrequently, much of their data is up-

dated regularly on an annual, quarterly, monthly or even

weekly basis through surveys and reports. Because of its

central importance as a source of detailed industrial data,

many business students will find it particularly rewarding

to become acquainted with the <u>Census of Manufactures</u>. Many of the statistical series which appear in this census are updated either in the Annual Survey of Manufactures, or in the series of Current Industrial Reports which appear monthly, quarterly, or annually. The Census of Retail Trade will also prove to be especially useful for many types of business research.

Statistical Periodicals

Many government agencies which compile statistical information publish it in the form of a monthly periodical. Students may already be familiar with several of these titles: Business Conditions Digest, Economic Indicators, the Federal Reserve Bulletin and the Monthly Labor Review (see Appendix for complete citations). Another periodical, the Survey of Current Business, is perhaps the most important source of current business statistics, both for its regularly appearing series and for its special issues:

U. S. Department of Commerce. Survey of Current Business. Washington, D. C.: U. S. Government Printing Office, 1921-.

Appearing in each monthly issue, the center blue section of the Survey includes both general economic statistics (general business indicators, commodity prices, employment, finance, trade, etc.) and industrial statistics for specific types of products. A subject index to these tables appears on the inside of the back cover. Special statistical reports appear at intervals ranging from quarterly to annually. The "National Income Issue," appearing in July, is the most important of these. The Survey also features articles which analyze the current business situation. These are indexed in the periodical indexes described in Chapter Nine. The statistical series are indexed

and described in ASI. Companion publications to the
<u>Survey</u> are <u>Business Statistics</u>, a weekly supplement,
and a biennial volume, also entitled <u>Business Sta-</u>
<u>tistics</u>, which provides historical data for the series
appearing in the <u>Survey</u>.

Chapter 7

COMPREHENSIVE STATISTICAL SOURCES

Assignment

1. The instructor in your marketing course has given an
    assignment that will involve finding statistical data
    on _____.
    She has suggested several sources, among them the
    periodical _____.
    Since it is a government statistical publication, you
    check the Index by Titles in the Index volume of Ameri-
    can Statistics Index, 1978 to see if this publication
    regularly publishes tables on your topic.

    a. To what ASI "accession number" are you referred?

    b. Turning to the Abstracts volume for 1978, what is the
        accession number for tables on your topic?
        *Note: Refer to Sample Abstract on page xxxiv at front
        of volume for clarification.*

    c. On what page did you find this information?

                *FINDING INFORMATION ABOUT
                COMPANIES AND INDUSTRIES*

2. You would like to get some idea of how much money cor-
    porations in your industry spend on advertising and,
    specifically, how this figure compares with their re-
    ceipts. When you consult the index of the Statistical
    Abstract of the United States, 1978 under "Advertising
    expenditures" you are referred to several pages where
    you find a table giving this data for 1974.

    a. What percentage of receipts was spent for advertising
        by industries dealing in or manufacturing _____.

    b. What source is given for these data?

3. You want to find current figures on average earnings for workers in your industry, so you turn to the <u>Handbook of Basic Economic Statistics</u>. Looking under the heading
_____,

    a. What were the average hourly earnings for _____
_____ in this <u>industry</u>
<u>in 1976</u>?

    b. What source is given for these data?

    c. On what page did you find this information?

4. To find _____
you consult <u>Standard & Poor's Statistical Service</u>. Turning to the "Basic Statistics" unit entitled _____
_____ (filed behind the "Business & Financial" tab), find an entry in its table of contents for _____
_____ and turn to the page <u>listed</u>.

    a. What figure is given for _____?

    b. What organization is given credit for compiling these figures?

5. You would like to find very current production or sales figures for your industry. You check the March, 1979, issue of the <u>Survey of Current Business</u> to see if its "Current Business Statistics" section includes such data. Using the _____ section of the index, find the page(s) giving statistics for _____
_____ and examine them.
Note: The abbreviation "do" stands for "ditto."

    a. What figure is given _____
_____
_____ in the month of (or the quarter ending in) September, 1978?

    b. On what page did you find this information?

6. To find other sources of statistics on your industry you
   check A Guide to Trade and Securities Statistics under the
   heading _____.
   To what source are you referred?
   *Note: Students should be aware when using this guide that
   one of the sources often referred to, Standard & Poor's
   Trade and Securities Statistics, is now called Standard &
   Poor's Statistical Service (described in this chapter).*

7. You are fairly sure that the U. S. government regularly
   collects statistics you need on your industry, but you
   weren't able to find them in the basic sources given in
   this chapter, so you turn to A. S. I.. Using the index
   volume for _____ you bypass the first index,
   the "Index by Subjects and Names," since you know that
   you want statistical series broken down by industry. You
   turn to the first page of the "Index by Categories,"
   which refers you to the section of the "Economic Break-
   downs" listing statistics broken down by industry. Looking under _____ in this sec-
   tion, you find a publication giving _____
   _____.

   a. What is the accession number given for this publica-
      tion?

   b. Using the abstract volume for the same year, use this
      number to find a description of this publication and
      the series of which it is a part. What is the title
      of the series?
      Note: Refer to Sample Abstract on page xxxv.

   c. What is the title of the individual report?

Chapter 8

MARKETING AND INDUSTRIAL STATISTICS

Objective 1: Given a topic, the student will use a guide to
statistical sources to locate a source for
data on that topic.
Objective 2: Given a topic, the student will use a marketing
guide to locate data on that topic.
Objective 3: Given an industry, the student will use a
source of industrial statistics described in
this chapter to locate data on that industry.

Marketing

Access to current statistical data is essential for those

engaged in market research. The marketing department of any

company attempting to determine sales potential, set sales

quotas, or establish effective sales territories will be

vitally interested in such factors as population, number of

households, age, sex, marital status, occupation, education

level, income, and purchasing power. Of course, many of these

data can be found in the U. S. government sources described

in the preceding chapter. Individual states also publish

such statistical series, often on a more timely basis than

the federal government. A publication which serves as a guide

to federal sources as well as to state publications which are

especially useful for those engaged in market evaluation is:

U. S. Department of Commerce. Measuring Markets: A
Guide to the Use of Federal & State Statistical Data.
Washington, D. C.: U. S. Government Printing Office,
1974.

Materials published by state and federal governments which are useful in marketing research are summarized using a tabular format. Sources for population, income, employment, sales statistics and some state taxes are included. Examples are provided which demonstrate the use of federal statistics in market analysis. There is no index, so access is through the table of contents.

Those involved in marketing research place a great deal of emphasis on obtaining the most current information possible, and a number of commercial publishers meet this need by providing estimates of many statistics broken down by those geographic units most likely to be useful to market researchers. Three widely used sources are:

Editor and Publisher Market Guide. New York: Editor and Publisher, 1884-.

Market data are provided for more than 1,500 United States and Canadian cities in which newspapers are published. Included are figures for population, households, principal industries and retail outlets. Estimates by county, newspaper city, and SMSA for such items as population, personal income, and total retail sales are also provided, arranged by state.

Survey of Buying Power Data Service. New York: Sales and Marketing Management, 1977-.

This service is a spin-off of the July statistical issue of Sales and Marketing Management magazine. It is arranged in three volumes. The first covers, by county and city, population characteristics, household distributions, effective buying income, total retail store sales, and various buying power indexes. The second volume includes retail sales by individual store groups and merchandise line categories for the current year. Volume three contains TV market data as well as metro area and county projections for population, effective buying income, and retail sales.

Commercial Atlas and Marketing Guide. Chicago: Rand McNally, 1884-.

This annual publication includes maps for each state in the United States and a shorter section for maps of foreign countries. Marketing statistics for states and some worldwide data, such as airline and steamship distances, are provided. Also included are population statistics and figures for retail sales, bank deposits, auto registration, etc., for principal cities.

Industry Statistics

A great many research projects in business involve gathering statistical and/or investment data on a particular industry or industries. All of the comprehensive sources described in the preceding chapter are very suited to this purpose. In addition to providing useful statistics on leading industries, the following publications analyze current trends and future projections:

Standard & Poor's Corp. Industry Surveys. 2 vols. New York: 1973-.

This service analyzes the performance and operating environment of more than 65 leading U. S. industries. "Basic Surveys" for each industry are updated three times a year by "Current Surveys." A brief "Trends and Projections" section on the economy as a whole appears monthly. Indexes by industry and company appear at the front of the first volume.

U. S. Department of Commerce. U. S. Industrial Outlook. Washington, D. C.: U. S. Government Printing Office, 1973-.

This publication offers a five year forecast of business prospects for 200 U. S. industries. In addition, statistics showing the industry's competitive trade position and growth history in key areas are summarized. A separate table for each industry or service area provides basic statistics for seven years, including estimates for the year immediately past and a forecast for the current year (the Outlook appears in January of each year). Terms used in tables are explained in the section, "How to Get the Most out of this Book." An index by industry includes SIC Codes.

A number of publications discussed in other chapters are also excellent sources of statistical information on industries. To summarize:

1. Industrial factbooks, yearbooks, almanacs, etc., often published by trade associations. Identify these publications through guides: Daniells' Business Information Sources or Encyclopedia of Business Information Sources (Chapter One) or through a directory of associations: Encyclopedia of Associations (Chapter Four).

2. Investment services covered in the preceding chapter, especially the center blue sections of Moody's Manuals.

3. Periodical and newspaper articles. Identify through periodical indexes and abstracts and newspaper indexes (Chapters Nine and Eleven).

4. Special issues of periodicals. Identify through guides, or through Guide to Special Issues of Periodicals (Chapter Eleven).

Chapter 8

MARKETING AND INDUSTRIAL STATISTICS

Assignment

1. In your course in Marketing Methods you have been given
    an assignment which involves establishing sales quotas
    by county in the state of _____.
    Since it would be very helpful if you could find recent
    sales statistics from that state broken down by county,
    you turn to Measuring Markets, a Guide to the Use of
    Federal and State Statistical Data to determine what
    sources of sales statistics are available for that state.

    a. What is the title of the first publication listed
        for that state?

    b. Are counties included in its geographic coverage?

    c. On what page did you find this information?

2. For your advertising methods class you must plan an
    advertising campaign for a department store in _____
    _____.
    In order to develop your plan you need to determine the
    number of households in that metropolitan area with an
    effective buying income of $15,000-$24,999 annually. You
    consult the Survey of Buying Power Data Service, 1979.

    a. How many households in this community had an income
        in this range during the preceding year?

    b. In what section and on what page did you find this
        information?

3. For your Marketing II course, each student has been asked to gather current population and sales data for specific counties in Wisconsin. You have been assigned _____ county. Using the 1979 Rand McNally Commercial Atlas and Marketing Guide,

    a. What were the food store sales for 1977 in your county?

    b. What were the drug store sales for 1977 in your county?

    c. What were the total retail trade sales in 1977 for your county?

4. On your first assignment in your new marketing job, your supervisor has informed you that the company is about to market a new electric household utensil in selected areas of the country. She would like you to measure the potential market for this item in _____. Using the 1979 Editor and Publisher Market Guide,

    a. How many residences have electric meters in this area?

    b. What are the major retail outlets (department stores) in this area?

FINDING INFORMATION ABOUT
COMPANIES AND INDUSTRIES

5. To find composite statistics on your industry which include
    data on leading companies within the industry, you turn to
    Standard & Poor's Industry Surveys. Yours is a major
    company and individual statistics for it may be included
    in the Surveys, so you use the "Index to Companies." This
    will refer you to a section and page of a "Current Analy-
    sis" giving very recent statistics on your company.

    a. Looking in the corresponding "Basic Analysis" pamphlet
        (immediately following the "Current Analysis"), find
        a table giving "Composite Industry Data" for your
        particular industry (each "Basic Analysis" may cover
        several related industries). What was the profit
        margin for this industry in 1976? (If figure is not
        available, so state).

    b. Referring to the "Comparative Company Analysis" tables
        which follow, how does your company compare to _____
        _____ in terms of _____
        _____ in 1976? Which had the higher
        figures?

6. In order to find statistics on trends and projections for
    your industry, you consult the index to the U. S. Industrial
    Outlook under the heading _____
    to find a chapter including information on your industry.

    a. Consulting the appropriate "Trends and Projections"
        table in this chapter, what figure is given for
        _____
        in 1976?

    b. On what page did you find this information?

Chapter 9

PERIODICAL INDEXES AND ABSTRACTS

Objective 1: The student will identify the basic difference
              between indexes and abstracts.
Objective 2: The student will identify the basic difference
              between a topical index and a citation index.
Objective 3: Given business topics, the student will use an
              index, an abstract, and a citation index to
              locate references to articles on those topics.
Objective 4: The student will examine an issue of Current
              Contents: Social and Behavioral Sciences and
              will describe a situation in which it would
              be useful.

Periodical indexes and abstracts are finding aids which

enable researchers to systematically identify journal articles

on individual topics. The Readers' Guide to Periodical Lit-

erature (see Appendix for complete citation), which lists

articles in general magazines, is an index familiar to most

students. More specialized indexes and abstracts list ar-

ticles published in business periodicals. For business stu-

dents these finding aids are important because the articles

they identify often update information found in books, and

in some instances, constitute the only published treatments

of certain topics.

The standard citation for articles in indexes includes

the author's name, the article's title, the name of the

journal, the volume, number and the date of the journal in

which the article appears, and its page numbers. Among the

indexes which identify articles in business journals are:

Public Affairs Information Service. Bulletin. New York: 1915-.

This publication, often referred to as PAIS, indexes some 1,000 periodicals on a selective basis, as well as a few books, pamphlets, yearbooks, directories and government documents. The scope is broad in that it gives international coverage to the fields of public administration, economics and other social sciences. It is published weekly, with quarterly and annual cumulations. Many entries have brief explanatory annotations.

Business Periodicals Index. New York: Wilson, 1958-.

Business Periodicals Index (BPI) is a subject index to business periodicals in the English language. An index to book reviews, by author, follows the subject index. It is published monthly, except August, with a bound annual cumulation.

Funk and Scott Index of Corporations and Industries, United States. Cleveland: Predicasts, 1960-.

This index, which appears weekly with monthly and annual cumulations, is an excellent finding aid for information on companies and industries. It indexes a wide variety of periodicals, services and newsletters that cater to business, industrial and financial organizations. Articles on industries (yellow pages) are arranged by SIC numbers. Articles on companies (white pages) are arranged alphabetically by company name. Many of the entries refer to very brief articles, so it should be noted that a black dot precedes citations for substantial articles.

Another type of index available to researchers is a relatively new type of finding aid. Citation indexes identify articles which have cited previous research by a particular author. When one looks up a given author, one is referred to later research that has "cited" particular works by that author. Thus, the citation index will lead one to material which was based, to some degree, upon the works written by that given author. An advantage of this type of index is that a researcher can find articles without depending on a subject classification system. A disadvantage is that this type of indexing does not clearly define the relationship of the later articles to the cited work. Those articles must be located in order to determine their usefulness. This type of index is useful for determining the quality of a specific key research paper, or for tracing the developments in theory and methods which were stimulated by this key paper. A student can determine the number of times a key article has been used, as well as the names of the researchers who have cited it. The citation index useful to business students, particularly to those in the field of management science, is:

Social Sciences Citation Index. Philadelphia: Institute for Scientific Information, 1972-.

This service enables the user to identify recent articles that refer to earlier works. Each issue is divided into three parts. The "Citation Index," arranged alphabetically by cited author, lists references to articles in which a particular work was cited. The "Source Index" lists alphabetically the authors who are citing the original work and gives bibliographic information for each article which cites the original work. The "Permuterm Subject Index" lists articles by all significant words in the title. The index is issued three times a year and cumulates annually.

Like indexes, abstracts provide a complete citation for each article. They also include a brief summary of its contents. This summary, or "abstract," often enables researchers to determine whether or not a scholarly article is pertinent to their purposes without having to spend time locating and reading it. The resulting economy of effort can be especially important when researchers are working in a library with a small periodical collection and must depend on interlibrary loan to acquire a number of journal articles. Among the abstracts useful in business research are Personnel Management Abstracts (see Appendix for complete citation) and:

Work Related Abstracts. Detroit: Information Coordinators, 1972-.

    This abstract lists articles, dissertations and books covering labor, personnel and organizational behavior. It is published in loose-leaf format and is arranged by subject in twenty broad sections. There is a detailed subject index in the front. A subject headings list, published annually, facilitates its use.

Still another type of indexing service is especially designed for those who want to stay absolutely up-to-date with the literature in their field. It is basically a compilation of the tables of contents of journals selected from a particular subject area and appears frequently (usually weekly) in a format which permits researchers, busy executives, and others with limited time to keep abreast of what is being published in areas of interest to them.

This type of publication provides the only systematic access to periodical articles between the time they are published and the time indexing for them appears in periodical indexes and abstracts. In a field as fast changing as business, these current awareness tools have an important function. An index of this type which is often used by those in business is:

Current Contents: Social and Behavioral Sciences.
Philadelphia: Institute for Scientific Information,
1961-.

    This weekly publication reproduces the tables
of contents of the most important journals in business, management, economics, computer applications
and other disciplines in the social and behavioral
sciences. Coverage is worldwide and includes more
than 1,330 journals. Each issue has a key word
subject index, author index, address directory and
a publishers' address index.

Chapter 9

PERIODICAL INDEXES AND ABSTRACTS

Assignment

1. What is the basic difference between indexes and abstracts?

2. What is the basic difference between a topical index
    such as Business Periodicals Index and a citation index?

3. Examine any recent issue of Current Contents: Social and
    Behavioral Sciences.

    a. What is the date, volume, and issue number of this
        issue?

    b. Examine the table of contents (called "In this Issue").
        On what page does the section devoted to Management
        begin?

    c. Turn to the "Weekly Subject Index" and read the
        section which explains its use. If you were looking
        for recent articles on management by objectives and
        you found the following entry in this index, how
        would you go about finding the article to which the
        entry refers?

                    MANAGEMENT-O
                    BJECTIVES
                     92   329

4. To update the information in your text for your course in advanced marketing techniques, the instructor has assigned each student a topic to report on. Your topic is _____ _____.
Since periodicals will contain the most recent materials, you consult several periodical indexes, among them the PAIS Bulletin. You begin with the most recent issue and are now using _____.

   a. What is the complete citation for the first English language article? (A complete citation consists of the author, title, and the journal name, volume, issue, pages and date.)

   b. On what page did you find this information?

5. You are preparing a paper on _____.
You have identified several books on the topic and would now like to bring your research up-to-date with periodical articles. You begin with the latest issue of Business Periodicals Index and have progressed to the cumulative annual index for 1974-75. What is the complete citation for the first article listed on your topic?

6. You are doing some preliminary reading for an independent study project. You find an article by _____ _____ which appeared in _____.
Since this article deals with issues specifically on your topic, you want to see if any additional research has been completed which uses this article as a basis. You begin with the most recent issue of Social Sciences Citation Index and have progressed to 1978. Who is the author and what is the title of the first article which refers to the article you have already located?
Note: You must use both the citation and source indexes to answer this question. For clarification, consult explanations found inside the front and back covers of each volume.

7. You have been assigned a research paper on _____
    _____. In order to save
    search time you would like to find summaries of the work
    done on this topic, so you consult Work Related Abstracts.
    Using the 1976 volume, give a complete citation for the
    first article listed on your topic.

*FINDING INFORMATION ABOUT
COMPANIES AND INDUSTRIES*

8. Referring back to Chapter Four, question 3c, give the
    SIC number for the industry you were assigned earlier.

    a. SIC _____

    b. Using this SIC number, locate a listing of articles
        dealing with your industry in the 1978 volume of
        Funk and Scott's Index. Give the complete citation
        of the first article listed.

9. Using the name of the company you were assigned earlier,
    locate a listing of articles on this company in the
    1978 volume of Funk and Scott's Index. Give the com-
    plete citation of the first article listed on your
    company.

Chapter 10

BIBLIOGRAPHIES

Objective 1:   After reading this chapter, the student will
               describe situations in which bibliographies
               are useful for study and research in business.
Objective 2:   Given a subject, the student will use a bibli-
               ography to identify a book on that subject.
Objective 3:   Given an industry, the student will identify a
               useful subject heading used in a standard bibli-
               ography.

To utilize study and research time effectively, students

must rely on sources which identify print materials relevant

to their topics. Bibliographies constitute an important

category of such finding aids. Business researchers will en-

counter bibliographies which list any or all of the following:

books, government documents (both published and unpublished),

and periodical articles. The focus of the discussion in this

chapter is on bibliographies as finding aids primarily for

books other than reference books and, secondarily, for ar-

ticles. Whenever students use a bibliography that does not

list journal articles as well as book titles, they should

also consult a periodical index or abstract (see Chapter Nine)

in order to compile a comprehensive reading list on a topic.

For the books and articles listed, some bibliographies

provide only citations; others provide annotations as well.

The standard bibliographic citation for books, for example,

includes author, title, place of publication, publisher, and

date of publication. This information is usually sufficient to enable the researcher to locate the item. Annotated bibliographies provide the additional service of affording students a basis for deciding whether an individual entry might be useful. An annotation consists of a brief summary of the article or book's content and may include a comment on its quality.

Whether annotated or not, bibliographies can appear in one of two different formats: some are relatively brief and are appended to articles or books; others are book-length. The purpose of the appended bibliographies is to identify titles either cited in or otherwise relevant to the topic of the article or book. They play an integral role in the information gathering process, often providing invaluable leads for both getting started on and following through the various steps of a research project. Students should learn to check for the existence of appended bibliographies whenever consulting reference works such as subject encyclopedias at the start of a project or examining books and articles already gathered. The existence of appended bibliographies is often noted in citations found in abstracts, indexes and other bibliographies and is noted on catalog cards, making it possible for students to focus on those materials most likely to provide further research leads.

The scope of book-length bibliographies is ordinarily wider than that of appended bibliographies. Examples of book-length bibliographies available for several functional areas of business are listed in the Appendix. For comprehensive

bibliographies on particular topics through the subject section
of the card catalog. Bibliographies will be listed under the
Library of Congress heading for that topic with the added subdivision: "--Bibliography." (See Chapter Fourteen for a more
detailed description of this procedure.)

Many bibliographies are at least somewhat selective, and
thus may save students' time by pointing out those works judged
to be particularly authoritative and/or useful.

    Core Collection: An Author and Subject Guide.
    Boston: Baker Library, Harvard Business School,
    1970/71-.

        This very selective listing includes the approxi-
    mately 4,000 titles which make up the Core Collection
    of Baker Library at the Harvard Business School. Com-
    puter-produced entries are in abbreviated form and
    books by more than one author are usually listed only
    under the name of the first author.

A bibliography which is not at all selective but is none-
theless valued for being both current and comprehensive is:

    Books in Print. New York: Bowker, 1948-.
    Subject Guide to Books in Print. New York: Bowker, 1957-.

        Books in Print is a non-selective listing of books
    limited in its coverage to those currently available from
    major United States publishers and University presses. It
    consists of separate two volume author and title indexes.
    The Subject Guide is also two volumes and uses Library of
    Congress subject headings and cross references.

A bibliography which is nearly universal in its subject
focus may be used as a substitute when more specialized bibliographies are not available. It should be used as a supple-

ment when it is more up-to-date than available specialized

bibliographies. A prestigious national library, such as the

British Library or the Library of Congress, houses copies of

most of the important books on all topics, and in many lan-

guages, that are available in the country. Therefore, the

subject catalog of the Library of Congress, available in most

college and university libraries, can be used as a reason-

ably comprehensive current bibliography on most topics.

> U. S. Library of Congress. Subject Catalog; A
> Cumulative List of Works Represented by Library
> of Congress Printed Cards. Washington, D. C.:
> 1950-.
>
> Published in quarterly, yearly, and five-year
> cumulative editions since 1950, the Subject Catalog
> lists books catalogued by the Library of Congress
> and other major libraries in the United States.
> Each edition offers the single most comprehensive
> bibliography of works on every subject, excluding
> works of fiction, and from all parts of the world,
> which have become available during the period it
> covers. Subject headings are cross-referenced.

Chapter 10

BIBLIOGRAPHIES

Assignment

1. Describe a situation in which bibliographies are useful for business research.

2. You will be doing a research paper on _____ _____ and want to do some preliminary reading. For a selective list of books on the topic you consult the 1977-78 edition of Baker Library's <u>Core Collection</u>.

    a. What is the title of the first book on your topic?

    b. On what page did you find this information?

3. For your senior project you have decided to submit a report on some aspect of _____ and want to determine how many books might be available. You have consulted more specialized sources and are now using a current general bibliography discussed in this chapter which includes all copyrighted material published in the United States, as well as a number of titles published in other countries. You begin your search with the most recent editions and have now reached the 1970-74 edition.

    a. What is the complete citation (author, title, place, publisher and copyright date) for the first English language title?

    b. What are the title and pages of the source where you found this information?

WB 86

FINDING INFORMATION ABOUT
COMPANIES AND INDUSTRIES

4. In the course of consulting your library's card catalog
    under the subject heading _____
    you have identified only one book. In order to see if
    there are other books available on your industry, you
    use the same heading to consult a non-selective bibli-
    ography which lists all books currently available from
    major publishers in the United States. What is the
    first additional heading to which you are referred by
    a "see also" reference?

Chapter 11

PERIODICALS

Objective 1:   After reading this chapter, the student will
               describe the principal uses of professional
               business periodicals, and trade and scholarly
               journals for research in business.
Objective 2:   Given a specific issue of a periodical, the
               student will answer questions about its con-
               tent and format.
Objective 3:   Given the name of a journal, the student will
               use Magazines for Libraries to identify an
               index or abstract which covers that journal.
Objective 4:   Given a specific industry, the student will
               identify a periodical that publishes spe-
               cialized data on a continuing basis for
               that industry.

Given a topic for study or research, students generally
turn first, and often solely, to book-length treatments of
that topic. The purpose of this chapter is to suggest the
considerable utility of three types of business periodicals --
professional, scholarly, and trade journals. The currency of
articles, book reviews, and statistics contained in these
journals makes them especially valuable sources of information. Students should consider the possible use of all three
types to ensure a broad and varied perspective on a given
topic.

A periodical article may deal with a topic that has not
yet been treated and may never be treated in a book-length
publication, or it may contain new information about, or a
new interpretation of, a subject already covered in book-
length publications. In either case, students interested in

compiling a well-rounded and up-to-date reading list on a topic can often insure those qualities only by seeking out articles in periodicals.

The book reviews in business periodicals also serve a very important function. Suppose, for example, that a student wants to compile a reading list on management-by-objectives or performance appraisal and has identified a number of book-length treatments of those subjects. In terms of the quality of their research and presentation, some of the books may be very good, some mediocre, and some unreliable. Book reviews summarize content and evaluate quality, providing a basis for making a decision about a book's utility. When faced with a choice among several books, researchers will save time, and will make judgments that are as informed as possible, if they consult book reviews. Because reviews themselves vary in quality, it is advisable to consult more than one review of a particular book. Those found in scholarly journals will usually be found to be the most authoritative.

Articles in professional business periodicals provide a broad overview of areas of interest to those in commerce and industry. They do not, however, address themselves to the kinds of specialized or technical topics and problems normally commented upon in scholarly and trade journals. An example of a professional business periodical designed to appeal to executives as well as business students and which deals with topics of general interest is:

Fortune. New York: Time, 1930-.

     Among the varied topics addressed by this periodical are new products and industries, political questions, and world affairs. Biographical information provided in the "Businessmen in the News" section often gives facts that cannot be found elsewhere. During each year, Fortune contains various lists of largest companies: May - the 500 largest industrial corporations in the U. S.; June - the second 500 largest industrial corporations in the U. S.; July - the largest non-industrial corporations in the U. S.; and August - the top foreign corporations. This journal is indexed in Funk and Scott Index, Business Periodicals Index, and PAIS Bulletin.

A few other widely circulated business periodicals of professional interest are Business Week, Dun's Review, Forbes, Nation's Business and the Economist.

Scholarly periodicals are an important research source for business students researching certain types of topics, particularly those of a theoretical nature. The articles in scholarly journals are generally written by subject specialists and are critically evaluated by other scholars prior to being accepted for publication. Scholarly business periodicals found in most college and university libraries are the Academy of Management Journal, Administrative Science Quarterly, Business Horizons, California Management Review, Journal of Finance, Journal of Marketing, and Journal of Business. Most of these journals are excellent sources of authoritative book reviews. One business journal which is exceptional in being acceptable to scholars, yet widely read by practicing professionals is:

Harvard Business Review. Boston: Harvard University Pr., 1922-.

This journal, considered by many to be an outstanding publication on professional management, contains lengthy articles by recognized authorities on trends and developments in business. It includes such special features as "Thinking Ahead," which lists and discusses the future outlook for specific industries and "Keeping Informed," notes on new publications. It is indexed in Business Periodicals Index, Funk and Scott Index, and PAIS Bulletin.

The third type of periodical that is of particular interest to persons in business is the trade journal. Whereas the professional business periodical is broad in scope and attempts to cover many facets of the business world, the trade journal is generally restricted to covering a specific trade or industry. It differs from the scholarly business journal in that scholarly journals usually emphasize theoretical concepts as voiced by scholars in the field while trade journals emphasize the practical applications of those theories in the world of work. Articles in trade journals are generally written by persons actually engaged in business, often specialists experienced in the application of the subject matter at hand. Trade journals are also an excellent source of news items, descriptions of new goods, products and manufactured articles, patents and statistical data pertinent to a particular industry or trade.

An example of a popular trade journal of interest to a wider audience than most is:

Industry Week. Cleveland: Penton Publishing Co.,
1882-.

    This journal attempts to cover the areas of mar-
keting, sales, production, purchasing, administration,
finance and engineering. Each March issue features a
"Financial Analysis of Industry," which provides profiles of seventeen manufacturing industries. Indexed
in Funk and Scott Index, Business Periodicals Index
and Work Related Abstracts, it is useful to the
business student for up-to-date reports on trends
and technology in industrial management.

Examples of other popular trade journals are Advertising
Age, American Machinist, Coal Week, Construction Review,
Hardware Retailing, Metals Week, Modern Plastics and Stores.

The professional, trade, and scholarly journals just described are only a small fraction of the periodicals students
will encounter when engaged in research and independent study.
Students can find brief descriptions of major business journals, as well as those of other academic disciplines, by consulting:

Katz, William. Magazines for Libraries. 3rd ed. New
York: Bowker, 1978.

    This work contains publication information as well
as descriptive and evaluative annotations for over
6,500 periodicals and newspapers. Titles are organized
into approximately 100 subject areas with business journals being divided into the following categories: accounting, advertising, marketing, finance, and management. The index may be used to locate individual titles.

Many professional and trade journals publish issues that
contain specialized data, some on a continuing quarterly,
semi-annual or annual basis. For instance, the June issue of
Fortune includes a list of the 500 largest industrial cor-

porations in the United States. Another special issue of
wide interest is Business Week's "Executive Compensation"
list, which gives the salaries of top executives of major
companies, arranged by industry classification. These are
only two examples of the many specialized lists found in
business periodicals. A tool designed to help users keep
track of which list is published where and when is:

>   Devers, Charlotte M. Guide to Special Issues and
>   Indexes of Periodicals. 2nd ed. New York: Special
>   Library Association, 1976.
>
>   This guide attempts to lead users to the vast
>   amount of specialized information published in the
>   special issues of 1,256 periodicals. It lists, in
>   alphabetical order, periodicals which publish special
>   feature articles, supplementary issues, editorial
>   indexes, and advertiser indexes. There is a clas-
>   sified list of periodicals by industry at the front
>   and a detailed subject index in the back.

Chapter 11

PERIODICALS

Assignment

1. Distinguishing between each type, describe the principal
    uses of professional, trade, and scholarly business
    periodicals.

In your business resources and methods course, your instructor
wants each student to become familiar with the format of some
of the more important business journals. As an exercise, he
gives each student a list of several journals and a set of
questions about each issue. You have been assigned the following:

2. Harvard Business Review, _____:

    a. What is the title of an article by _____
        _____?

    b. Where is the author employed?

3. Fortune, _____:

    a. Who is the author of an article entitled _____
        _____?

    b. Who is featured in the "Businessmen in the News" section
        of the above issue?

    c. Where is he or she employed?

4. Industry Week, _____ :

   a. Using the table of contents of this issue, locate a special feature entitled "Emerging Technologies." What is the first topic discussed in this section?

   b. Locate the "Advertiser Index" in this issue. On what page is a product by _____ featured?

   c. What is the advertising agency for this firm?

5. You are interested in subscribing to a journal that will keep you abreast of current developments in your major field. Your instructor has suggested two titles which he thinks are equally good, but you would like some assistance in evaluating which of the two would better suit your needs. To do this, you consult Katz's Magazines for Libraries. The title of one of the journals is: _____

   Note: See page IX for an explanation of "How to Use This Book."

   a. Are book reviews available in this journal? If yes, what kinds?

   b. For what type of audience is this journal suited?

   c. Where is this journal indexed?

*FINDING INFORMATION ABOUT
COMPANIES AND INDUSTRIES*

6. You are interested in identifying special issues of journals that provide current data on your industry. Using Devers' Guide to Special Issues and Indexes of Periodicals,

   a. Give the title of the first periodical listed in the "Classified List of Periodicals" section at the front under the heading _____.

   b. What is the journal's special feature during the month of _____ ?

Chapter 12

NEWSPAPERS

Objective 1: After reading this chapter, the student will
describe the principal uses of newspapers in
business.
Objective 2: Given a topic and a time period, the student
will identify the date, page, column, and summary information for a newspaper article using
the New York Times Index.
Objective 3: Consulting Ayer Directory of Publications, the
student will identify a newspaper published in
a specific city.
Objective 4: Given a topic and a time period, the student
will identify the date, page, column, and
summary information for a newspaper article
using the Wall Street Journal Index.

Newspapers are regularly issued publications which report

events and discuss topics of current interest. Types of news-

paper information which business students may find useful are:

news items; factual reporting of events; feature articles

which may represent extensive investigation into a topic;

columns, often written by well-known economists and financial

analysts who comment on or report current issues and events;

and many types of current business and financial statistical

data. Persons in business read newspapers in order to be

well-informed about local, national and international news in

general and about the current financial picture and business

trends in particular.

Persons in business have available to them a number of

newspapers which are national in scope and which specialize

in business and/or finance. The most important of these and

an essential source for virtually all business persons is the
Wall Street Journal. The New York Times also gives excellent
coverage to business and economic news and is the most comprehensive source of news on more general topics as well. Indexes are available for both of these newspapers:

Wall Street Journal Index. New York: Dow Jones,
1958-.

     The Wall Street Journal offers a complete report
on current business. It includes feature articles on
business and economic topics, news of individual companies, Dow Jones and other averages, commodity and
stock market quotations, and other data. The Index
is published monthly and cumulates annually. It is
a subject index in two parts: general news and corporate news.

New York Times Index. New York: New York Times,
1913-.

     This index provides subject access to news stories,
editorials, and other features. Published every two
weeks, it is cumulated annually. Each entry begins
with a subject, followed by references to other relevant sections of the index (if there are any). Each
article is summarized. Citations identify the month
by one or two letters, followed by the date, a roman
numeral for the newspaper section and an arabic page
number, and sometimes a column number, preceded by a
colon. The year is identified on the cover and title
page and should be included by researchers when copy-
ing citations. One important item to note in using
this index is that the cross-references which directly follow the subject in each entry must be checked
in the index to obtain complete citations. The user
cannot identify the exact location of the articles
noted in this section without doing so.

Many local newspapers enjoy good reputations for city or
regional news coverage and can be valuable sources of business
news on these levels. Indexes are published for a few of
these. To identify newspapers published in a particular

state or region, consult the Ayer Directory of Publications.
This source is also the source used most often by those
wishing to find trade journals published for particular industries.

Ayer Directory of Publications. Philadelphia: Ayer
Pr., 1880-. (Formerly titled N. W. Ayer and Son's
Directory of Newspapers and Periodicals.)

This volume lists newspapers and periodicals
published four or more times yearly in the United
States, Canada, the Bahamas, Bermuda, and the Re-
publics of Panama and the Philippines. In the main
section, publications are listed by location. Information includes, in the case of newspapers: date
of establishment, frequency of publication, political
identity (Democrat, Republican, Independent), circulation, address, editor, publishing company, and
advertising rates. The volume includes sections
listing publications by type and by subject orien-
tation. The most important of these for business
researchers is the section listing "Trade, Technical
and Class Publications." An "Index by Classifica-
tions" provides subject access. The listings in
these sections as well as the alphabetical index
at the end of the volume indicate place of publication to which the user should turn for a more comprehensive description of the publication.

Chapter 12

NEWSPAPERS

Assignment

1. You are involved in a marketing research project and are
    attempting to construct a profile of _____
    _____. To find
    information about the local newspapers you consult the
    latest edition of the Ayer Directory of Publications.

    a. What is the name of the daily newspaper in this
        city?

    b. When was it founded?

2. In your international marketing seminar you are research-
    ing the ways in which the political environment of a par-
    ticular country may affect the business climate. You have
    been asked to summarize the major events in _____
    _____ for the year _____.
    One of the works you use to compile a list of references is
    the New York Times Index. On a separate card you take down
    the summary and citation for news stories you think you may
    want to consult.

    a. What is the subject of the first story listed under
        your topic?

    b. What is the complete citation for that story: month,
        day, year, section (if Sunday), page, column?

FINDING INFORMATION ABOUT
COMPANIES AND INDUSTRIES

3. To find information on developments within your company
    and industry, you consult the Wall Street Journal Index.
    You start with the most recent cumulations and have
    reached 1977.

    a. Using the corporate index, what is the subject of
        the first story listed under your company?

    b. What is the complete citation for that story: month,
        day, year, page, column?

    c. Using the general index, what is the subject of the
        first story listed under the heading: _____
        _____?

4. To find a very complete list of trade journals relevant
    to those in your industry, you consult the "Trade, Tech-
    nical and Class Publications" section of the 1979 edition
    of the Ayer Directory of Publications. Consulting that
    portion of the Table of Contents found under the heading,
    "Classified Lists," find the entries for the "Index to
    Classifications" and for "Trade, Technical and Class
    Publications." The "Index to Classifications" serves
    as the subject index to all of the classified lists.

    a. Consulting this index under the heading _____
        _____, what is the first
        page in the "Trade, Technical and Class Publications"
        section to which you are referred?
        *Note: This index refers to other lists as well, so
        the first page given may not be the correct answer.*

    b. Turning to that page, what is the first trade journal
        listed in _____?

Chapter 13

GOVERNMENT PUBLICATIONS

Objective 1:   After reading this chapter, the student will
               describe a situation in which a person in
               business would want to gain access to govern-
               ment publications.
Objective 2:   Using a source discussed in this chapter, the
               student will identify a United States govern-
               ment publication on a specified business topic.
Objective 3:   Using a source discussed in this chapter, the
               student will identify a congressional publica-
               tion on a specified business topic.

The term "government publications" refers to the public

documents of governments at all levels: local, state, and

federal, as well as foreign. In this chapter, however, em-

phasis is placed on the federal publications of the United

States.

The United States government is the world's largest pub-

lisher. Federal publications not only provide source ma-

terials about the government and its activities, but also

provide coverage of many other fields. In the field of busi-

ness, the reports released by the various departments and

agencies of the government are often the most extensive in-

formation sources available for a given topic or problem

area. Students who learn how to gain access to these publi-

cations will find that there are few topics on which some

governmental agency, department, or congressional committee

has not published valuable information in the form of a re-

port, hearing, statistical compilation, bibliography or other

document.

Gaining access to these various kinds of information may
be essential to the solution of many everyday business problems. An executive deciding whether his company should increase production will surely want to be aware of broad economic trends in employment, prices, credit, and so on. Faced
with a decision on whether to move into a new market, he or
she will be vitally interested in relevant demographic factors. The most comprehensive source for data of this sort
is the federal government, with a few departments originating
the bulk of the information most useful for business, among
them the Department of Commerce, the Department of Labor, and
the Department of Agriculture. Much of this information is
statistical in nature, and methods of gaining access to a
large portion of it have already been described in those
chapters devoted to statistical sources. However, different
types of reference tools are generally needed to identify
the many non-statistical publications of these and other
agencies.

Another important aspect of business-government relations is that of regulation. A major task of the federal
government today is the establishment of rules and regulations
that govern businesses in their dealings with other businesses and with the public. The number of laws regulating
business increases daily and the government has begun to
enforce them more stringently. Companies that have failed
to comply have found the penalties to be severe, and ignorance

not accepted as a defense. Some of the independent regulatory agencies of which business executives should be cognizant are the Federal Trade Commission (FTC), the Securities and Exchange Commission (SEC), the Federal Reserve System, the National Labor Relations Board (NLRB), and the Occupational Safety and Health Board. Topical law reporters, described in Chapter Five, "Services," are used by many business executives to keep themselves informed about government regulations affecting them. Since regulatory agencies are responsible for keeping the public informed, they also publish many useful explanatory works. Reference materials which can be used to identify these, as well as other government publications, are the subject of the remainder of this chapter.

A guide used for identifying government publications of particular interest to persons in business is:

> Business Services and Information: The Guide to the
> Federal Government. Philadelphia: Management In-
> formation Exchange, 1978.
>
> This source facilitates the task of gaining
> access to the wealth of business-oriented infor-
> mation published by the U. S. government. The
> guide is divided into four parts: Part A - the
> Introduction; Part B - the body of the text, which
> is an annotated list of publications arranged by
> subject; Part C - the Appendix, contains telephone
> numbers and agency addresses; and Part D - the Index.

A basic index which students should know how to use in order to identify federal documents covering all subject areas is:

U. S. Superintendent of Documents. <u>Monthly Catalog of United States Government Publications</u>. Washington, D. C.: Government Printing Office, 1885-.

     This index, published by the government itself, is the most complete catalogue of federal documents available. The detailed indexes--subject, author/agency, and title--refer users to individual items by entry number. The subject index uses Library of Congress subject headings. Entries identify personal author (if any), pagination, date, illustration notes, series, title, and the Superintendent of Documents number. United States documents are arranged by this number in many libraries, especially those that are federal depositories.

Since the <u>Monthly Catalog</u> normally cumulates only annually, retrospective searches can be time-consuming. An index which is useful in such cases is the <u>Cumulative Subject Index to the Monthly Catalog of U. S. Government Publications, 1900-1971</u>.

In the course of its work, the Congress of the United States generates an array of publications which is amazing in both its variety and scope. Most legislation under consideration is researched in committees which then publish reports, prints, documents and hearings, many of which are useful for persons researching assorted business topics. These publications, as well as resulting legislation, are indexed and abstracted in:

<u>CIS/Index to Publications of the United States Congress</u>. Washington, D. C.: James B. Adler, 1970-.

     The <u>CIS/Index</u> is a basic source for the working papers of Congress. It provides information in the form of abstracts of congressional documents, and microfiche copies of the documents themselves. It covers the entire range of congressional publications, which is to say approximately 400,000 pages a year of hearings, committee prints, House and Senate reports and other congressional documents.

The CIS/Index is issued in two sections, the indexes and abstracts, and is cumulated quarterly and annually. To locate specific materials or information on a specific topic, first turn to the index section. Key word titles are listed in the index with entry numbers which can be used to locate the abstract and the microfiche copy of the publication.

Because the federal government distributes its publications to a network of libraries across the country called "depositories," and because many university libraries maintain government document collections, federal publications, once identified, are generally accessible to business researchers, either locally or through interlibrary loan.

For a more detailed discussion of federal publications and appropriate finding aids, students may consult Lawrence F. Schmeckebier's Government Publications and Their Use (see Appendix for complete citation).

Publications of state, local, and international governments may also be needed to research some topics in business. While not as well indexed or accessible as federal documents, finding aids do exist. Students wishing to locate appropriate reference sources should consult Government Publications: A Guide to Bibliographic Tools by Vladimir M. Palic (see Appendix for complete citation).

Chapter 13

GOVERNMENT PUBLICATIONS

Assignment

1. Describe a situation in which government publications would be useful in business research.

2. In your new job you have been given responsibility for
   _____.
   Your background is not strong in this area, and following your hunch that the federal government has probably published something on the topic, you check Business Services and Information.

   a. Using the index, what is the first item number to which you are referred?

   b. What is the title of the first publication to which the number refers?

3. For your Government and Business course, you are interested in locating several congressional publications on the topic of _____.

   a. Using the 1977 CIS Annual Index, what is the accession number for the first publication listed on this topic?

   b. Give the name of the major congressional committee (not a subcommittee) responsible for this report.
   Note: Refer to sample abstract on page xxi at front of abstract volume for clarification.

   c. How many pages are in this report?

4. A congressional report published in 1977 with the title
    _____
    has been assigned as reading material for a course you
    are presently taking. Using the 1977 CIS Index, find
    the accession number for this title.

                    FINDING INFORMATION ABOUT
                    COMPANIES AND INDUSTRIES

5. Since you want to identify government documents on your
    industry which may have been published by any part of
    the United States government, you consult the Monthly
    Catalog. Its subject index uses Library of Congress
    subject headings so you start with the same headings
    which have proven useful to you in finding materials
    in your library's card catalog and in Books in Print
    (Chapter Ten).

    a. Under the heading _____
        in the 1978 index, what is the title of the first
        publication listed?

    b. What entry number is given for this title?

    c. What government agency authored this publication?
        Note: Refer to the sample entry in the "User's
        Guide" at the front of the January-March volume
        for clarification. The author is that part of
        the entry referred to as the "main entry."

Chapter 14

RESEARCH REPORTS
MECHANICS AND METHODOLOGY

Objective: After reading this chapter, the student will
utilize the techniques and strategies presented
to accomplish the preparatory work for a research paper, up to and including the compilation of a bibliography.
Specifically, the student will:
a)   identify and use reference works such as
encyclopedias for background information;
b)   develop a list of appropriate subject
headings to use in indexes, abstracts,
the subject catalogue, etc.;
c)   identify and use appropriate indexes,
abstracts, bibliographies;
d)   utilize other resources to full advantage, for example by exploiting bibliographies and footnotes in books and
articles and the information on a
catalogue card;
e)   locate needed background data in appropriate reference tools;
f)   locate appropriate sources of information outside the library;
g)   maintain a search record; and
h)   prepare bibliography cards, using
standard citation forms.

Business students may be called upon to submit several

different types of research projects, depending on their area

of specialization and the wishes of a particular instructor.

A research project may simply be a term paper of the type

required in many other subject areas. Or, it may be a case

study in which some information is supplied and the student

is expected to find additional information, develop plans,

draw conclusions, etc. Finally, students may be expected to

submit a report on the model of reports routinely written in

the business world. Such a report might explore the possibility of manufacturing a new product line, consider marketing considerations, weigh plant locations, etc. Research methods for each of these purposes will vary, but researchers will want to be able to exploit a full range of research resources, regardless of which type of research they are doing. Research methodology which would be used for a comprehensive research project will be described in detail in the first half of this chapter. Subjects to be discussed include: choosing a topic, using generalized research strategies for locating books and periodicals, supplementing with facts and figures from reference sources, and locating sources of information outside the library. The second half of the chapter will focus on research mechanics, such as compiling a subject headings list and keeping a research record. Attention paid to these mechanics will enable researchers to use their time efficiently.

Research Methodology

CHOOSING A TOPIC

When given the opportunity to choose a research topic, students should do so with care. It is a good idea to plan to spend some time on this preliminary phase of a project before becoming committed to a particular topic. The following questions should be asked:

1. Can the topic be investigated well?

For most research papers, this reduces to the question of whether there is sufficient research material relevant to

the topic available locally--either housed in area libraries
or easily obtained through interlibrary loan.

2. Can the project be <u>done</u> well?

An important objective factor to consider here is the
scope of the research topic. A topic that is too large en-
courages superficial research, and, inevitably, an incom-
plete treatment.

How does the student tell if there is either too little
or too much material available? There is no substitute for
doing a little preliminary research. Following the first
few steps outlined below for both book and periodical search-
ing should help students decide whether their topic is one of
those which will yield a suitable number of sources.

In deciding whether a project may be done well, there
are subjective factors to consider as well. It is advisable
for students to select a topic about which they have some
knowledge and that will hold their interest. In addition,
topics should allow for evaluation, the formation of judgments, and the development of conclusions. When these factors
are taken into consideration in choosing a topic, the resulting paper is likely to be more satisfying both to the
student and the instructor.

GETTING STARTED

The most frequent error made by students involved in a
research project is to begin their investigation by turning
first to the subject section of their library's catalogue.

A library catalogue is primarily an author, title, and subject list of the book holdings of that library. Because the budgets in individual libraries are limited and the subject emphasis of institutions differs, no library owns a comprehensive collection (or even a collection of all the best publications) on every topic. Thus, students who limit themselves to the holdings of a particular library are likely to miss some important sources. At the same time, since the card catalogue is not an evaluated list of books, students may waste a good deal of time determining which titles of those available are actually relevant.

In addition, the subject headings used by most libraries are general in nature and limited in number for any given book. Therefore, it is important for students involved in research to recognize that the library's catalogue is not generally the best place to begin a research project but rather is ordinarily a tool to be consulted in the specific circumstances described on the following pages.

STEP 1: *FIND A GENERAL SOURCE.*

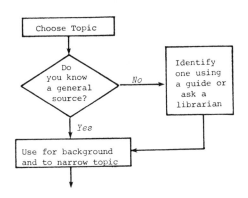

A general source will supply background information which will enable you to define your topic precisely. Subject encyclopedias (Chapter Three), handbooks (Chapter Two), and textbooks are examples of publications useful at the start of a project. If you do not know a general source, attempt to identify one by consulting a guide (Chapter One). Your instructor or a librarian may also be able to help you identify a general source. Most general sources include a bibliography, in which case you have a head start on the next step.

STEP 2: *FIND A BIBLIOGRAPHY*

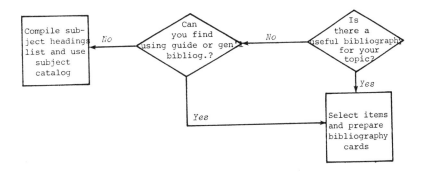

If there is no bibliography in the general source, locate one by using a guide (see Chapter One), or one of the general business bibliographies discussed in Chapter Eight; consult with your instructor or a librarian; or consult your library's subject catalogue. To do this, you will first need to compile a list of subject headings using the Library of Congress Subject Headings (see page 123 under "Research Mechanics" for more information on this). If your library owns a specialized bibliography on your topic, it will be listed under the subject with a subdivision for bibliography, e.g. Sales forecasting--Bibliography.

You will be looking for a fairly recent bibliography which will provide you with a list of recommended books and/or articles on your topic. Even a bibliography which is somewhat out-of-date will be useful if it provides you with a list of basic sources which can be updated in subsequent steps.

STEP 3: *PREPARE BIBLIOGRAPHY CARDS FOR SELECTED ITEMS.*

Having located a suitable bibliography, select books and articles which seem appropriate, and make bibliography cards using complete citations (see page 122 under "Research Mechanics" for format).

LOCATING BOOKS

STEP 4: *CHECK AUTHOR OR TITLE CATALOGUE.*

Determine whether your library owns the materials you identified through your previous efforts. If the library does not own some of the materials you need, request the materials through interlibrary loan (ask a librarian about procedures).

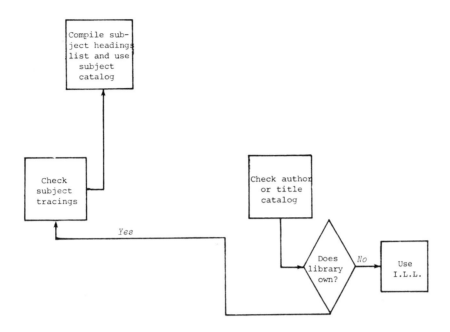

Also, check the catalog card to see if the books you selected have bibliographies. Note this information on bibliography cards.

STEP 5: *IF OWNED, CHECK THE SUBJECT TRACINGS.*

Subject "tracings" are subject headings printed at the bottom of each catalog card (see page 124 for examples). Use these subject headings to start a master list or add them to your existing list.

STEP 6: *USE THE SUBJECT CATALOGUE.*

Using your master list of subject headings, consult the library's subject catalogue to determine whether it has books relevant to your topic published since the bibliography you used. If some are found, copy complete citations, list pertinent notes, and look for any new subject tracings that would be useful headings. If at this point you feel your bibliography is inadequate, see a librarian or your instructor to evaluate your research to this point.

STEP 7: *RETRIEVE BOOKS AND BROWSE FOR OTHERS.*

Once you have identified relevant items owned by the library, go to the shelves, and, while gathering your books, examine others nearby for which you have no citations but whose titles indicate they might deal with your topic.

STEP 8: *CHECK BIBLIOGRAPHIES.*

As you begin using the books you have selected, check the bibliographies. If you do not have citations for some of the items you find, you may want to make additional bibliography cards and attempt to locate these materials later.

LOCATING PERIODICAL ARTICLES

You probably came across some periodical articles while using a general source under "Getting Started" (Step One). If so, go on to Step Eleven to find out if the library owns the needed journals. To locate other articles which will update those sources already identified:

STEP 9: *CONSULT APPROPRIATE ABSTRACTS AND INDEXES.*

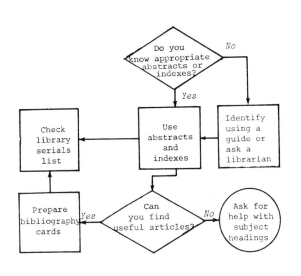

If you are not sure which abstracts or indexes would be useful, review Chapter Seven and its Appendix, and consult a guide (see Chapter One), a librarian, or your instructor. Use your master list of subject headings to get started. Since subject headings often differ from source to source, you will probably need to follow-up a number of cross-references. Add new headings to your master list. Maintain a research record card for each index and abstract used (see page 125).

If you don't find useful articles, ask a reference librarian for assistance. You may be using inappropriate subject headings.

STEP 10: *PREPARE BIBLIOGRAPHY CARDS FOR ARTICLES SELECTED.*

Be sure to copy complete citations (see page 121).

STEP 11: *CHECK SERIALS LIST.*

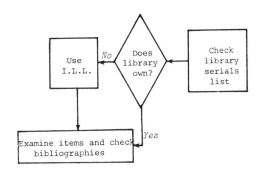

To determine whether the library owns the journals containing the articles you wish to consult, check the serials list or file which identifies the jour-

nals owned by that library. If the library does not own the
material, request it on interlibrary loan.

STEP 12: *CHECK BIBLIOGRAPHIES.*

As you begin reading the articles you have selected,
check the bibliographies. If you do not have citations for
some of the items you find, you may want to make additional
bibliography cards and attempt to locate these materials later.

FINDING FACTS AND FIGURES

STEP 13: *FIND AND UPDATE STATISTICAL INFORMATION AND OTHER DATA.*

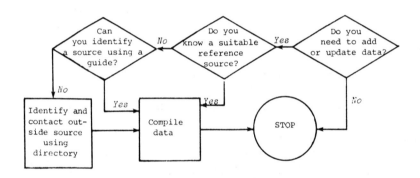

After books and articles have been gathered and an outline
of the report has been developed, you will probably find that
some areas of your report would be strengthened by additional
data. Also, statistical information gathered from book and
periodical sources will often need to be updated. Sources introduced in Chapters Five through Eight and used for the assignment on "Finding Information About Companies and Industries"
should be useful for this purpose. If you do not readily find
a source for the information you need, consult a general business

guide or one of the special guides to statistics. If you are still unable to locate needed data, it may be necessary to:

STEP 14: *LOCATE SOURCES OF INFORMATION OUTSIDE THE LIBRARY.*

You should not feel restricted to using only resources found in a library. The information needed to complete a research project in business is sometimes simply not available there. Directories, yearbooks and almanacs, guides or even the source notes often supplied in statistical works will help you locate sources such as trade and professional organizations, government agencies, chambers of commerce, or industrial research organizations, which may be able to supply the information you need.

The flow chart on the following page is a graphic summary of the strategy that has been developed in Steps One through Fourteen. Following these steps may initially seem to be a needlessly complicated way of finding books and articles, and, of course, not all of these steps will always be needed. In some cases, for example, articles may be the only available sources of information. The intention is to provide the researcher with a wide overview of the information gathering process and an appreciation for the role different types of sources play in forming a bibliographic network. The result of tying in to this network and using its linking mechanism is a generally higher percentage of relevant citations gained in a shorter period of time and a much higher likelihood of finding key sources.

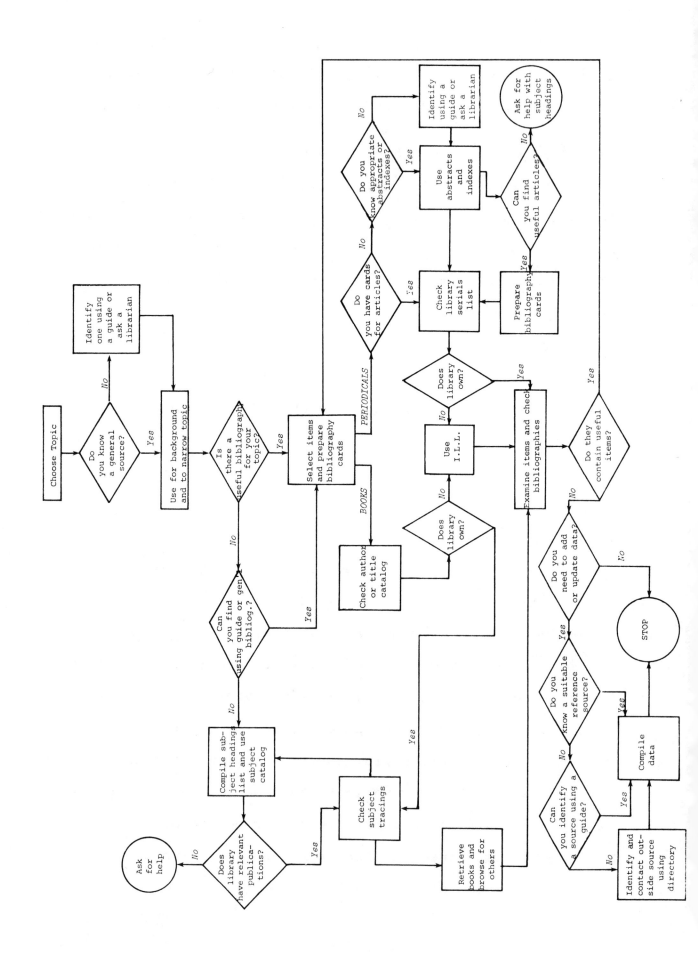

Research Mechanics

In the preceding discussion of research methodology, references have been made to bibliography cards and to a subject heading list. These are record keeping devices which, if maintained consistently and accurately, will greatly increase the efficiency of the research, and decrease some common frustrations. Another recommended record is one which keeps track of the various steps involved in a particular research project. All three of these records can conveniently be kept on three by five cards. The mechanics of doing so will be described in the following sections.

1. Bibliography Cards

Using complete citations in keeping a record of possible sources will enable researchers to save time by avoiding a lot of back-tracking. One technique is to copy, in correct form and on separate cards, complete citations for every book, article, etc., for which a reference is found and which is, or might be, consulted. Among other things, this procedure will: (1) afford a complete, current record of sources which have been or will be used; (2) eliminate retracing steps later to find necessary bibliographic information on sources which have been used; (3) afford a record of sources which weren't available during the initial search; (4) allow requests for interlibrary loan to be filled out without having to return to the source of the citation for complete bibliographic information. Finally, at the end, no source will have to be rechecked for precise title, author, publication data, and other information necessary to prepare an accurate bibliography for the completed paper.

When citing books, articles, pamphlets, government publications, etc., it is often recommended that business students use the forms suggested in Student's Guide for Writing College Papers by Kate Turabian (see Appendix for complete citation).

Books

> Gordon, Robert A. Business Fluctuations.
> 2d ed. New York: Harper, 1961.

Articles

> Wolf, R. J. "Group Management--an Experiment
> That Has Worked." Research Management
> 13 (November 1970): 445-9

Newspaper Articles

> Wall Street Journal, 12 December 1977.

Government Publications

> U. S. Department of Commerce. Domestic and
> International Business Administration.
> A Business Guide to the European Common
> Market. Overseas Business Reports OBR76-13,
> by J. Robert Wilson. Washington, D. C.:
> U. S. Government Printing Office, 1976.

2. Subject Headings List

During the initial stages of research, students should develop a list of the subject headings they will use when consulting the card catalogue, bibliographies, indexes and abstracts. An inclusive list of possible headings is advanta-

geous because not all of these reference sources use the same
subject headings for indexing. Thus, the more topical categories students have listed, the more likely they are to locate useful material in all of the reference sources they consult. For example, a student writing on direct-mail advertising may find books and articles listed under:

    Mail-order business
    Sales letters
    Junk mail
    Circular letters

The Library of Congress Subject Headings (see Appendix for
complete citation) is a useful source for quickly identifying
a number of subject heading alternatives. This two-volume work
contains a list of the headings which are used in the subject
catalogues of most libraries. When beginning a research project, students should note the subject headings listed in this
source and then, as the research proceeds, add new headings
which seem appropriate. The following excerpt from this work
is given to demonstrate the way it lists related headings:

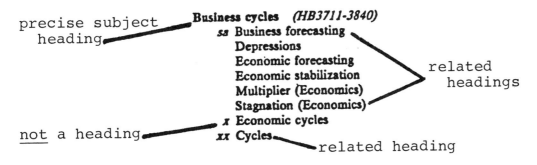

    The precise Library of Congress subject heading listed
here is "Business Cycles." Related headings are all of those
listed after "sa" and "xx." Terms listed after "x" are not
Library of Congress subject headings and will not be used in
a card catalog, but are synonymous terms which may very well
be used in an index or abstract.

Use of Catalogue Card Information

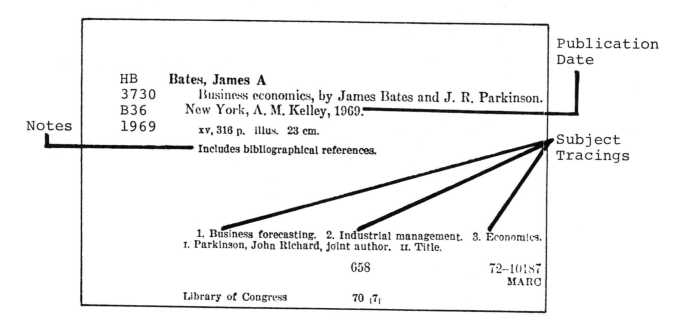

In addition to the call number, cards in the library's
card catalogue provide other useful information which may be
used to supplement the subject headings list or noted on
bibliography cards. The date of publication, of course, indicates how current the book is. If a book has a bibliography
or bibliographical footnotes, a brief note in the center of
the card indicates this and sometimes indicates the pages of
the book on which the bibliography will be found. This information should be included on the bibliography card the
student prepares for the book. Books with bibliographies
should be examined first; the bibliographies may lead directly to useful sources and save a great deal of research time
using more general reference sources.

The subject tracings on catalogue cards identify all the
subject headings under which the book is listed in the subject

section of the card catalogue. For the book in the example, cards are filed under Business forecasting, Industrial management, and Economics. The student who finds that the Bates book is useful for a particular research project may find additional useful titles by checking the library's subject catalogue under these headings. Subject heading tracings as they are identified should be added to the "Subject Headings List" suggested above.

3. Search Record

In research projects carried out over a period of time, students often redo some search work or miss valuable sources. To save time and insure a thorough search, a research record should be kept. This can be done conveniently on cards--one for each step in the research plus a general card that lists together, in abbreviated form, all sources used. An individual card should indicate one source (index, abstract, bibliography, etc.) and the subject headings and dates covered in that source during the research. As an example:

```
Business Periodicals Index

Volumes Searched:  v. 12 (1969-70) to v. 20
                   no. 1 (1978)

Topic:  Rating of Employees

Headings Used:
        Ability Testing
        Executives--Rating
        Performance Standards
        Salesmen--Rating
        Self-evaluation
```

Chapter 14

RESEARCH REPORTS
MECHANICS AND METHODOLOGY

Assignment

Select a topic and obtain approval for it. Prepare and turn in:

1. Bibliography. This should include enough sources to
    support a 20-page research report. It should be on
    three by five cards using the style suggested in this
    chapter. Each bibliography should include:

    a. basic sources for the topic;

    b. the major publications dealing with the topic;

    c. publications dealing with the most recent research,
        trends, or developments;

    d. sources of statistical information, if relevant
        to the topic; and

    e. sources of information outside the library which
        could supply additional information.

2. Search record cards. Include both a general card listing
    all sources used plus an individual card for each finding
    aid.

3. Subject headings list.

4. "Journal" or "log" of your research work. Write down each
    step you take as you take it and explain why you decided
    to take that step. For example, when you consult a ref-
    erence work, record its title, your reason for consulting
    it and what, if any, use it was to you.

APPENDIX

Chapter 1 - Guides to the Literature

Demarest, Rosemary R. Accounting: A Guide to Information Sources. Detroit: Gale Research, 1970.

Daniells, Lorna M. Business Reference Sources; an Annotated Guide for Harvard Business School Students. Cambridge, Mass: Baker Library, Graduate School of Business Administration, Harvard University, 1979.

Melnyk, Peter. Economics: Bibliographic Guide to Reference Books and Information Resources. Littleton, Colo.: Libraries Unlimited, 1971.

Carter, Ciel. Guide to Reference Sources in the Computer Sciences. New York: Macmillan Information, 1974.

Johnson, H. Webster. How to Use the Business Library, With Sources of Business Information. 4th ed. Cincinnati: Southwestern, 1972.

Shabacker, J. C. Small Business Information Sources. Milwaukee: National Council for Small Business Management Development, University of Wisconsin-Extension, 1976.

Coman, Edwin T. Sources of Business Information. Berkeley: University of California Pr., 1964.

White, Carl M., and Associates. Sources of Information in the Social Sciences: A Guide to the Literature. 2nd ed. Chicago: American Library Association, 1973.

Vernon, K. D. C., ed. Use of Management and Business Literature. London and Boston: Butterworths, 1975.

Brownstone, David M. and Gorton Carruth. Where to Find Business Information. New York: Wiley, 1979.

Chapter 2 - Handbooks

Moore, R. F., ed. AMA Management Handbook. New York: American Management Association, 1970.

Casey, W. J. Accounting Desk Book. 5th ed. Englewood Cliffs, N. J.: Institute for Business Planning, 1977.

Wixon, Rufus, Walter G. Kell, and Norton M. Bedford, eds. Accountant's Handbook. 5th ed. New York: Ronald Pr., 1970.

Baughn, W. H., and C. E. Walker. The Bankers' Handbook. Rev. Homewood, Ill.: Dow Jones-Irwin, 1978.

Britt, Stewart H., ed. The Dartnell Marketing Manager's Handbook. Chicago: Dartnell, 1973.

Minor, R. S., and C. W. Fetridge. The Dartnell Office Administration Handbook. Chicago: Dartnell, 1975.

U. S. Bureau of Labor Statistics. Dictionary of Occupational Titles. Washington, D. C.: U. S. Government Printing Office, 1965-.

Levine, S. N. Financial Analyst's Handbook. Homewood, Ill: Dow Jones-Irwin, 1974.

Vancil, Richard F., ed. Financial Executive's Handbook. Homewood, Ill.: Dow Jones-Irwin, 1970.

Cashin, James A., ed. Handbook for Auditors. New York: McGraw-Hill, 1971.

Davidson, S., and R. L. Weil, eds. Handbook of Cost Accounting. New York: McGraw-Hill, 1978.

Mixon, S. R. Handbook of Data Processing Administration, Operations, and Procedures. New York: AMACOM, 1976.

Harrison, T. J., ed. Handbook of Industrial Control Computers. New York: Wiley-Interscience, 1972.

Ferber, Robert, ed. Handbook of Marketing Research. New York: McGraw-Hill, 1974.

Burington, R. S. Handbook of Mathematical Tables and Formulas. 5th ed. New York: McGraw-Hill, 1973.

Davidson, Sidney, ed. Handbook of Modern Accounting. 2nd ed. New York: McGraw-Hill, 1977.

Buell, Victor P., ed. Handbook of Modern Marketing. New York: McGraw-Hill, 1970.

Rock, M. L., ed. Handbook of Wage and Salary Administration. New York: McGraw-Hill, 1972.

Lawson, J. W. How to Develop a Personnel Policy Manual. Chicago: Dartnell, 1978.

Lund, H. F. Industrial Pollution Control Handbook. New York: McGraw-Hill, 1971.

McFarlan, F. Warren, and Richard L. Nolan, eds. Information Systems Handbook. Homewood, Ill.: Dow Jones-Irwin, 1975.

Brady, G. S., and H. R. Clauser. Materials Handbook. 11th ed. New York: McGraw-Hill, 1977.

U. S. Bureau of Labor Statistics. Occupational Outlook Handbook. Washington, D. C.: U. S. Government Printing Office, 1949-.

Portfolio of Accounting Systems for Small and Medium-sized Businesses. Rev. Englewood Cliffs, N. J.: Prentice-Hall/National Society of Public Accountants, 1977.

Carson, Gordon B., Harold A. Bolz, and Hewitt H. Young. Production Handbook. 3rd ed. New York: Ronald Pr., 1972.

Craig, Robert L. Training and Development Handbook. New York: McGraw-Hill, 1976.

Chapter 3 - Subject Dictionaries and Encyclopedias

Sippl, Charles J., and Charles P. Sippl. Computer Dictionary and Handbook. 2nd ed. Indianapolis: Howard W. Sams, 1972.

Kohler, E. L. A Dictionary for Accountants. 5th ed. Englewood Cliffs, N. J.: Prentice-Hall, 1975.

Urdang, Laurence, ed. Dictionary of Advertising Terms. Chicago: Tatham-Laird & Kudner Advertising, 1977.

Seide, Katharine, ed. A Dictionary of Arbitration and its Terms. Dobbs Terry, N. Y.: Oceana Publications, 1970.

Ammer, Christine. Dictionary of Business and Economics. New York: Free Pr., 1977.

Davids, Lewis E. Dictionary of Business and Finance. Totowa, N. J.: Rowman and Littlefield, 1978.

Rosenberg, Jerry M. Dictionary of Business and Management. New York: Wiley, 1978.

Sloan, Harold S., and A. J. Zureker. Dictionary of Economics. New York: Barnes and Noble, 1970.

Kendall, Maurice G., and William R. Buckland. A Dictionary of Statistical Terms. 3rd ed. New York: Hafner, 1971.

Lindemann, A. J., Earl F. Lundgren, and H. K. von Kaas. Encyclopaedic Dictionary of Management and Manufacturing Terms. 2nd ed. Dubuque, Ia.: Kendall-Hunt Publishing Co., 1974.

Graham, Irvin. Encyclopedia of Advertising. 2nd ed. New York: Fairchild Publications, 1969.

Munn, Glenn G. Encyclopedia of Banking and Finance. 7th ed. Boston: Bankers Publishing Co., 1973.

Ralston, Anthony, and Chester L. Meek. Encyclopedia of Computer Science. New York: Petrocelli/Charter, 1976.

Bittel, Lester. Encyclopedia of Professional Management. New York: McGraw-Hill, 1978.

Encyclopedia of the Social Sciences. New York: Macmillan, 1935.

Rodgers, Harold A. Funk & Wagnalls Dictionary of Data Processing Terms. New York: Funk & Wagnalls, 1970.

Gross, Jerome S. Illustrated Encyclopedic Dictionary of Real Estate Terms. Englewood Cliffs, N. J.: Prentice-Hall, 1978.

Greenwald, Douglas. The McGraw-Hill Dictionary of Modern Economics; A Handbook of Terms and Organizations. 2nd ed. New York: McGraw-Hill, 1973.

Skrapek, Wayne A., et al. Mathematical Dictionary for Economics and Business Administration. Boston: Allyn and Bacon, 1976.

Chapter 4 - Directories

Broadcasting Yearbook. Washington, D. C.: Broadcasting Publications, 1935-.

Classified Directory of Wisconsin Manufacturers. Milwaukee: Manufacturers Association, 1921-.

Datapro Directory of Software. Delran, N. J.: Datapro Research, 1975-.

Angel, Juvenal L., ed. Directory of American Firms Operating in Foreign Countries. 8th ed. New York: Simon & Schuster, 1975.

Trzyna, Thaddeus C. Directory of Consumer Protection and Environmental Agencies. Orange, N. J.: Academic Media, 1973.

Directory of Corporate Affiliations of Major National Advertisers: Who Owns Whom. Skokie, Ill.: National Register Pub. Co., 1967-.

Directory of European Associations. Part 1, National Industrial, Trade and Professional Associations. Beckenham, Kent, England: EBD Ltd., 1971.

Arpan, Jeffrey S., and David A. Ricks, eds. <u>Directory of Foreign Manufacturers</u>
     <u>in the United States</u>. Atlanta, Ga.: School of Business Administration,
     Georgia State University, 1975.

<u>Europe's 5000 Largest Companies</u>. New York: Bowker, 1975-.

<u>Jane's Major Companies of Europe</u>. London: Jane's Yearbooks, 1970-.

<u>Kelly's Manufacturers and Merchants Directory</u>. Kingston Upon Thames, Surrey,
     England: 1880-.

Dun & Bradstreet. <u>Million Dollar Directory</u>. New York: 1959-.

<u>National Trade and Professional Associations of the United States and Canada</u>
     <u>and Labor Unions</u>. Washington, D. C.: Columbia Books, 1966-.

<u>Polk's World Bank Directory: North American Section</u>. Nashville: R. L.
     Polk, 1971-.

Chamber of Commerce of the United States. <u>Sources of State Information and</u>
     <u>State Industrial Directories</u>. Washington, D. C.: Chamber of Commerce
     of the United States, 1974.

<u>Sources of State Information on Corporations</u>. Washington, D. C.: Washing-
     ton Researchers, 1978.

<u>Standard Directory of Advertisers</u>. Skokie, Ill.: National Register Pub-
     lishing Co., 1964-.

<u>Standard Rate and Data Service: Business Publication Rates and Data</u>.
     Skokie, Ill.: 1919-.

<u>Thomas Grocery Register</u>. New York: Thomas Publishing Co., 1966-.

Crowley, Ellen E., ed. <u>Trade Names Dictionary</u>. 2nd ed. Detroit: Gale
     Research, 1979.

<u>United States Government Manual</u>. Washington, D. C.: Office of the Federal
     Register, General Services Administration, 1935-.

<u>Who's Who in America: A Biographical Dictionary of Notable Living Men and</u>
     <u>Women</u>. Chicago: Marquis, 1899-.

Chapter 5 - Services

Standard & Poor's Corporation. <u>Analysts Handbook</u>. New York: 1964-.

Standard & Poor's Corporation. <u>Bond Guide</u>. New York: 1939-.

Moody's Investor Service. Bond Record: Municipals, Corporates, Governments, Convertibles and Preferred Stock Ratings. New York: 1931-.

Moody's Investor Service. Bond Survey. New York: 1936-.

Commerce Clearing House. Congressional Index. Chicago: 1937-.

Commerce Clearing House. Consumerism. Chicago: 1971-.

Moody's Investor Service. Dividend Record. New York: 1930-.

Commerce Clearing House. Employment Safety and Health Guide. Chicago: 1971-.

Bureau of National Affairs. Environment Reporter. Washington, D. C.: 1970-.

Standard & Poor's Corporation. Fixed Income Investor. New York: 1973-.

Weisenberger Investment Companies Service. Investment Companies. New York: 1941-.

Bureau of National Affairs. Labor Relations Reporter. Washington, D. C.: 1937-.

Standard & Poor's Corporation. The Outlook. New York: 1922-.

Commerce Clearing House. State Tax Reporter. Wisconsin. Chicago: 1950-.

Standard & Poor's Corporation. Trendline Stock Chart Services. New York: 1962-.

Value Line Investment Survey. New York: A. Bernhard, 1936-.

Wall Street Transcript; a Professional Publication for the Business and Financial Community. New York: Richard A. Holman, 1963-.

Chapter 6 - Yearbooks and Almanacs

American Institute of Certified Public Accountants. Accounting Trends and Techniques. New York: 1946-.

Brewers' Almanac; the Brewing Industry in the United States. Washington, D. C.: United States Brewers Association, 1940?-.

Broadcasting Yearbook. Washington, D. C.: Broadcasting Publications, 1935-.

Europa Year Book. London: Europa Publications, 1959-.

The Municipal Yearbook. Washington, D. C.: International City Management
       Association, 1934-.

Pick's Currency Yearbook. New York: Pick Publishing Corp., 1955-.

United Nations. Statistical Yearbook. New York: 1963-.

Whitaker's Almanack. London: J. Whitaker and Sons, 1869-.

World Almanac. New York: Newspaper Enterprise Association, 1868-.

United Nations. Yearbook. New York: Columbia University Pr./United
       Nations, 1946/47-.

International Labour Office. Yearbook of Labour Statistics. Geneva:
       International Labour Office, 1976-.

                 Chapter 7 - Comprehensive Statistical Sources

U. S. Bureau of the Census. Annual Survey of Manufactures. Washington,
       D. C.: U. S. Government Printing Office, 1949/50-.

U. S. Bureau of Economic Analyses, Department of Commerce. Business
       Conditions Digest. Washington, D. C.: U. S. Government Printing
       Office, 1961-.

U. S. Department of Commerce. Business Statistics. Washington, D. C.:
       U. S. Government Printing Office, 1921-.

U. S. Bureau of the Census. Catalog of Publications. Washington, D. C.:
       U. S. Government Printing Office, 1974.

U. S. Bureau of the Census. Census of Agriculture. Washington, D. C.:
       U. S. Government Printing Office, 1860-.

U. S. Bureau of the Census. Census of Construction Industries. Washing-
       ton, D. C.: U. S. Government Printing Office, 1967-.

U. S. Bureau of the Census. Census of Governments. Washington, D. C.:
       U. S. Government Printing Office, 1957-.

U. S. Bureau of the Census. Census of Housing. Washington, D. C.: U. S.
       Government Printing Office, 1960-.

U. S. Bureau of the Census. Census of Manufactures. Washington, D. C.:
       U. S. Government Printing Office, 1810-.

U. S. Bureau of the Census. Census of Mineral Industries. Washington,
       D. C.: U. S. Government Printing Office, 1840-.

U. S. Bureau of the Census. Census of Population. Washington, D. C.:
    U. S. Government Printing Office, 1780-.

U. S. Bureau of the Census. Census of Retail Trade. Washington, D. C.:
    U. S. Government Printing Office, 1948-.

U. S. Bureau of the Census. Census of Selected Service Industries.
    Washington, D. C.: U. S. Government Printing Office, 1948-.

U. S. Bureau of the Census. Census of Transportation. Washington, D. C.:
    U. S. Government Printing Office, 1963-.

U. S. Bureau of the Census. Census of Wholesale Trade. Washington, D. C.:
    U. S. Government Printing Office, 1948-.

U. S. Bureau of the Census. County and City Data Book. Washington, D. C.:
    U. S. Government Printing Office, 1947-.

U. S. Bureau of the Census. County Business Patterns. Washington, D. C.:
    U. S. Government Printing Office, 1943-.

U. S. Council of Economic Advisers. Economic Indicators. Washington,
    D. C.: U. S. Government Printing Office, 1948-.

U. S. Bureau of the Census. Enterprise Statistics. Washington, D. C.:
    U. S. Government Printing Office, 1954-.

U. S. Board of Governors of the Federal Reserve System. Federal Reserve
    Bulletin. Washington, D. C.: U. S. Government Printing Office, 1915-.

U. S. Bureau of the Census. Historical Statistics of the United States,
    Colonial Times to 1970. Washington, D. C.: U. S. Government
    Printing Office, 1976.

U. S. Bureau of Statistics. Monthly Labor Review. Washington, D. C.:
    U. S. Government Printing Office, 1915-.

U. S. Office of Management and Budget, Executive Office of the President.
    Standard Industrial Classification Manual. Washington, D. C.: U. S.
    Government Printing Office, 1972.

Wasserman, Paul, ed. Statistics Sources. 5th ed. Detroit: Gale
    Research, 1977.

Chapter 8 - Marketing and Industrial Statistics

Troy, Leo. Almanac of Business and Industrial Financial Ratios. Engle-
    wood Cliffs, N. J.: Prentice-Hall, 1972-.

Robert Morris Associates. Annual Statement Studies. Philadelphia: Robert
    Morris Associates, 1922-.

Broadcasting Yearbook. Washington, D. C.: Broadcasting Publications,
     1935-.

Dun & Bradstreet. Key Business Ratios. New York: 1931-.

Bureau of Mines. Minerals Yearbook. Washington, D. C.: U. S. Govern-
     ment Printing Office, 1932/33-.

U. S. Federal Trade Commission. Quarterly Financial Report for Manu-
     facturing, Mining, and Trade Corporations. Washington, D. C.:
     U. S. Government Printing Office, 1947-.

Ward's Automotive Reports. Detroit: Ward's Communications, 1924-.

United Nations, Statistical Office of the United Nations. Yearbook of
     Industrial Statistics. New York: 1976-.

Chapter 9 - Periodical Indexes and Abstracts

Accountant's Index. New York: American Institute of Certified Public
     Accountants, 1921-.

Accounting Articles. Chicago: Commerce Clearing House, 1965-.

Applied Science and Technology Index. New York: Wilson, 1913-.

Computing Reviews. New York: Association for Computing Machinery, 1960-.

Conference Board. Cumulative Index. New York: 1963-.

Dissertation Abstracts International. Section A: The Humanities and the
     Social Sciences. Ann Arbor, Mich.: Xerox University Microfilms, 1938-.

Index to Legal Periodicals. New York: Wilson, 1908-.

"Marketing Abstracts." Journal of Marketing. Chicago: American Marketing
     Association, 1936-.

Management Contents. Skokie, Ill.: G. D. Searle, 1975-.

U. S. Civil Service Commission. Personnel Literature. Washington, D. C.:
     U. S. Government Printing Office, 1941-.

Personnel Management Abstracts. Ann Arbor, Mich.: Graduate School of
     Business Administration, University of Michigan, 1957-.

Psychological Abstracts. Washington, D. C.: American Psychological
     Association, 1927-.

Quarterly Bibliography of Computers and Data Processing. Phoenix, Ariz.:
     Applied Computer Research, 1971-.

Readers' Guide to Periodical Literature. New York: Wilson, 1905-.

Sage Public Administration Abstracts. Beverly Hills, Calif.: Sage Publications, 1974-.

Social Sciences Index. New York: Wilson, 1974-.

Sociological Abstracts. New York: Sociological Abstracts, 1952-.

Topicator: Classified Article Guide to the Advertising/Communications/ Marketing Periodical Press. Littleton, Col.: Thompson Bureau, 1965-.

Chapter 10 - Bibliographies

Demarest, Rosemary R. Accounting Information Sources. Detroit: Gale Research, 1970.

Hills, William G., ed. Administration and Management; A Selected and Annotated Bibliography. Norman: University of Oklahoma Pr., 1975.

Ferber, Robert, et al. A Basic Bibliography on Marketing Research. (A. M. A. Bibliography No. 20) 3rd ed. Chicago: American Marketing Association, 1974.

Bibliographic Index. New York: Wilson, 1937-.

Brealey, Richard A., and Connie Pyle, comps. A Bibliography of Finance and Investment. Cambridge, Mass.: MIT Pr., 1973.

Bibliography of Publications of University Bureaus of Business and Economic Research. Morgantown, W. Va.: Bureau of Business Research; College of Business and Economics, West Virginia University/Association for University Business and Economic Research (various publishers), 1956-.

Marke, Julius J., and Edward J. Bander. Commercial Law Information Sources. Detroit: Gale Research, 1970.

Christian, Portia. Ethics in Business Conduct: Selected References from the Record -- Problems, Attempted Solutions, Ethics in Business Education. Detroit: Gale Research, 1970.

Hanson, Agnes O., ed. Executive and Management Development for Business and Government: A Guide to Information Sources. Detroit: Gale Research, 1976.

Vara, Albert C. Food and Beverage Industries: A Bibliography and Guidebook. Detroit: Gale Research, 1970.

Thomas, Ray Edwin. Insurance Information Sources. Detroit: Gale Research, 1971.

International Bibliography of Economics. Prepared by the International Committee for Social Science Information and Documentation. Chicago: Aldine, 1952-.

Bakewell, K. G. B. Management Principles and Practice: A Guide to Information Sources. Detroit: Gale Research, 1977.

U. S. Small Business Administration. Small Business Bibliography Series. Washington, D. C.: U. S. Government Printing Office, 1963-.

Videolog: Programs for Business and Industry. New York: Esselte Video, 1979.

Chapter 11 - Periodicals

Academy of Management Journal. Mississippi State, Miss.: Mississippi State University, 1958-.

Accounting Review. Sarasota, Fla: American Accounting Association, 1926-.

Administrative Science Quarterly. Ithaca, N. Y.: Graduate School of Business, Cornell University, 1956-.

Advertising Age. Chicago: Crain Communications, 1930-.

Banker's Magazine. London: Waterlow & Sons, 1844-.

Barron's; National Business and Financial Weekly. New York: Dow Jones, 1921-.

Business Horizons. Bloomington, Ind.: Indiana University, School of Business, 1958-.

Business Week. New York: McGraw-Hill, 1929-.

California Management Review. Berkeley: Graduate School of Business Administration, University of California, 1958-.

Coal Week. New York: McGraw-Hill, 1975-.

Computers and People. Newtonville, Mass.: Berkeley Enterprises, 1951-.

Conference Board Record. New York: The Conference Board, 1939-.

Construction Review. Washington, D. C.: U. S. Dept. of Commerce, 1955-.

Data Management. Park Ridge, Ill.: Data Processing Management Association, 1964-.

Data Processing Digest. Los Angeles: Data Processing Digest, 1955-.

Datamation. Los Angeles: Technical Publishing Co., 1957-.

Dun's Review. New York: Dun-Donnelly, 1893-.

Economist. Leiden, Netherlands: H. E. Stenfett Kroese, 1852-.

Financial Executive. New York: Financial Executive Institute, 1932-.

Forbes. New York: 1917-.

Hardware Retailing. Indianapolis: National Retail Hardware Association, 1901-.

Industrial and Labor Relations Review. Ithaca, N. Y.: Cornell University, 1947-.

International Management. New York: McGraw-Hill, 1947-.

Journal of Business. Chicago: University of Chicago Pr., 1928-.

Journal of Economic Literature. Nashville, Tenn.: American Economic Association, 1963-.

Journal of Finance. New York: American Finance Association, 1946-.

Journal of Management Studies. Oxford: Basil Blackwell and Mott, 1964-.

Journal of Marketing. Chicago: American Marketing Association, 1936-.

Journal of Systems Management. Cleveland, O.: Association for Systems Management, 1950-.

MSU Business Topics. East Lansing, Mich.: Graduate School of Business Administration, Michigan State University, 1953-.

Management Accounting. New York: National Association of Accountants, 1919-.

Tega, Vasile G. Management and Economics Journals: A Guide to Information Sources. Detroit: Gale Research, 1977.

Management Review. New York: American Management Association, 1923-.

Management Science. Providence, R. I.: Institute of Management Sciences, 1954-.

Metals Week. New York: McGraw-Hill, 1930-.

Modern Plastics. New York: McGraw-Hill, 1923-.

Nation's Business. Washington, D. C.: Chamber of Commerce of the United
States, 1912-.

Operations Research. Baltimore, Md.: Operations Research Society of
America, 1952-.

Personnel Journal. Santa Monica, Cal.: Personnel Journal, 1922-.

Personnel Psychology. Durham, N. C.: Personnel Psychology, 1948-.

Quarterly Review of Economics and Business. Urbana, Ill.: Bureau of
Economic and Business Research, University of Illinois, 1961-.

Sales and Marketing Management. New York: Sales Management, 1918-.

Chapter 12 - Newspapers

Chicago Tribune Index. Wooster, O.: Newspaper Indexing Center, Bell
and Howell, 1972-.

Journal of Commerce. New York: Twin Coast Newspapers, 1827-.

NewsBank; Urban Affairs Library. Greenwich, Conn.: 1975-.

Washington Post Index. Wooster, O.: Newspaper Indexing Center, Bell
and Howell, 1972-.

Chapter 13 - Government Publications

King, Richard L., ed. Business Serials of the U. S. Government; A Selective Annotated Checklist of Reference Titles. Chicago: American
Library Association, 1978.

U. S. Superintendent of Documents. Catalogue of Public Documents of the
...Congress...and of all Departments of the Government of the United
States.... Washington, D. C.: U. S. Government Printing Office,
1896-1940.

Commerce Clearing House. Congressional Index. Chicago: 1937-.

Congressional Quarterly Almanac. Washington, D. C.: Congressional
Quarterly, 1945-.

Cumulative Subject Index to the Monthly Catalog of U. S. Government
Publications, 1900-1971.

Palic, Vladimir M. Government Publications: A Guide to Bibliographic Tools. Oxford: Pergamon Pr., 1977.

Schmeckebier, Laurence F., and Roz B. Eastin. Government Publications and Their Use. 2nd rev. ed. Washington, D. C.: The Brookings Institution, 1969.

Andriot, John L. Guide to U. S. Government Publications. McLean, Va.: Documents Index, 1976-78.

U. S. Library of Congress. Popular Names of U. S. Government Reports. Washington, D. C.: U. S. Government Printing Office, 1976.

United States Government Manual. Washington, D. C.: Office of the Federal Register, General Services Administration, 1935-.

Chapter 14 - Research Reports Mechanics and Methodology

United States Library of Congress. Library of Congress Subject Headings. 8th ed. Washington, D. C.: U. S. Government Printing Office, 1975.

Turabian, Kate L. Student's Guide for Writing College Papers. 3rd ed. Chicago: University of Chicago Pr., 1976.